# THE FATHERS
# OF THE CHURCH

A NEW TRANSLATION

VOLUME 118

# THE FATHERS
# OF THE CHURCH

A NEW TRANSLATION

# ST. CYRIL OF ALEXANDRIA

## FESTAL LETTERS 1–12

*Translated by*

PHILIP R. AMIDON, S.J.
*Creighton University*

*Edited with introduction and notes by*

JOHN J. O'KEEFE
*Creighton University*

THE CATHOLIC UNIVERSITY OF AMERICA PRESS
Washington, D.C.

The paper used in this publication meets the minimum requirements of the
American National Standards for Information Science—Permanence of Paper
for Printed Library Materials, ANSI z39.48-1984.

LIBRARY OF CONGRESS CATALOGING-IN-PUBLICATION DATA
Cyril, Saint, Patriarch of Alexandria, ca. 370–444.
[Correspondence. English. Selections]
Festal letters 1–12 / St. Cyril of Alexandria ; translated by Philip R. Amidon ;
introduction and notes by John J. O'Keefe.
p. cm. — (The Fathers of the church : a new translation ; v. 118)
Includes bibliographical references and indexes.
ISBN 978-0-8132-0118-4 (cloth : alk. paper)   1. Cyril, Saint, Patriarch
of Alexandria, ca. 370–444—Correspondence.   2. Christian saints—Egypt—
Alexandria—Correspondence.   3. Christian life—Early works to 1800.
4. Theology, Doctrinal—Early works to 1800.   I. Title,   II. Series.
BR65.C952E5 2008
270.2092—dc22
2008029287

# CONTENTS

# ABBREVIATIONS

FL   *Festal Letters.*

*Ep.*   Epistle.

*JTS*   *Journal of Theological Studies.*

PG   Patrologia Graeca, ed. J.-P. Migne. Paris.

SC   Sources Chrétiennes. Paris: Cerf.

# SELECT BIBLIOGRAPHY

## Primary Sources

Azéma, Yvan, ed. *Théodoret de Cyr, Correspondance.* 3 vols. SC 40, 98, 111. Paris: Cerf, 1955–1965.

Burguière, Paul, and Pierre Évieux, eds. *Cyrille d'Alexandrie: Contre Julien, Tome 1, Livres I–II.* SC 322. Paris: Cerf, 1985.

Durand, G. M., ed. *Cyrille d'Alexandrie: Deux Dialogues Christologiques.* SC 97. Paris: Cerf, 1964.

———, ed. *Cyrille d'Alexandrie: Dialogues sur la Trinité,* Tomes 1–3. SC 231, 237, 246. Paris: Cerf, 1976–1978.

Évieux, Pierre. *Cyrille d'Alexandrie: Lettres Festales I–XVII.* Sources Chrétiennes, 372, 392, 434. Paris: Cerf, 1991–1998.

McEnerney, John I. *St. Cyril of Alexandria Letters 1–110.* The Fathers of the Church, vols. 76, 77. Washington: The Catholic University of America Press, 1987.

Migne, J.-P., ed. *Patrologia cursus completus.* Series Graeca, vols. 68–77.

Pusey, P. E., ed. *Sancti Patris Nostri Cyrilli Archiepiscopi Alexandrini.* 7 vols. Oxford, 1868. Reprint. Bruxelles, 1965.

Socrates. *Ecclesiastical History.* PG 67.

Sophronius. *Laudes in SS. Cyrum et Joannem.* PG 87: 3411–13.

Wickham, Lionel R., ed. *Cyril of Alexandria: Select Letters.* Oxford, 1983.

## Secondary Sources

Boulnois, Marie-Odile. *Le paradoxe trinitaire chez Cyrille d'Alexandrie: Herméneutique, analyse philosophique et argumentation théologique.* Paris: Institut d'études Augustiniennes, 1994.

Boyarin, Daniel. *Intertextuality and the Study of Midrash.* Bloomington, IN: Indiana University Press, 1994.

———. *Dying for God: Martyrdom and the Making of Christianity and Judaism.* Stanford: Stanford University Press, 1999.

Cameron, Averil. *Christianity and the Rhetoric of Empire: The Development of Christian Discourse.* Berkeley: University of California Press, 1991.

Casiday, A. M. *Evagrius Ponticus.* London and New York: Routledge, 2006.

Chadwick, Henry. "Eucharist and Christology in the Nestorian Controversy." *JTS N.S.* 2 (1951): 145–64.

Clark, Elizabeth. *The Origenist Controversy: The Cultural Construction of an*

*Early Christian Debate*. Princeton, NJ: Princeton University Press, 1992.

Dawson, David. *Allegorical Readers and Cultural Revision in Ancient Alexandria*. Berkeley: University of California Press, 1992.

Dysinger, Luke. *Psalmody and Prayer in the Writings of Evagrius Ponticus*. Oxford: Oxford University Press, 2005.

Evagrius of Pontus. *The Praktikos & Chapters On Prayer*. Translated by John Eudes Bamberger. Kalamazoo: Cistercian Studies, 1981.

Frankfurter, David. *Religion in Roman Egypt: Assimilation and Resistance*. Princeton, NJ: Princeton University Press, 1998.

Gorday, Peter. *Principles of Patristic Exegesis: Romans 9–11 in Origen, John Chrysostom, and Augustine*. New York: Edwin Mellen, 1983.

Guillaumont, Antoine. *Aux Origines du Monachisme Chrétien. Spiritualité Orientales*, no. 30. Abbaye de Belle Fontaine, 1979.

Haas, Christopher. *Alexandria in Late Antiquity: Topography and Social Conflict*. Baltimore and London: The Johns Hopkins University Press, 1997.

Hardy, E. R. "The Further Education of Cyril of Alexandria (412–444): Questions and Problems." *Studia Patristica* 17, vol. 1 (1982): 116–22.

Harmless, William. *St. Augustine and the Catechumenate*. Collegeville, MN: Liturgical Press, 1995.

———. *Desert Christians: An Introduction to the Literature of Early Monasticism*. New York: Oxford University Press, 2004.

Hirshman, Marc. *A Rivalry of Genius: Jewish and Christian Biblical Interpretation in Late Antiquity*. Albany, NY: State University of New York Press, 1996.

Hurtado, Larry W. *One God, One Lord: Early Christian Devotion and Ancient Jewish Monotheism*. Edinburgh: T&T Clark, 1998.

Jones, A. H. M. *The Later Roman Empire*. Vol. 2. Baltimore: Johns Hopkins University Press, 1986.

Jouassard, G. "L'activité littéraire de saint Cyrille d'Alexandrie jusqu'à 428: Essai de chronologie et de synthèse," in *Mélanges E. Podechard*. Lyon, 1945.

Kelly, J. N. D. *Golden Mouth: The Story of John Chrysostom, Ascetic, Preacher, Bishop*. Ithaca, NY: Cornell University Press, 1995.

Kennedy, G. *Greek Rhetoric under Christian Emperors*. Princeton: Princeton University Press, 1983.

Kerrigan, Alexander. *St. Cyril of Alexandria: Interpreter of the Old Testament*. Rome, 1952.

Koen, Lars. *The Saving Passio: Incarnational and Soteriological Thought in Cyril of Alexandria's Commentary on the Gospel according to St. John*. Uppsala: Acta Universitatis Upsaliensis, 1991.

Liébaert, J. *La doctrine christologique de Cyrille d'Alexandrie avant la période nestorienne*. Lille, 1951.

———. "Saint Cyrille d'Alexandrie et la culture antique." *Mélanges de Science Religieuse* 12 (1955): 1–21.

Malina, Bruce. *Christian Origins and Cultural Anthropology*. Atlanta: John Knox, 1986.

Malley, W. J. *Hellenism and Christianity: The Conflict between Hellenic and*

*Christian Wisdom in the* Contra Galilaeos *of Julian the Apostate and the* Contra Julianum *of St. Cyril of Alexandria.* Rome, 1978.

Mango, Cyril. *Byzantium: The Empire of New Rome.* New York: Scribner, 1980.

Manoir, Hubert du. *Dogme et Spiritualité chez Saint Cyrille d'Alexandrie.* Paris, 1944.

McGuckin, John A. *St. Cyril of Alexandria: The Christological Controversy: Its History, Theology, and Texts.* Leiden: E. J. Brill, 1994.

————. *Cyril of Alexandria: On the Unity of Christ.* Crestwood, NY: St. Vladimir's Seminary Press, 1995.

McKinion, Steven. *Words, Imagery, and the Mystery of Christ: A Reconstruction of Cyril of Alexandria's Christology.* Leiden and Boston: Brill, 2000.

Meunier, Bernard. *Le Christ de Cyrille d'Alexandrie: L'humanité, le salut et la question monophysite.* Paris: Beauchesne, 1997.

Neusner, Jacob. *Judaism and Christianity in the Age of Constantine: History, Messiah, Israel, and the Initial Confrontation.* Chicago: University of Chicago Press, 1987.

O'Keefe, John J. "Impassible Suffering? Divine Passion and Fifth-Century Christology." *Theological Studies* 58 (1997): 39–60.

————. "'A Letter that Killeth': Toward a Reassessment of Antiochene Exegesis, or Diodore, Theodore, and Theodoret on the Psalms." *Journal of Early Christian Studies* 8, no. 1 (2000): 83–104.

O'Keefe, John J., and R. R. Reno. *Sanctified Vision: An Introduction to Early Christian Interpretation of the Bible.* Baltimore: Johns Hopkins University Press, 2005.

Prestige, G. L. *Fathers and Heretics.* SPCK, 1940.

Quasten, Johannes. *Patrology,* vol. 3. Westminster, MD: Christian Classics, 1986.

Russell, Norman. *Cyril of Alexandria.* The Early Church Fathers. New York: Routledge, 2000.

————. *The Doctrine of Deification in the Greek Patristic Tradition.* Oxford: Oxford University Press, 2004.

Schäublin, Christoph. *Untersuchungen zu Methode und Herkunft der Antiochenischen Exégèse.* Cologne and Bonn: Peter Hanstein, 1974.

Simon, Marcel. *Verus Israel.* Translated by H. McKeating. Oxford, 1986.

Simonetti, Manlio. *Biblical Interpretation in the Early Church: An Historical Introduction to Patristic Exegesis.* Translated by John A. Hughes. Edinburgh: T&T Clark, 1994.

Smith, Jonathan Z. "What A Difference A Difference Makes." In *To See Ourselves as Others See Us.* Edited by Jacob Neusner and Ernest S. Frerichs. Chico, CA: Scholars Press, 1985.

Stark, Rodney. *The Rise of Christianity: A Sociologist Reconsiders History.* Princeton, NJ: Princeton University Press, 1996.

Vaggione, Richard Paul. *Eunomius of Cyzicus and the Nicene Revolution.* Oxford: Oxford University Press, 2000.

Visotzky, Burton. *Fathers of the World: Essays in Rabbinic and Patristic Literatures.* Tübingen: J. C. B. Mohr, 1995.

Wilken, Robert. *John Chrysostom and the Jews: Rhetoric and Reality in the Late 4th Century.* Berkeley: University of California Press, 1983.

———. *Judaism and the Early Christian Mind: A Study of Cyril of Alexandria's Exegesis and Theology.* Reprint of 1971 edition. Eugene, OR: Wipf & Stock, 2004.

Young, Frances. "The Rhetorical Schools and their Influence on Patristic Exegesis." In *The Making of Orthodoxy: Essays in Honour of Henry Chadwick,* edited by Rowan Williams. Cambridge: Cambridge University Press, 1989.

———. *Biblical Exegesis and the Formation of Christian Culture.* Cambridge: Cambridge University Press, 1997.

———. *The Art of Performance: Towards a Theology of Holy Scripture.* London: Darton, Longman and Todd, 1990.

# INTRODUCTION

# INTRODUCTION

## I. The Festal Genre and St. Cyril of Alexandria

When Cyril of Alexandria was consecrated patriarch of Alexandria in A.D. 412, he inherited a style of leadership that was already venerable and old. Reaching back more than two hundred years to the time of Demetrius, the traditions of the Alexandrian see were well established, and the influence of the city's bishop on the affairs of church and empire was rivaled only by the bishops of other patriarchal cities such as Rome, Constantinople, and Antioch. Cyril, then thirty-five years old,[1] having been groomed for this role from his youth, was one of the most powerful men in the Christian Empire. He would continue in this role for the next thirty-two years. These years were, of course, punctuated with the controversies for which many remember him. He allegedly stood by while the philosopher Hypatia was murdered by a Christian mob. He presided over the expulsion of the Jews from the city of Alexandria, and he engineered the condemnation and exile of Nestorius. These, and other incidents that were never reported, prompted many to breathe a sigh of relief when Cyril finally died in A.D. 444. One famous and often-quoted letter sums up this sentiment:

At last with a final struggle the villain has passed away. . . . Observing that his malice increased daily and injured the body of the Church, the Governor of our souls has lopped him off like a canker. . . . His departure delights the survivors but possibly disheartens the dead; there is

---

1. We do not know the exact year of Cyril's birth. P. Évieux suggests that it was between 375 and 380; *Cyrille d'Alexandrie: Lettres Festales I–IV*, Sources Chrétiennes 372, 11. Henceforth all references to the Sources Chrétiennes series will be designated by SC. Évieux, in SC 372, 11–135, has written one of the best introductions to Cyril available in any modern language. References to this introduction will be designated simply as Évieux.

some fear that under the provocation of his company they may send him back again to us. . . . Care must therefore be taken to order the guild of undertakers to place a very big and heavy stone on his grave to stop him coming back here. . . . I am glad and rejoice to see the fellowship of the Church delivered from such a contagion; but I am saddened and sorry as I reflect that the wretched man never took rest from his misdeeds, but died designing greater and worse.[2]

These are strong words, and, although they are likely an exaggeration, they do witness indirectly to the power and impact of the man.

Cyril was a towering figure of enormous influence both theologically and politically. Like those of most patristic theologians, Cyril's theological insights emerged from close readings of the Bible. Seven of the ten volumes devoted to him in Migne's *Patrologia* contain works of exegesis,[3] and all of his writings, indeed his entire theological project, are built upon the backbone of an encyclopedic knowledge of the biblical text. He wrote several important doctrinal treatises, including a major treatise on the Trinity, in which he argued forcefully in defense of Nicene doctrine.[4] He is, of course, most famous for his doctrinal works on Christology, especially his short treatise *That Christ is One* and the letters to Nestorius, which were immortalized in the proceedings of the Councils of Ephesus and Chalcedon. These texts, especially, earned Cyril an honored place in the history of Christian theology.[5]

2. Theodoret, *Ep.* 180, as quoted by G. L. Prestige, *Fathers and Heretics* (SPCK, 1940), 150. Azéma, SC 40, 10, says, "Les lettres à Jean d'Antioche (P.G. 83, col. 1489 et suiv.) sur la mort de saint Cyrille . . . sont certainement apocryphes." Thus classified as of dubious authorship, *Ep.* 180 survives only in Latin.

3. A number of Cyril's commentaries survive. *The Adoration and Worship of God in Spirit and in Truth* and the *Glaphyra*, or "Elegant Comments," deal with excerpted passages from the Pentateuch. We also have his commentaries on Isaiah, the Minor Prophets, John, and Luke. Fragments of commentaries preserved in catenae survive on Kings, Psalms, Proverbs, Song of Songs, Jeremiah, Ezekiel, Daniel, Matthew, Romans, 1 and 2 Corinthians, and Hebrews.

4. Cf. *Dialogues sur la Trinité*, SC 231, 237, 246. He also wrote a major treatise against the emperor Julian, PG 76 and SC 322.

5. See Cyril of Alexandria, *On the Unity of Christ*, trans. John McGuckin (Crestwood, NY: St. Vladimir's Seminary Press, 1995). For the critical edition see *Deux Dialogues Christologiques*, SC 97, and L. Wickham, ed., *Cyril of Alexandria: Select Letters* (Oxford, 1983).

Few students of Cyril, however, would include on a list of critical texts the twenty-nine *Festal Letters* that comprise the contents of the two volumes of which this is the first. Like so many of Cyril's exegetical works, these letters have never been translated into English, and until fairly recently they have never been translated into any modern language at all.[6] As a result, they have been the subject of virtually no published studies or scholarly investigation. This is unfortunate. These letters will not revolutionize scholarly understanding of Cyril's Christology, but they are uniquely able to reveal how Cyril presented his theological ideas pastorally. Twenty-nine in all, they cover, in uninterrupted succession, all but three of Cyril's years as bishop.[7] Because they can be so easily dated, the letters offer scholars a rare opportunity to witness development in one of Christian antiquity's most significant thinkers.

But what exactly are these letters? In brief, Cyril's *Festal Letters* are his own adaptation of an Alexandrian tradition that began during the episcopate of Demetrius (188–230). Bishops Peter (300–311), Alexander (311–328), Athanasius (328–373), and Theophilus (385–412) all continued the practice and developed the genre further.[8] They are a unique literary genre that should not be confused with other forms of writing associated with the Christian paschal celebration, such as Easter sermons or the festal greetings extended from one bishop to another.[9] Festal letters functioned primarily as a vehicle for announcing the beginning of Lent and the proper date for the celebration of Easter. They also served an important catechetical purpose by providing the patriarch with an annual opportunity to present his flock with a pastoral version of the theological issues that found more formal and complex expression elsewhere. Thus Cyril's *Festal Letters* offer the modern reader a glimpse of the issues that Cyril himself

6. The only other modern language translation is the SC edition in French. Currently volumes 372, 392, and 434 have appeared; they contain letters 1–17. This translation uses the SC edition when available.

7. We have no letters for the years 413, 443, or 444.

8. Évieux, 94–106, surveys the development of the festal genre in Cyril's predecessors.

9. Évieux, 94–95. Cf. Johannes Quasten, *Patrology*, vol. 4 (Westminster, MD: Christian Classics, 1986), 553.

considered important enough to proclaim to the entire diocese and a sample of how he prepared these ideas for reception by a less sophisticated audience. Still, the primary purpose of the letters was to announce the date of Easter.

The dating of Easter was a notoriously tricky undertaking in the early church. Theological and astronomical complexities stood in the way of arriving at a common date for the entire church. What exactly did the Christian version of Pascha celebrate? Was it a celebration of Christ's Passover, Christ's Passion, or Christ's Resurrection? Should it coincide with the Jewish celebration of the feast on the fourteenth of the lunar month Nisan, or should it be observed on the following Sunday? All of these questions had to be answered, and a regular rhythm for the Easter celebration had to be created, including Lent and Holy Week itself. Changes in Rabbinic Judaism's method of calculating Passover, as well as disagreements about how to adjust the lunar calendar correctly so that Pascha would remain a spring feast, further ensured that there would be confusion about when to celebrate the Christian holy day.[10] Despite the efforts of the Council of Nicaea to stabilize the date, differences remained throughout the fourth century and beyond.[11] Nevertheless, in general, it appears that the Fathers at Nicaea managed to bring a certain degree of unanimity to the celebration. They also delegated responsibility for calculating Pascha to the church of Alexandria, which was recognized for its expertise in this area. The Bishop was to send the calculations to Rome for further promulgation.[12] The general rule was that Christian Pascha would take place the Sunday following the paschal moon, which was the first full moon following the vernal equinox. The date of the equinox was fixed at March 21, and this date was eventually observed by the whole church. In this role, then, the Alexandrian patriarch had an important responsibility. The festal genre was the

10. According to the Jewish tradition, Pascha falls on 14 Nisan, a lunar date. Since the lunar year is about 11 and ¼ days shorter than the solar year, without correction a lunar month will migrate around the solar year, causing any associated holidays to migrate with it. Such, for example is the case with the Muslim month of Ramadan. Évieux, 74–75.

11. Évieux, 88–92.

12. Ibid., 80–88.

particular form that the patriarchs of Alexandria developed to disseminate the required dates to their home diocese. By the time of Cyril, the genre was well established. Written during the previous autumn, the letters were copied by scribes and sent off to the various churches and monasteries of Egypt to arrive in time for oral presentation on or around the feast of the Epiphany.[13]

Internal evidence suggests that the audience for the letters included monks and other clerics.[14] Cyril, however, also seems to have the laity in mind as well. The letters contain references to farmers and to crop failures;[15] they record concerns about a rise in rural gang violence, and even about a growing problem with piracy on the Nile.[16] The letters are also remarkably human. Cyril writes, seemingly from personal experience, about the need to control one's anger.[17] He seems to appreciate good food, and frequent references to sea travel, to favorable winds, and to the pleasure of pleasant seas suggest that the patriarch personally enjoyed his many voyages.

So then, although the official reason for composing these letters was to publicize the date on which to celebrate Easter, it is quite clear that they served a larger purpose. Indeed, a careful reading reveals to the scholar of patristic literature a number of recurring themes or questions.

How do we read and understand the Bible?

What is the enduring meaning of the Old Testament?

What is the value of the ascetical way of life, especially in the wake of the Origenist crisis?

Why do the Jews continue to prosper?

How are we to understand the significance of the becoming human of the Word of God?

When we consider Cyril's doctrinal corpus it is quite clear that these were questions of deep concern to Cyril the theologian, but when we see them recur year after year in the pages of the *Festal Letters*, we recognize that these were also the very themes

13. Ibid., 108.
14. Ibid., 109–10.
15. Cf. FL 2 and 8.
16. Cf. FL 7 and 8.
17. Cf. FL 11.

and questions that motivated his pastoral agenda and that dominated his thinking throughout his life. In order to understand this agenda a bit better, we would do well to step back for a moment and set it in the context of Cyril's life.

## II. Cyril's Life and the Content of the *Festal Letters*

We know little about the early life of Cyril. He was probably born between 375 and 380 in Theodosiou, about 120 kilometers east of Alexandria. His mother was the sister of the powerful patriarch Theophilus, who quickly took responsibility for young Cyril's education and religious formation. Cyril himself claims to have studied the Scriptures from early childhood,[18] and by the time he was a teen he would have memorized vast quantities of the biblical text. Later in life this early work of memorization would serve him well as he effortlessly connected various parts of the Bible together in a series of massive biblical commentaries. Because Cyril was the nephew of Theophilus, we can reasonably speculate that he could have had contact with the likes of Jerome, Rufinus, and even Didymus the Blind. Cyril would have participated in the exegetical discussions that went on in the circles associated with his uncle. The figure of Origen and his interpretive methods would have been a frequent focus of this conversation until the eruption of the Origenist controversy at the turn of the fifth century and beyond it.

When he was still in his teens, Cyril probably spent as long as five years with the monks in Nitria, where his training in biblical interpretation continued and where he also absorbed the values and practices of the ascetical life. He could easily have met the famed Macarius (d. 394) and even Evagrius of Pontus himself (d. 399). He certainly would have had contact at least with Evagrius's entourage,[19] all of whom were at the time in the good graces of Theophilus. These years in the desert were critical for Cyril's intellectual development. The biblical commentaries, as

18. Évieux, 12.

19. For a discussion of what Palladius calls "the Entourage of Ammonius and Evagrius," see William Harmless, *Desert Christians: An Introduction to the Literature of Early Monasticism* (New York: Oxford University Press, 2004), 314.

well as the *Festal Letters* themselves, are filled with the fruits of this early training.

## A. *Cyril the Exegete*

In his introduction to Cyril's writings, Johannes Quasten offers the following assessment:

[Cyril's] exegetical works form the greater but not the better part of his literary output. His interpretation of the Old Testament is strongly influenced by Alexandrian tradition and therefore highly allegorical though he differs from Origen because of the emphasis with which he insists that not all the details of the Old Testament yield a spiritual signification. His New Testament exegesis is more literal but, nevertheless, betrays a disinclination to the historico-philological approach.[20]

Quasten speaks for many others who believe that the Christian Church would have been better off had Cyril not bothered to write commentaries on the Bible at all. According to this view, Cyril was a good theologian but a poor exegete, and he should have stayed with his strengths.

This is a remarkable thing to say. As noted above, seven of the ten volumes of Migne's *Patrologia* devoted to Cyril contain exegetical works. It is equally astonishing to note how scriptural interpretation provided the basis for everything of significance that Cyril wrote, including his celebrated doctrinal treatises. Quasten's view, sadly, remains widespread even today, although it seems to have begun to wane. Indeed, for decades students of patristic exegesis have distinguished sharply between the historically-minded Antiochenes and the "allegorizing" Alexandrians. The exegetical works of Alexandrian theologians like Cyril have been dismissed because of what was believed to be the "a-historical" nature of their commentary. Fortunately this way of understanding ancient exegesis has been seriously challenged. Not only is it misleading to distinguish rigidly between Antioch and Alexandria, but it is also anachronistic; there was no historical criticism in antiquity, and no ancient exegete approached a text asking questions analogous to those asked by a modern scholar trained in historical criticism. The recognition that all ancient commentary was pre-

20. Johannes Quasten, *Patrology*, vol. 3 (Westminster, MD: Christian Classics, 1984), 119.

modern has prompted a reconsideration of texts previously considered to be nothing more than historical curiosities, including, one might argue, these *Festal Letters*.[21]

The key to understanding the patristic approach to the Bible is the concept of "economy." While modern readers associate this term with the system of goods and services that defines modern life, in Christian theology "economy" is a technical term with no exact English equivalent. Put succinctly, "economy" refers to the entire scope of God's plan for the redemption of the world through Christ. It is a shorthand term that covers everything from creation to apocalypse and the entire saving work of Christ in between. From the point of view of the Fathers, the primary source for detailed knowledge about the economy was the Bible. For them, the economy is the subject of the Bible. This assumption is quite different from that of modern interpreters who tend to think the primary subject matter of the Bible is its historical content, both narrative and theological. Modern readers trained to think in historical-critical categories tend to look to the Bible to provide information about the context that produced it, the ancient theologies it was trying to convey, and the historical knowledge that can be gleaned from its careful study. Ancient readers did not seek these things. One might say that they looked for meaning within the economy of the Christian narrative rather than within the historical economy of modernity.

Although ancient readers assumed that the entire Bible was

---

21. For a complete introduction to patristic interpretation see John J. O'Keefe and R. R. Reno, *Sanctified Vision: An Introduction to Early Christian Interpretation of the Bible* (Baltimore: Johns Hopkins University Press, 2005). For technical discussions of the difference between Antioch and Alexandria, see Christoph Schäublin, *Untersuchungen zu Methode und Herkunft der Antiochenischen Exegese* (Cologne and Bonn: Peter Hanstein, 1974); Frances Young, *Biblical Exegesis and the Formation of Christian Culture* (Cambridge: Cambridge University Press, 1997). See also Young's article "The Rhetorical Schools and their Influence on Patristic Exegesis," in *The Making of Orthodoxy: Essays in Honour of Henry Chadwick*, ed. Rowan Williams (Cambridge, 1989), and my own articles "Impassible Suffering? Divine Passion and Fifth-Century Christology," *Theological Studies* 58 (1997): 39–60, and "'A Letter that Killeth': Toward a Reassessment of Antiochene Exegesis," *Journal of Early Christian Studies* 8 (2000): 83–104. Also noteworthy is David Dawson, *Allegorical Readers and Cultural Revision in Ancient Alexandria* (Berkeley: University of California Press, 1992).

about the economy of Christ, they knew from simple observation that it was not always obviously so. For example, it is not immediately clear how the story of the exodus of the Israelites from slavery in Egypt was relevant to those who would follow Christ. Nor was it immediately clear how the love poetry of the Song of Songs should be interpreted as revelation by the Christian community. In each case, some technique other than a literal reading was required to allow the interpreter to see the "spiritual meaning" of the text and, in so seeing, to understand how that text fit within the larger framework of the Christian economy. The exegetical techniques of typology and allegory were used in such situations to allow the "economic" meaning of the text to emerge. For example, in the story of the Exodus, ancient Christians generally saw the Israelite crossing from slavery to freedom as a "type" of the crossing of the Christian from death in sin to new life in Christ. Similarly, the eroticism characteristic of the Song of Songs became, through the application of allegory, passionate poetry about the soul's relationship to Christ.

Another technique common in patristic interpretation resembles what modern readers might think is a kind of free association. Texts were often chosen because an image or an event triggered the memory of a verse; the original context was unimportant. For example, Cyril in one place in the *Festal Letters* recalls Ps 103.14 (LXX)—"You make grass spring up for the cattle"—and effortlessly deploys it to support a reflection on the coming of spring and God's care for the farmer and the fields.[22] In other words, Cyril and his flock inhabited a world in which the Bible and biblical allusion formed a database of shared memories that could be accessed at will. From their point of view, because the Bible as a whole was about the economy, any part of it could be used to interpret any other part or any experience.

Many modern readers who have been exposed to historical-critical methods recoil at the patristic approach to the Bible. From their point of view, building typologies, spinning allegories, and playing free association word games with the Scriptures may be acceptable in the loosest form of personal reflection, but it hardly qualifies as good interpretation. Without the control of

22. FL 2.3.

history, how can we think of these ancient interpretations as anything but the fanciful whimsy of creative, but nonetheless misguided, readers? The ancients, if given a chance to understand this modern objection, would have responded that the control on their reading was doctrine. The rule of faith, or the basic theological affirmations of the Christian community, rather than an historical timeline, determined the aptness of a particular reading. Concretely, this means that, in Cyril's day, as long as his interpretation did not contradict the theological convictions of the Nicene Creed, it would likely be considered a legitimate interpretation (but not necessarily a good one).

Despite the resistances that these methods evoke, moving past them, at least as a thought experiment, is required if we are to appreciate Cyril's approach to the Bible in these letters. Modern readers encountering this interpretive world for the first time will likely misread Cyril's exegetical style as arbitrary and unsophisticated. Such a reading would be wrong. The networks of biblical allusion that fill the *Festal Letters* are an intertextual reflection on the Christian economy within the limits of Nicene orthodoxy. They are not arbitrary strings of references and proof-texts. Thus in these letters, when Cyril engages in theological reflection on Christ, redemption, or the human condition, he does so as an ancient interpreter steeped in ancient methods of reading. This interpretive world is the frame within which the larger themes of the *Festal Letters* are presented.

### B. Cyril, Politics, and the Origenist Controversy

Biblical interpretation, however, was not all that Cyril learned under the patronage of the powerful Theophilus. It seems that in 399, at the outbreak of the Origenist controversy, Theophilus recalled Cyril to Alexandria.[23] The next few years, like those spent in the desert, would also prove to be critical as the future patriarch was inducted into the political machinery of the Alexandrian see. The first crisis to which Cyril was a witness erupted after his uncle published his own festal letter for 399. In it, he attacked a group of monks, dubbed "anthropomorphites," who were in the habit of imagining that God possessed human fea-

23. Évieux, 20–29.

tures and human form. These monks tended to be less educated and more literal-minded in their approach to the Bible, but they were also numerous and politically powerful. Apparently they reacted violently against Theophilus's letter and accused the patriarch of Origenism.[24] This in turn set off a chain of events that forced Theophilus to condemn Origen, to turn his back on former friends who were admirers of Origen, to deny his own attachment to Origenist ideas, and eventually, in 403, to engineer the condemnation of John Chrysostom at the infamous "Synod of the Oak."[25] Cyril, who accompanied his uncle to the synod, may have been personally involved in the decisions leading to the condemnation itself.

Several things are noteworthy here. First, it is quite clear that Theophilus was fighting a political battle and that his rejection of Origenist ideas was motivated by his desire to survive politically; he needed to placate the anthropomorphite monks. It also seems that he used the controversy as an opportunity to enhance his own power in the empire by causing the humiliation of his rival in Constantinople, John Chrysostom. Theophilus's political motivations seem even clearer when we note that Origenist thought continued to influence his writing even after the controversy had begun to wane. Still, it would be a mistake to reduce all Theophilus's motives to the level of politics.

Elizabeth Clark, in her study of Origenism, has argued that significant theological disagreements ran to the heart of the Origenist debate. In particular, Theophilus and his entourage especially resisted Origenist tendencies to denigrate reproduction and to spiritualize resurrection.[26] The key player in all of this was not Origen himself, but the monk Evagrius of Pontus (d. 399). It would be difficult to exaggerate the impact that Evagrius had not only on the desert circles in which he operated, but also on the subsequent development of Christian monasticism and Christian spirituality. On one level the popularity of Evagri-

24. Ibid., 22–23.
25. See J. N. D. Kelly, *Golden Mouth: The Story of John Chrysostom, Ascetic, Preacher, Bishop* (Ithaca, NY: Cornell University Press, 1995), 218–27.
26. Elizabeth Clark, *The Origenist Controversy: The Cultural Construction of an Early Christian Debate* (Princeton, NJ: Princeton University Press, 1992), 116–17.

us's teaching can be traced to its practical application. He developed a method by which the aspiring ascetic could work toward *apatheia,* or "freedom from passions." *Apatheia* is often explained as a Christian appropriation of Stoic detachment that resembles Buddhist freedom from craving. Some modern interpreters of this tradition, however, suggest that "freedom to love" better captures the spirit of this ambition.[27] Evagrius's *Praktikos* is especially powerful both in its insight into the human problem and in its ability to offer a cure. Consider, for example, this masterful description of *acedia,* "the noonday demon":

> The demon of *acedia*—also called the noonday demon—is the one that causes the most serious trouble of all. He presses his attack upon the monk about the fourth hour and besieges the soul until the eighth hour. First of all he makes it seem that the sun barely moves, if at all, and that the day is fifty hours long. Then he constrains the monk to look constantly out the windows, to walk outside the cell, to gaze carefully at the sun to determine how far it stands from the ninth hour, to look this way and now that to see if perhaps one of the brethren appears from his cell. Then too he instills in the heart of the monk a hatred for the place, a hatred for his very life itself, a hatred for manual labor . . .[28]

It was not this more ascetical side of Evagrius that caused problems. Rather, Cyril, his uncle, and other anti-Origenists were far more concerned with Evagrius's adaptations of the speculative and cosmological dimensions of Origen's thought, especially in those areas dealing with the pre-existence of souls and the ultimate superfluity of human bodily life. Anti-Origenists, influenced by a more literal reading of Genesis and Revelation, insisted not only that the human was a single creation of God, body and soul, but also that the body, with all its parts, had to have a place in the heavenly Jerusalem. Cyril's own Christology—with its strong emphasis on the reality of Christ's bodily life and its insistence on the actual fact of the Word's Incarnation—was refined in this context. In other words, there were serious theological issues involved, but they were unavoidably bound up with the politics of the early fifth century.

27. Harmless, *Desert Christians,* 348.

28. John Eudes Bamberger, ed. and trans., *The Praktikos & Chapters On Prayer* (Kalamazoo: Cistercian Studies, 1981), 18–19. See the discussion in Harmless, *Desert Christians,* 324–27.

For our purposes here, we need only note that traces of these years of controversy have found their way into the pages of the *Festal Letters*. The letters clearly contain an ascetical agenda. There are frequent references to the value of fasting, to the goal of passionlessness, and to the transforming possibilities associated with monastic discipline. Of course, the pre-Lenten context of the letters easily explains the prominence of these themes. It is significant, however, that Cyril avoided any language implying that the body, in the end, did not participate in a real resurrection, and that he displays no interest in the possible cosmological implications of these ascetical ideas. Such speculation was precisely the problem that caused Origenist thinkers so much difficulty and that worried men like Cyril.[29] In the *Festal Letters* the context of the ascetical language is Lenten, but the form of the language stems from the Origenist controversy. Consider the following example from the letter for 427, which is typical.

In the early part of *Letter* 15, just after the opening greeting, Cyril launches into an unusual reading of Nm 10.9–10:[30]

And if you shall go forth to war in your land against your enemies that are opposed to you, and you sound the trumpets, you will be had in remembrance before the Lord, and you will be saved from your enemies. And in the days of your gladness, and on your feasts, and on your new moons, you shall sound the trumpets at your holocausts and at the sacrifices of your altars, and there shall be a remembrance for you before your God. I am the Lord your God.

On the one hand, the text is chosen because the references to festivals and trumpets connect it to the festal topic of the letters. On the other, Cyril selects it to advance a point about the ascetical life.

These words, he explains, are a "type" of future things. He then gives a history lesson and explains that the Jews were constantly threatened by external enemies. In contrast, he then cites

29. Cf. Luke Dysinger, *Psalmody and Prayer in the Writings of Evagrius Ponticus* (New York: Oxford University Press, 2005), 1–47, and Harmless, *Desert Christians*, 359–63.

30. The liturgical use of the image of the "trumpet blast" to mark the beginning of Lent seems to have been widespread in the ancient Church. See the discussion of William Harmless, *Augustine and the Catechumenate* (Collegeville, MN: Liturgical Press, 1995), 94–95; 251–60.

2 Cor 10.4 to explain that "the weapons of our warfare are not carnal"[31] and claims that this text must, in a Christian context, point to our battle with the passions of the flesh. The "trumpet" calls us to the spiritual battle of the season. This image brings to mind a passage from Joel: "Sanctify a war, rouse the fighters, advance and go up, all you men of war; beat your plowshares into swords, and your sickles into spears. Let the weak say: I am strong."[32] Cyril says we could read this literally as a command to turn our farm equipment into weapons and head to battle, but, he says, this is not the best reading. Since, according to Paul, our relationship to the Law is one of having been "justified in Christ" and "sanctified in the Spirit,"[33] we must set this text from Joel, and the other from Numbers, in the context of both the Christian battle against the passions and the pursuit of virtue. We, like the warriors in Joel, are perfectly equipped for our battle. As proof he quotes Eph 6.14–17, with its references to "loins girt with truth," (v. 14), "the breastplate of justice" (v. 14), "the shield of faith" (v. 16), and "the sword of the Spirit" (v. 17). So equipped, the Christian can enter the battle of Lent.

While one could easily add more examples, this one sufficiently illustrates the influence of ascetical ideas on Cyril's thought. The monastic worldview was becoming a standard that many, including Cyril, were beginning to present, in an adapted form, as the Christian way of life *par excellence*. Clearly, the very forces that were causing the great explosion of monastic life at this time heavily influenced the young Cyril. Other forces, however, were also afoot, and they, too, left their mark on the *Festal Letters*.

### C. Cyril, Egypt, the Old Testament, and the Jews

Let us return, then, to the environment in which Cyril came of age both as a young Christian cleric and as bishop. We have already seen how the traces of the monastic life and the anti-Origenist agenda impacted the *Festal Letters*. I will now briefly

31. Translations of biblical passages as quoted by Cyril are original throughout this volume, but were prepared in consultation with the RSV.

32. Jl 3.9–10.

33. Gal 2.17; Rom 15.16.

consider two other realities that characterized Alexandria in the early fifth century and that influenced the content of our text, namely, the continued presence of pagans and Jews. A great deal of Christian energy in the years following the conversion of the emperor Constantine went toward the elimination of tradition-al religion. This process was slow in all regions of the empire, and the former religious practices proved to be tenacious. Egypt was no exception. In a study of religion in Roman Egypt, David Frankfurter has demonstrated exactly how slow this process was and how Christian devotion and practice overlapped with an-cient forms for centuries.[34] Cyril continued policies put in place by his uncle that were designed to weaken and destroy these an-cient forms.

It is, of course, this aspect of Cyril's legacy that many modern readers find extremely troubling. The church historian Socrates reports a notorious mob attack that resulted in the death of the pagan philosopher Hypatia.[35] As one modern commentator ex-plains, we do not know if Cyril was the direct instigator, but the results were horrific:

On that fateful day, Hypatia was riding grandly through the city. . . . She was pulled from her carriage. . . . After dragging her through the streets, the enraged mob tortured her in the Great Church of the Cae-sarion—the former temple of the imperial cult and the site of the pa-gan riots of 356. Her mangled body was then taken to another location where it was burnt on a pyre of brushwood. The manner of her death suggests that her attackers viewed her as a disruptive element in the city's recently established structure of authority which revolved around the prefect and the patriarch.[36]

Socrates also mentions a string of other outrages, including the expulsion of Jews from the city of Alexandria, and a riot of out-

---

34. David Frankfurter, *Religion in Roman Egypt: Assimilation and Resistance* (Princeton, NJ: Princeton University Press, 1998).

35. Socrates, *H.E.* 7.15. E. R. Hardy, "The Further Education of Cyril of Al-exandria," *Studia Patristica* 17, 1 (1982): 117, says that this incident probably took place in 415. For Cyril's attitude toward Greek wisdom, see W. J. Malley, *Hellenism and Christianity: The Conflict between Hellenic and Christian Wisdom in the* Contra Galilaeos *of Julian the Apostate and the* Contra Julianum *of St. Cyril of Alex-andria* (Rome, 1978), 399–417.

36. Christopher Haas, *Alexandria in Late Antiquity: Topography and Social Con-flict* (Baltimore and London: The Johns Hopkins University Press, 1997), 313.

raged monks against the imperial prefect, Orestes. Cyril's relationship with the prefect was strained, to say the least.[37] These
incidents may have resulted in an imperial edict of 416 "which
reduced the number of *parabalani,* the guild of orderlies who
could serve as an ecclesiastical militia, to 400 and transferred
appointment from the bishop to the prefect." Two years later
the number was increased again and control restored to the
bishop.[38] One contemporary student of Cyril suggests that "to
this [early] period belongs the translation of the bones of Saints
Cyrus and John to the ancient seat of Isis at Menouthis."[39] An
angel, it is said, prompted Cyril in a dream to transfer the remains of the two saints from Alexandria to the Shrine of the
Holy Evangelists, which had been dedicated by Theophilus at
that site in an effort to assert Christian dominance. The power of the saints was intended to counteract the influence of
the idols and demons of that place.[40] The success of uncle and
nephew must have been mixed because years later, Zacharias
of Mitylene, writing of Alexandria at the end of the fifth century, describes a secret temple at Menouthis, "a building covered with hieroglyphs and housing a huge assortment of idols
of dogs, cats, and monkeys in wood, bronze, and stone."[41]

Yet, despite this clear evidence of conflict between pagans and
Christians, the *Festal Letters* show little of it. We could mention *Festal Letter* 6 for 418, where there is a long refutation of Greek no-
tions of chance and fate, a common topic in the Fathers. We
might also note scattered references to the shedding of idola-
trous practices, such as we find in *Festal Letter* 11.4, but, in general, Cyril did not devote much attention in the *Festal Letters* to lingering pagan practices. Although Frankfurter argues convincingly
that overlap between traditional and Christian religious practices
continued into the late fifth century, Haas may also be correct
when he notes that paganism in Alexandria had suffered a crush-

---

37. Socrates, *H.E.* 7.13–16.          38. Hardy, "Education," 117.
39. Wickham, *Letters,* 17.
40. Sophronius, *Laudes in SS. Cyrum et Joannem,* PG 87: 3411–13.
41. As quoted by A. H. M. Jones, *The Later Roman Empire,* vol. 2 (Baltimore:
Johns Hopkins University Press, 1986), 941. Zacharias, of course, wrote after
Cyril's death. The example is intended to demonstrate the tenacity of pagan
worship in Egypt.

ing blow in 391 and that in Cyril's day "the Jewish community was the only major group remaining in the city that challenged the complete hegemony of the church and its patriarch."[42]

The *Festal Letters* seem to support such a view. Indeed, one of the most striking—and troubling—aspects of the twenty-nine letters is the constant stream of anti-Jewish rhetoric. Cyril was preoccupied with the Jews and profoundly concerned about their continued existence. The worst comments appear in the letters composed during the early years of Cyril's episcopacy when, we know from other sources, he was involved in a bitter struggle with Alexandria's Jewish community, which resulted in the expulsion of a significant number of Jews from the city of Alexandria.[43] The anti-Jewish language permeates all the letters, and it always leads to the same conclusion: the Jews, by hardening their hearts, have failed to recognize that Jesus has offered them the key to understanding the promises of God hidden in the Law as types and shadows. Consider the following example.

For the mentality of the Jews is really quite full of every uncleanness, nor is there any wickedness which is not held by them in high esteem. They do not want to know the divine Law, and they even reject the commandment given them, and so they continue disobedient and unbelieving. It is for these reasons that God accuses them, crying out through the prophet, "To whom shall I speak and make my declaration? Who will listen? Behold, their ears are uncircumcised, and they cannot hear; behold, the word of the Lord has become a reproach for them, and they wish to hear none of it."[44]

It is easy to add to this a litany of citations reflecting Cyril's conviction that the Jewish people have absolutely failed to follow God and have therefore been left behind. The Jews "ignored the prophets" (FL 1). They cling to worship in type (FL 2). They have betrayed the call of Abraham (FL 3). They cling to a literal interpretation of circumcision, not recognizing that it refers to the eschatological circumcision of the heart on the eighth and

42. David Frankfurter, *Religion in Roman Egypt: Assimilation and Resistance* (Princeton: Princeton University Press, 1998), 15–36. See also Haas, 126. Readers interested in a detailed discussion of the Jewish community in ancient Alexandria should consult Haas, 91–127.

43. Haas, 303–9.

44. FL 1.5.

last day (FL 6). The prophets knew of the Incarnation in advance, but the Jews hardened their hearts (FL 18). The Law is but a shadowy anticipation of the evangelical way of life (FL 20). The Jews falsely imagine themselves to be the guardians of the Law (FL 21). The Old Covenant brought nothing to completion and has been abrogated (FL 22). The message is clear enough. According to Cyril, the Jews had not just failed to understand their own books, but they had failed utterly and completely. Such language can only indicate a deep and long-standing tension between the Christian and Jewish communities in Alexandria.

The presence of this language requires explanation. One approach is to understand Cyril's anti-Jewish language in the context of his wider effort to read the Old Testament as Christian Scripture. More than thirty years ago Robert Wilken noted that two New Testament passages captivated Cyril's theological imagination.[45] The first was Mt 5.17–18: "Do not think that I have come to abolish the law or the prophets; I have come not to abolish but to fulfill. For truly I tell you, until heaven and earth pass away, not one letter, not one stroke of a letter, will pass from the law until all is accomplished." The second text was Jn 4.23–24: "But the hour is coming, and is now here, when the true worshipers will worship the Father in spirit and truth, for the Father seeks such as these to worship him. God is spirit, and those who worship him must worship him in spirit and truth." According to Wilken, the collision between Cyril and ancient Jews makes sense only if we keep these texts in mind: the tension with the Jewish community follows from unresolved questions about the relationship between Church and Synagogue that first emerge in the New Testament. Fundamentally the question is this: why do the Jews still exist in Christian times?

Exactly the same issue, of course, comes up in Romans 9–11; these chapters could be added to any list of Cyril's favorite passages.[46] From Cyril's point of view, if Matthew 5 and Romans

45. Robert Wilken, *Judaism and the Early Christian Mind: A Study of Cyril of Alexandria's Exegesis and Theology* (reprint of 1971 edition: Eugene, OR: Wipf & Stock, 2004), 69 ff.

46. It is worth noting that in Cyril's time the Christian Church had largely forgotten that Paul's theology of gentile inclusion was written by a Jew and for Jews.

9–11 raise the question, then John 4 offers a solution: the Law is fulfilled "in spirit," not "in letter." Moreover, the notion of worship in Spirit and in truth is, for Cyril, further controlled by the ideas of Hebrews 8–10, which speak of the Law as a shadow of things to come. Throughout the *Festal Letters* there are clear links between the ideas about the endurance of the Law in Matthew 5 and Romans 9–11, the Johannine notion of worship in spirit and in truth, and the ideas in the Epistle to the Hebrews about the replacement of the old with the new. As noted above, for Cyril theological problems were biblical problems and should be solved biblically. A problem evoked by one text could always be resolved in the light of another text. As he understood it, the Law had not passed away (Matthew's and Paul's problem), but it was being fulfilled and honored now purely and faithfully by the Christian community (John's solution). From this point of view, the presence of anti-Jewish language can be explained, at least in part, by referencing Christianity's efforts to make sense of its own texts in the presence of a Jewish community that remained influential.

A second reason for the extreme rhetoric is more cultural than theological. For several decades New Testament scholars who have applied social-scientific models to biblical texts point to linguistic markers used by ancient authors to differentiate clearly one group from another, especially groups that overlap a great deal.[47] Scholars have become increasingly aware that the years after the peace of Constantine were critical for the emergence of orthodox Christianity and for early rabbinic Judaism. Some scholars even suggest that the fourth century is really the first in which we can speak clearly about two different religions.[48] Christians and Jews were engaged in a battle over the legacy of the past, indeed, over the Bible itself. They were, in a way, close cousins engaged in a blood feud. We should also re-

47. For example, Bruce Malina, *Christian Origins and Cultural Anthropology* (Atlanta: John Knox, 1986). See also Jonathan Z. Smith, "What A Difference A Difference Makes," in *To See Ourselves as Others See Us*, ed. Jacob Neusner and Ernest S. Frerichs (Chico, CA: Scholars Press, 1985).

48. See the discussion of this in Boyarin, *Dying for God: Martyrdom and the Making of Christianity and Judaism* (Stanford: Stanford University Press, 1999), 2–21.

member that at the turn of the fifth century Christians had only recently come to outnumber Jews in the general population.[49] In the middle of the fourth century Christians in Antioch still seem to have felt connected enough to the Jewish community that they occasionally worshiped in the synagogue. John Chrysostom preached a series of homilies against such Christians,[50] and Cyril himself may have faced a similar situation.[51] Indeed, the *Festal Letters* presume a familiarity with Jewish practices and with Jewish readings of the Bible.

We also need to remember that under Theodosius II the empire itself was moving steadily in the direction of religious uniformity and greater intolerance for diverse religious practice. "Violence against Jewish citizens and their property was on the rise in the early fifth century, [and] frequent reiteration of imperial laws prohibiting these assaults betrays the ineffectiveness of legislation designed to protect the Jews."[52] Yet, at the same time, the empire was gradually working to exclude Jews from participation in public life.[53] Some scholars believe that the legislation of 418 was a turning point for Jews within the empire. We have clear evidence that violence between Christians and Jews was on the rise in Alexandria, especially in the years 414–

49. Rodney Stark, *The Rise of Christianity: A Sociologist Reconsiders History* (Princeton, NJ: Princeton University Press, 1996), 49–71.

50. The best study of the sermons is Robert Wilken, *John Chrysostom and the Jews: Rhetoric and Reality in the Late 4th Century* (Berkeley: University of California Press, 1983).

51. In his commentary on Malachi, Cyril asks, "Since it is possible to bear fruit spiritually in the church of Christ, what reason could there be for wanting to be in communion with profane synagogues?" P. E. Pusey, ed., *Sancti Patris Nostri Cyrilli Archiepiscopi Alexandrini: In XII Prophetas,* vol. 2, 584, 20–23. See also the similar language in the *Commentary on Isaiah,* PG 70: 36B–C.

52. Kenneth Snyder, "For the Salvation of Souls or Personal Gain? Examining Motives for Anti-Jewish Violence in the Early Fifth Century" (unpublished paper, 2001), 3. Laws against physical attacks on synagogues begin in the last decade of the fourth century and are frequently repeated in the fifth century. *Cod. Theod.,* 16.8.9 (393, Theodosius); 16.8.12 (397, Arcadius); 8.8.8 or 2.8.26 (412, Honorius); 16.8.20 (412, Honorius); 16.8.21 (420, Theodosius II); 16.8.25, 26 (423, Theodosius II).

53. Laws against Jews holding civil or military offices are in *Cod. Theod.* 16.8.16 (404); *Cod. Theod.* 16.8.24 (418); *Sirm. Const.* 6 (425); *Nov. Theod.* 3.2 (438).

415, when a series of riots between the two groups resulted in injury and death. Eventually some of the Jews were expelled from the city altogether.[54] This did not destroy the Jewish community in Alexandria, but it did weaken it significantly.[55]

While the strength of the rhetoric may incline us to label the *Festal Letters* as anti-Semitic, this would be an overstatement. Cyril's language is anti-Jewish, but not yet anti-Semitic. We need first to remember that the term "anti-Semitic" carries with it the memory of centuries of Christian abuse of the Jews that culminated in the genocide of the Holocaust of the mid-twentieth century. In the first decades of the fifth century these events had yet to occur. We should also remember that at the turn of the fifth century, there was much less distance religiously between Jews and Christians than there would be even at the beginning of the sixth. Moreover, the "rhetoric of abuse" was a part of the cultural world that Cyril inhabited.[56] Good speakers were expected to insult their enemies, and Christian rhetoricians regularly used this classical technique against other Christians with whom they disagreed. Although Cyril may not have always been motivated by Christian charity, he was at least a man of his age. Cyril's "anti-Judaism" should, therefore, be read in the context of emerging imperial Christianity in the fifth century and its quest to dominate public life and classical culture.[57] This culture would eventually contribute to the rise of modern anti-Semitism, but in the fifth century that darkness had yet to emerge.

Given this information, it becomes easier to understand why Cyril was so preoccupied with the Jews: he perceived them as both a political and a religious threat. We can also understand why texts like Matthew 5 and Romans 9–11 raised such an urgent question and why these particular texts rose to such prominence within the intertextual matrix of his thought. Cyril found the answer to the question in the confluence of John 4 and Hebrews 8. The Church, not the Jews, possessed true worship. The Christians, not the Jews, were the legitimate heirs to the promis-

---

54. Haas, 303–7.      55. Ibid. 304.

56. Wilken, *John Chrysostom and the Jews*, 123–27.

57. See Averil Cameron, *Christianity and the Rhetoric of Empire: The Development of Christian Discourse* (Berkeley: University of California Press, 1991).

es God made to Abraham.[58] We could say, then, that denuncia-
tion of the Jews was one way in which Cyril used the *Festal Letters*
to assert Christian ownership of the Old Testament and to affirm
Christian dominance over a Jewish community that was still
strong and vibrant.

Yet, if we focus our attention only on the negative aspects of
the anti-Jewish rhetoric of these letters and fail to take into account the theological and cultural circumstances just described,
it will be difficult to perceive the pastoral lessons that are embedded in these tensions. In these letters Cyril used his skills as an
interpreter to offer Christian readings of key texts that may have
been confusing to his flock. Beyond the rhetoric, the *Festal Letters* show us what Cyril thought average Christians needed to
know about the meaning of the Bible. Two examples will help to
illustrate Cyril's mindset.

Standing in a long line of interpreters reaching back through
Origen to Paul and Philo, Cyril offers a reading of Genesis 22,
which contains the story of the sacrifice of Isaac.[59] The pre-
sumed question is what this text—so markedly about the destiny
of the Jews—has to do with the Church. To answer it, Cyril must
use all his skills as an interpreter. He begins by retelling the story of Abraham and Sarah's sterility and how Abraham had sexual relations with Hagar. (Reflecting his monastic formation, he
notes that Abraham, virtuous man that he was, did not enjoy this
sexual encounter.) He describes the birth of Ishmael and then
finally the begetting and birth of Abraham's legitimate son,
Isaac. Cyril then turns to Gal 4.22–26 and, with Paul, reminds
his hearers that the present Jerusalem is the Jews and that the
Church has inherited the promise through Isaac. The next step
is to show how Isaac was also a type of Christ himself.

Cyril begins by focusing on God's words to Abraham in Gn
17.16: "I will bless her," God said of Sarah, "and give you a son of
her, and I will bless him, and he shall become nations, and kings
of nations shall come from him." Since, Cyril argues, the Jews

58. See the classic study by Marcel Simon, *Verus Israel: A Study of the Relations
between Christians and Jews in the Roman Empire,* trans. H. McKeating (Oxford,
1986).

59. Cf. SC 372, 315, n. 2; 317, n. 1. The following summary is of FL 5.3–7.

are but one nation, and since the promises of God must be fulfilled, the only way to understand the promise that Isaac will be "nations" is in the light of Jer 38.31: "Behold, the days are coming, says the Lord, when I will make a new covenant with the house of Israel, and with the house of Judah." This in turn is read in the light of Heb 8.13: ". . . what is becoming obsolete and growing old is ready to vanish away." The promises of God to Abraham and Sarah through Isaac are fulfilled only in the new covenant of Christ, which, says Cyril, returning to Paul, is accessible only through faith rather than blood inheritance.

Since the promise points to Christ, Cyril reintroduces Isaac himself to examine the way in which we can now, in the illuminating light of the New Covenant, understand the spiritual meaning of the sacrifice of Isaac. Perhaps, if they listen to this, Cyril suggests, the Jews may yet be moved to obey the Law. Cyril explains that Abraham's taking his "beloved son" is a reminder of the sacrifice of the Father for us and for the world. The boy being offered by his father symbolizes the truth that Jesus was offered by the will of the Father, not by human power, confirming what Jesus said to Pilate in Jn 19.11: "You would have no power over me, if it had not been given you from above." Isaac does not speak against Abraham just as Jesus "humbled himself" before the Father (Phil 2.8). When the story speaks of Abraham leaving behind the two young men (Gn 22.5), the text is hinting at those who are not yet ready for the wisdom of Holy Baptism and must remain behind under the tutelage of the catechism. The wood of the holocaust is the wood of the cross. Cyril concludes with a Christological insight: the ram who was killed instead of Isaac shows that the Lord himself did not suffer because he was passionless, even though he made the body's sufferings his own.

The second example is taken from *Letter* 30, written near the end of Cyril's life. Though not as detailed and carefully constructed as the interpretation of the sacrifice of Isaac, it does show that even at the end of his career Cyril was still worried about issues of biblical relevance. Here, as he does frequently in the letters, he opens by reminding his hearers that the foundation for the Pascha is to be found in the commands of the Old Testament itself. This time he quotes Ps 81.4–5: "Blow the trumpet at the new moon on the fortunate day of our festival, for it is a statute of Israel and an ordinance by the God of Jacob." This reminds him, in keeping with his exegetical training, of Ps 118.27: "The Lord is God and he has shone upon us. Join a festival with shady branches up to the horns of the altar." This, in turn, evokes a question: "What does [the psalmist] mean by 'shady branches up to the horns of the altar'?" Cyril answers that this is a reference to the tabernacle. He explains that the ancient tabernacle had two parts. In one, worship in types and shadows was carried on through animal sacrifices. The second, inner tabernacle was for prayer and was separated by a veil; it was called "the Holy of Holies." "There the altar was a type of Christ, with cherubim shading it with their wings." Cyril then invokes Hebrews 9 and explains that only the high priest could enter the inner tabernacle once a year because it had not yet been thrown open by Christ. The outer worship was to continue as long as the inner tabernacle remained veiled. Since Christ has removed the veil, the first sacrifice is no longer necessary; we can finally fulfill the promises of the psalm and "rush into the Holy of Holies" with "shady branches" like the Cherubim and offer the bloodless sacrifice of the Eucharist and the spiritual sacrifice of moral purity.

Clearly, dealing with the Jews and offering instruction in how to read the Bible correctly were two of Cyril's major concerns as he set out each year to compose a new festal letter. The former occupied his attention especially in the earlier years of his episcopate, but both issues, which are present in all twenty-nine letters, worried him throughout his life.

## D. "That Christ is One"

Let us return one final time to the context of these letters. Cyril is, of course, most celebrated in the Christian tradition for his contribution to the articulation of Christological orthodoxy. His most significant work in this area came after his conflict with Nestorius began in 428, and it was immortalized in the councils of Ephesus (431) and Chalcedon (451). Yet, if we take 375 as the year of Cyril's birth, he was already 53 years old when the so-called "Christological controversy" began. Cyril was certainly interested in Christology long before 428, and dating his treatises is notoriously tricky.[60] Significantly, Cyril's earliest doctrinal tracts were conceived as expositions of the issues of Nicaea. Arianism of the Eunomian variety still seems to have been an issue for him, and dealing with these heresies seems to have been a part of his intellectual formation.[61] This is hardly surprising, since in the early years of the Christological controversy bishop theologians were slow to recognize that these issues were distinct from those of Nicaea and that some doctrinal formulation beyond that of Nicaea would be necessary to begin to resolve them. We know, then, that Cyril was interested in Christology long before he had wranglings with Nestorius. We also know that before 428 his Christology was immature, when considered against the language of Chalcedon. Do the *Festal Letters* offer any insight into the evolution of Cyril's Christological thought? The answer is yes.

The letters are, of course, not doctrinal tracts, nor are they particularly sophisticated theologically. They do, however, have the advantage of being easy to date and, because they are occasioned by Easter, they all must deal explicitly with Christ and the impact of Christ. What we can see, if we read carefully, is that the essence of the Christology that Cyril brought to the Council of Ephesus in 431 was already present in his thinking at the very beginning of his episcopacy. With remarkable consistency, during the thirty years they cover, Cyril relied upon the same set of texts whenever he wrote about Christ, namely, Jn 1.14, the Epistle to the Hebrews (especially Heb 1.3), and Phil 2.14–17.[62] The basic contours of Cyril's Christology follow the same pattern as that established by Athanasius and are determined by his soteriological vision. Christ is the Son of God, the second person of the Trinity, understood in a thoroughly Nicene framework. By a

60. For discussions of the dating of Cyril's work, see G. Jouassard, "L'activité littéraire de saint Cyrille d'Alexandrie jusqu'à 428: Essai de chronologie et de synthèse," in *Mélanges E. Podechard* (Lyon, 1945): 172–78, and Wickham, *Letters*, xvii–xviii.

61. See *Letter* 8, n. 10. Cf. Norman Russell, *Cyril of Alexandria* (New York: Routledge, 2000), 21–23.

62. For a thorough discussion of how these texts functioned in the Christological controversy, see John J. O'Keefe, "Impassible Suffering? Divine Passion and Fifth-Century Christology," *Theological Studies* 58 (1997): 46–52.

selfless act of self-emptying (*kenosis*) and out of deep love for humanity (*philanthropia*), the Son descended, became incarnate of the Virgin Mary, and, by his death and resurrection, delivered humanity from corruption to incorruption. The critical text is Philippians 2 with its Pauline notion of *kenosis*. Cyril insisted that in Jesus the believer encountered none other than the second person of the Trinity himself. In the *Festal Letters* we can see that Cyril adheres to this pattern throughout his life. The letters, however, generally avoid using the more complex language that would characterize the Christological debates after 428. This suggests that Cyril wished to ensure that the content of the letters would remain accessible to a wider audience.

Here are a few examples. In his fourth letter (416), after a long discussion of the failure and disobedience of the Jews, Cyril finally arrives at the point in the letter where he characteristically sums up Christian teaching about the Incarnation. To press his point, Cyril relies upon the juxtaposition of Philippians 2, Hebrews 1, and John 1:

The Only-Begotten Word of God came to stay, therefore, he who is the exact impress of the Father's substance [Heb 1.3], who put on our likeness [Phil 2.7] and, having become a human being, "appeared on earth and lived among human beings" [Bar 3.37], as one of the wise has said. Seeing human nature running toward complete destruction and unable to accomplish anything good . . . he called everyone to salvation. . . . But since, as holy Scripture says, "it was not possible for him to be held" [Acts 2.24] by death, he rose again on the third day. . . . He also destroyed the power of death, having placed in us the Holy Spirit as our earnest of future hope, the pledge of the good things we expect. . . . For he stayed among us that he might make the human being a citizen of heaven. . . .[63]

This is the Christological vision that stayed with Cyril all his life; it was already present in 416. There is much that is not clear, and linguistic precision has yet to emerge, but the key themes and texts were already in place.

If we step ahead a few years to *Letter* 8 (dated to 420) we note a similar pattern. Sections five and six of the letter contain a sustained Christological lesson addressed to some unnamed heretics who deny the Christian claim that Jesus, who had lived so re-

63. FL 4.6.

cently, was the same as the Son of God who is eternal. Cyril responds with a reflection on the Incarnation that relies upon the intersection of the key texts already identified. He explains that the Word of God is the very one who is present in the world through the Incarnation. In support he alludes to the Epistle to the Hebrews: "Jesus Christ is the same yesterday, today, and forever."[64] The Word is joined to a complete humanity in an "inseparable and ineffable unity," and his flesh is his very own flesh. The union is so close that we divide the Word from his flesh only in our thoughts. This is what John meant when he said, "The Word became flesh." Likewise, Paul, in Philippians 2, tells us we should worship Jesus. He indeed is the one who opened up heaven for us. Cyril then finishes the letter with a standard doxological reflection on the results of the Incarnation. Here the key themes and texts that we observed in the earlier letter are present again.

Seven years later, while composing *Letter* 15 (427), Cyril was still thinking along the same lines. Beginning with a standard summary of the issues associated with Trinitarian orthodoxy, Cyril moves on to a discussion of Incarnation. The first text cited is from Philippians 2:

Accordingly, the one who is very distinguished indeed by the dignities of God the Father, through whom all things were brought into being, "did not consider being equal to God a thing to be clung to," according to the Scriptures, "but emptied himself, taking the nature of a slave, being made like us, and appearing in the form of a man, he humbled himself, becoming obedient unto death, even death on a cross."[65]

Cyril goes on to explain that the Word was not harmed or diminished by this *kenosis*. Instead, our human nature was transformed and redeemed. He acknowledges that this notion stretches the human ability to comprehend, and that it appears to assault the dignity of the godhead. He says he knows that even for the sake of *philanthropia*, the Incarnation seems to go too far. Then, as if responding to his critics, he writes: "It is certainly a demeaning thing for him to have become like us, but that is what *kenosis* means." In the end, he argues, it would have been less dignified of God not to intervene, for without that intervention, we would

---

64. Heb 13.8.                    65. FL 15.3.

remain lost. Here again the theme of Philippians 2, Hebrews, and John 1 continues to control Cyril's Christological thinking.

I draw a final example from *Letter* 17 of 429.[66] This letter shows clear evidence that the Christological controversies had begun. Even though there are refinements and new claims, however, the central elements and controlling texts remain constant. Cyril moves to the topic of the Incarnation directly from a discussion of the absolute impossibility of having virtue and vice coexist. Citing Dt 22.10–11, "You shall not plow with an ox and ass together," he urges his listeners not to mix things that cannot be mixed, namely, virtue and vice. The segué to Incarnation follows immediately:

[If we live morally, we will] dwell with Christ, who for our sake became poor though he was rich, that we might be enriched by his poverty [2 Cor 8.9]. For the Son, being the very image, the impress of God the Father, the reflection of his glory [Heb 1.3], begotten from him by nature, distinguished by equality in every respect, coexistent and co-eternal, equal in power and activity, equal in renown and sharing the same throne, "did not count equality with God a thing to be grasped," as is written. For he came into our condition, and underwent a voluntary emptying [Phil 2.7]; and, as John says in his wisdom, "he became flesh and dwelt among us" [Jn 1.14].[67]

Cyril continues along standard lines, but he adds more pointed language that probably reflects the growing conflict with Nestorius. Hence, Jesus is not "a God-bearing man," and Mary is Mother of God (here *Mētēr Theou* rather than *Theotokos*). He concludes by reminding his hearers that the Son did not despise human birth, as some have said. Even though the miracle of the Incarnation is "beyond explanation," it shows that God made "his own nature bearable even for the weakest."

Similar examples could be cited from the remaining letters. What is striking in all of this is not just that Cyril selected and employed basically the same set of scriptural passages to support his Christological vision through his entire episcopacy, but also that he gave Christological reflection so much pastoral energy; he wanted the people of Egypt to think rightly about the nature

66. The following examples are taken from FL 17.2.
67. FL 17.2.

of the Incarnation. On the other hand, it is also striking that Cyril generally kept technical language to a minimum. There are, for example, scarcely any references to the theopaschite implications of his Christology, and he avoided the use of technical language altogether.[68] In his conflict with Nestorius he had to address these issues in formal letters and treatises, but in this pastoral context the language is more generically biblical. In these letters, Cyril rests on the Scriptures alone. The debates about the meaning of the words *hypostasis, physis,* and *prosopon,* which characterized the wider controversy, are largely absent. Here a vision of Christ and his redemptive work is allowed to emerge from the confluence of texts, primarily Phil 2.14–17, Jn 1.14, and Heb 1.3.

## III. Conclusion

In this brief introduction I have discussed some of the key themes, both social and theological, that form the background of these festal letters. While Cyril treats these themes in more focused ways in his other writings, what strikes the modern reader here is the way in which the pastoral context of the festal genre delivers them in a single package for easy discernment. Like all theologians, Cyril has a vision of the Christian life. This vision included positive features, such as a deep reverence for the Son of God's philanthropic and kenotic entry into the corruptible world. Cyril used these letters to preach this vision relentlessly. He wanted his people to know that by the Incarnation, Christ had delivered them to a new life free from death and decay. This message never arrives as abstraction. Each theological nuance comes wrapped in biblical narrative and is developed through intertextual weaving. Cyril clearly wanted his people to think with the text such that the words of the Scriptures would enter deeply into mind and heart.

For Cyril, a biblical people was also a disciplined one. In Cyril's doctrinal works his ascetical side retreats, but here it emerges

68. The best study of the technical aspect of Cyril and the Christological debates is John A. McGuckin, *St. Cyril of Alexandria: The Christological Controversy: Its History, Theology, and Texts* (Leiden: E. J. Brill, 1994).

strongly. The ascetic life, with its call to renunciation and its promise of transformation, is here expressed in more practical form. The letters explain the transformative power of fasting and other forms of physical discipline. For Cyril, average people in their average lives should embrace, in some way at least, the very specific monastic goal of *apatheia* (passionlessness). The monasticization of popular religious practice was already well advanced in the Alexandria of Cyril's day.

Regrettably, Cyril's vision contained some darker features, in particular his (and his culture's) profound unease with the continuing existence of a rival claimant to the Law, namely, the Jews. The anti-Judaism of these letters is strong. Contextualizing it culturally and historically softens the impact somewhat, but not completely. With such strong language coming year after year from powerful bishops in the empire like Cyril, we should not be surprised that anti-Judaism embedded itself so deeply in subsequent Christian discourse. As cultural artifacts, these letters whitewash nothing.

During the entire twenty-nine-year period covered by the *Festal Letters,* these themes remained remarkably stable. They were, in short, at the very core of what Cyril believed to be the essence of the *economy.* On the one hand, these themes hardly surprise. Yes, of course, the seeds of his mature Christology would be present early. Yes, of course, Cyril was interested in the fulfillment of the promises of the Old Covenant. Yes, of course, he would have freely used the language of the ascetical tradition in which he was trained. Yet what makes these letters interesting and worthy of attention is not so much that they definitively illuminate obscurity in Cyril's theology, nor that they fill in hitherto unknown details about connections between monastery and patriarchate or Jew and gentile. What they offer instead is a glimpse into his pastoral world. It is easy to forget that twenty-nine years is also 10,585 days, and very few of these were spent in fighting directly with Nestorius; many more were spent in reading the Bible, reflecting on the Gospel, and ministering to the people of Alexandria.

# FESTAL LETTERS 1–12

# FESTAL LETTER ONE

## A.D. 414

THE BRIGHT LIGHT of our divine feast shines forth upon the whole world with such cheerful radiance, that it banishes all gloom and darkness for those wishing to celebrate the feast worthily. Thus the blessed apostle speaks as follows to such as these when he shows them how to proceed: "The night is advanced, and the day draws near; let us walk becomingly, as by day."[1] Thus guided by the unquenchable rays of our Savior's light, we may reach the Jerusalem above, where we shall dwell with the holy choirs of angels in heaven. Blessed David, then, in gathering us into such a fair company, bids us sing the song of victory to Christ, who became incarnate for our sakes and who destroyed the power of death through the cross;[2] he says, "Come, let us exult in the Lord, let us shout to God our Savior."[3] For he calls those who attend to the divine laws the Savior's choir, teaching them to form an assembly one in harmonious thought, rather than divided in mind and ideas, as they confess their faith in Christ, "in order that," as Paul says, "with one voice and one mind"[4] we may keep our confession of him firm and unwavering.

With the divine and inviolate festival bidding us, as it were, to ascend at last to the spiritual Jerusalem and stirring us to hasten to enter upon a life of piety, let us listen to what we hear through the prophet: "You who are saved, go out from the land, remember the Lord from afar, and let Jerusalem arise in your heart."[5]

---

1. Rom 13.12.                                    2. Cf. Heb 2.14.

3. Ps 95.1. Unless otherwise indicated, references to the Psalms follow the numbering system found in a modern English translation rather than the numbering of the Septuagint.

4. Cf. Rom 12.16.                                5. Jer 28.50 (LXX).

Since Paul thus cries, "Run so as to win the prize,"[6] and since our holy feast is rising over us like the sun, let us cast far away our fruitless laziness, overcome the heavy darkness of our idleness, and with brave and luminous hearts set ourselves to seek every virtue, repeating to each other the words, "Come, let us go up to the mountain of the Lord, and to the house of the God of Jacob, and he will announce his way to us, and we will walk in it."[7] For the Jews, who do not know how to abandon their figurative and corporeal form of worship,[8] hear the words, "What do your many sacrifices mean to me? says the Lord. I have had enough of holocausts of rams, and I do not want the fat of lambs and the blood of bulls and goats, not even if you appear before me."[9] But to those who have left such things far behind, and are concerned to show God the true circumcision of the heart through worship in the Spirit, the prophet cries, "Seek God, and when you find him, call upon him. But when he approaches you, let the ungodly forsake their path and the lawless their plans, and turn to the Lord, and they will find mercy, for he will remove your sins far away."[10]

Since therefore our Savior Christ has come near to us by becoming like us, let us put off the old man, as is written, and put on the new one who is being renewed according to the image of his Creator;[11] forgetting what is behind, let us press on to what lies ahead, going up in our purity to the divine festival. The prophet Jeremiah cries, "Thus he speaks to the men of Judah and to the inhabitants of Jerusalem: Plough fallow ground for yourselves, and sow not among thorns; be circumcised to God, and circumcise the hardness of your hearts, men of Judah and inhabitants of Jerusalem."[12] Let us, then, purify our minds with the fear of God, using it like fire to rid them of the impiety with

---

6. 1 Cor 9.24.　　　　　　　　　　7. Is 2.3.

8. Cyril frequently used figural forms of biblical interpretation to move from the letter to the spirit. Frequently in these letters, however, he accuses the Jews of dwelling in mere figures. By this he means reading the Bible without paying attention to its spiritual meaning. In other words, they read the figures literally and did not understand their true meaning.

9. Is 1.11–12.　　　　　　　　　　10. Is 55.6–7.

11. Cf. Eph 4.22–24; Col 3.10.

12. Jer 4.3–4.

which they are overgrown and barren, and receive the good
seed of our Savior,[13] who does not teach us to engage in merely
figurative worship, but who renews us for salvation with his good
teachings. Let us therefore show God the Jew who is hidden[14]
and the circumcision which is hidden, circumcising all vice from
our hearts, that it may be right that we should hear, "Celebrate
your feasts, Judah, and offer to the Lord God your prayers."[15]

2. Those therefore who are sent to announce this may well
feel deep fear at their task, and with good reason, for the punishment for neglecting it is hardly light. "Accursed is he," it says,
"who performs God's works carelessly."[16] That is easy to see if
one considers the blessed Jonah, and the sea which raged
against him, and the terrible, frightful sea-monster loosed
against him. I find as well that each of the saints feared the
greatness of the divine service. Moses, for instance, the teacher
of divine truths, when God bade him send the people out, reckoned up what was possible to human nature and saw that the
service of the proclamation was beyond it, and said, "I am hesitant in speech and slow of tongue."[17] The blessed Jeremiah, sent
to prophesy, speaks likewise when he cries, "Lord and Master,
You who are, behold, I do not know how to speak, for I am too
young!"[18]
Now even though the saints have left us a wonderful model
of reverence in speaking thus, nevertheless the sort of fear involved here results in a laziness which is neither inconsiderable
nor without peril to the weak. But God repeatedly asks us, and
bids us put away our fear, saying to Moses, "Who has given a
mouth to man, and who has made him deaf or dumb, or with or
without sight? Is it not I, the Lord God? Now go, and I will open
your mouth."[19] And to the blessed Jeremiah, "Say not, 'I am too
young'; for to all to whom I will send you, you shall go, and you
will say everything I command you."[20]

13. Cf. Mt 13.1–9; Lk 8.5–11, Mk 4.1–8.
14. Cf. Rom 2.29.
16. Jer 48.10.                          15. Na 1.15.
18. Jer 1.6.                            17. Ex 4.10.
20. Jer 1.7.                            19. Ex 4.11–12.

Since, then, the priestly office calls even my lowly self to the task of proclamation, and I fear the words, "Speak and be not silent,"[21] I am compelled to proceed to the writing of this letter. For our father Theophilus,[22] of renowned and wholly blessed memory, who was bishop (and whose account, known to the Steward of us all, I would not presume to give in writing), has, by God's decree, left this life virtuously and flown to the heavenly dwellings, and so the succession to the episcopacy has fallen to me, the least of all. And since I hear what Paul has written, "Woe to me if I do not proclaim the good news!"[23] I proceed then, fearfully, to the task of proclamation, beyond my powers though it be.

With our holy festival therefore shining forth and calling us to an unblemished and prescriptive sanctity, one must say to those still in the toils of vice, "Cleanse your hands, you sinners, and purify your hearts, you men of double mind!"[24] To those who have fled the shameful defilement of sin and embraced an honorable way of life, however, let the prophet announce the good news, as he says, "Shine forth, shine forth, Jerusalem, for your light has come, and the glory of the Lord has risen upon you."[25] For since all human beings under the sun, having become the "portions of foxes,"[26] as it is written, have been divided into every sort of vice, and, once conquered by the darkness of ignorance, have fallen into the depths of sin as into a pit, the Psalmist, in calling God the Word to us from heaven, was forced to say, "O Shepherd of Israel, give ear; you who lead Joseph like a sheep, who are seated upon the Cherubim, shine forth before Ephraim and Benjamin and Manasseh! Rouse your might and come to save us!"[27] When he realized how opportunely he was going to come to us when we had fallen and were prostrate, he again cried, "Why, Lord, have you kept far away, paying no attention whether in prosperity or tribulation?"[28] For our Savior, who had not yet assumed our likeness, had kept far away in respect to the Incarnation, since

---

21. Ezek 24.27.

22. Cyril's uncle Theophilus, the former bishop of Alexandria (from 385), died on October 15, 412. Cyril succeeded him a few days later.

23. 1 Cor 9.16.                     24. Jas 4.8.

25. Is 60.1.                        26. Ps 63.10.

27. Ps 79.2–3.                      28. Ps 9.22 (LXX).

the distance between human nature and that of God the Word is great indeed.[29] Concerning us, one of the saints said, "I am earth and ashes."[30] But concerning the existence of the Only-Begotten, Isaiah says, "Who shall relate his generation?"[31] It was opportunely, then, that the Savior shone upon us in our great tribulation when he was born of a woman in regard to the flesh, that he might save man born of a woman, and, having loosed him from the bonds of death, might teach him to say joyfully, "O death, where is your victory? Hell, where is your sting?"[32] For he does not only give us the gift of the resurrection; he also, in blunting hell's sting, the sin that stings us, tells us, "Behold, I have given you [authority] to tread upon serpents and scorpions, and over all the power of the enemy; and nothing shall harm you."[33] This is in addition to the other blessings coming from our Savior's coming. Holiness, therefore, reigns supreme upon earth, while the darkness [hiding] the truth has been driven out. The Psalmist, foreseeing this by the power of the divine Spirit, said, "Justice shall arise in his days, and fullness of peace, until the moon be no more!"[34] For "while we were enemies," as Paul says, "we were reconciled to God through the death of his Son";[35] then the fullness of peace shall arise for us. And this having happened, the moon must necessarily be utterly destroyed, meaning the devil, the ruler of night and darkness, who is here called "the moon" figuratively.[36]

The beams from these great and many [blessings] thus shine down upon us, and the light of our divine feast is rising. Once again the bright festival draws us to itself, its admonition that vice is to be abandoned sounding even more loudly in the following words, "Wash yourselves, be clean, remove the evil from your

---

29. At this early date Cyril's Christological thinking is still quite immature and largely derived from Athanasius. For a full discussion see the introduction.

30. Gn 18.27.                                    31. Is 53.8.

32. Hos 13.14; Cf. 1 Cor 15.55–56.

33. Ps 91.13; Lk 10.19.                          34. Ps 72.7.

35. Rom 5.10.

36. The editors of the SC edition of this text note that this particular interpretation seems to be unique to Cyril (see SC 372, 154, n. 1). He may, however, have been influenced by Clement of Alexandria (*Strom.* 1.15) or Eusebius (*Preparation for the Gospel* 4.5).

souls!"[37] For if the author of the Book of Proverbs speaks wisely when he says, "There is a season for everything, and a time for every matter,"[38] then it is certainly with reason that we acknowledge that this particular time is opposed to every evil, that it calls one to only such behavior as does honor to the divine law, and that it assures those who act accordingly that they will be regarded with affection. Now those who decide to become contest judges in this present life, and who purchase the title at heavy cost and make the youths sweat at the games, reward the winners with rich trophies; the satisfaction derived from the prizes is, however, little enough, and the enjoyment lasts only as long as this earthly life. But God, the contest judge of the just, grants to the pious "what eye has not seen, and ear has not heard, and the human heart has not conceived."[39] For those whose deeds reveal a character which surpasses what is natural, receive what they are given in a way that will rightly surpass human understanding. For, having led the kind of life unknown to the many because of its hardships, they will be rewarded meetly, and, having drawn to themselves their Master's boundless love, they will enjoy the bounties which surpass nature.

Let us too, therefore, call those devoted to piety to the annual contest of toil, and, since the prophet says, "Blow a trumpet in Zion, sanctify a fast, proclaim a service,"[40] let us sound the Church's sacred trumpet, making it resound piercingly. Let us make known the arrival of our holy feast with a proclamation clear and most conspicuous, and since the all-wise God says to Moses, the teacher of sacred truths, "Make for yourself two trumpets; you will make them of silver, and you will use them to summon and to dismiss the assembly,"[41] let us act in full accordance with the meaning of the words. He orders that there should be two trumpets, because the Church has two messages: one of them summons the ignorant to the right understanding of the sacred teachings, while the other warns against the defilement of wicked deeds. He commands the trumpets to be silver, since in both instances the message is bright and spotless, both when it keeps

---

37. Is 1.16.
38. Eccl 3.1.
39. 1 Cor 2.9; Cf. Is 64.4.
40. Jl 2.15.
41. Nm 10.2.

clear of error in teaching and when it presents what is to be chosen in one's actions.

Let our message, then, sprint from its starting-point, as it were; let it call those far from the Law as though to the tent itself; let it draw those still sundered by sin to the Legislator's will; let it sanctify a fast and proclaim a service, as the prophet says. How else could we do these things? How else could we fulfill the divine commandment, wholly avoiding what is evil[42] and keeping ourselves from what is utterly shameful, while striving to insist on the importance of what we know sanctifies those fasting? For thus it is that those who intend to celebrate the feast properly will worship our good God.

3. Let Christ's disciple, then, come into our midst; let him teach us how to fast, and we will hear him say, "A fast that is pure and undefiled before God and the Father is this: to visit orphans and widows in their affliction, and to keep oneself unstained from the world."[43] And how and in what way we may come by what is said, is easy to discover. For I think that the law of nature itself suffices for those of sound understanding when it teaches us to hate whatever seems contrary to the divine commandments, and urges that the Legislator's will should hold sway in us. But if it be thought that we need something clearer, let us listen to Paul's words, "Put to death what is earthly in you: fornication, impurity, passion, evil desire."[44] For it is not simply by abstaining from food and refraining from eating that we will find the truer grace of fasting, nor will we be completely pure and holy only by keeping from such things; this will happen rather when we banish from our spirit the things for which fasting was instituted as a remedy. Let us, then, obey the saint when he says, "Cleanse your hands, you sinners, and purify your hearts, you men of double mind!"[45] This is the right manner of fasting, and in these ways will we display the best works: do not feed your mind with licentious pleasures; let the sting of fornication remain idle in you;

42. Using the variant reading *kakon* instead of *kakoi;* see SC 372, 158, note on line 137.

43. Jas 1.27.                              44. Col 3.5.

45. Jas 4.8.

keep your spirit free from passion; avoid the company of the impure. This is how you will prove yourself to God; these are the works that will win you the crown of justice.

It is good, then, to abstain from superfluous food in due season, and to withdraw from the over-laden table, lest our self-indulgence in eating more than we need awaken the sin dormant in us. For the flesh, when it has battened upon delicacies, is irksome, and vigorously opposes the desires of the spirit. When it is weak, however, and unaided by overindulgence, it is forced to yield to the other. This is what blessed Paul teaches us when he says, "Even though our outer self is wasting away, yet the inner self is being renewed day after day."[46] For between those for whom friendship is impossible because they are so contrary in outlook and incompatible in manners, one may gain the advantage by being able to prevail over the other. But victory, I think all will agree, belongs to those who are superior. For what we will gain from the one would match the harm caused by the other, were the better side vanquished.

4. Let evil, then, be idle in us, and all luxury in diet depart! Let fasting come in to us, with its temperance and hostility to all sin; its beauty, dearly beloved, I have thought well to demonstrate from examples from of old, even though you know them. What was it, may I ask, that made the blessed Baptist such a great man? How was it that he received that marvelous declaration from Christ our Savior, who said of him, "Among those born of women there has risen no one greater than John the Baptist"?[47] Or what was it that prepared Moses, the teacher of divine truths, to enter into the darkness and stand before God?[48] Was it not fasting, which furnishes us the form of every virtue—fasting, which is the imitation of the angelic way of life, which is the fountain of temperance, the source of continence, the banishment of lust? Through it the three youths were found by the Babylonians to be fearsome and invincible; they asked to be fed from the seeds of the earth when they might have shared the royal table and its banquets of renown,[49] but yielded to the Babylonians on the field

---

46. 2 Cor 4.16.
48. Cf. Ex 24.12–18.

47. Mt 11.11; Lk 7.18.
49. Cf. Dn 1.12.

of fleshiness and the craving for meat, and bade them conquer where to be conquered is so good, since they loved a plain and simple diet.[50] But look at the result! They were granted divine visions, they proved stronger than fire,[51] they confounded the threats of the king, and they conquered lions, changing them to a gentleness quite unnatural.[52] And what was it that saved the Ninevites from the terrible threat hanging over them? For the prophet had announced, "Three more days, and Nineveh shall be destroyed!"[53] But they seized upon fasting as though it were an unassailable stronghold, mollified the divine wrath, and escaped the impending doom. And many indeed are the benefits of fasting which one might list. But to try to show its usefulness through a number of instances would, I think, be to little purpose, as it is obvious and well known to all, being self-evident.

Since, however, the beauty of fasting appears more clearly when set against its opposite, let us also display the misfortunes resulting from self-indulgence, unfold the tale of what has befallen people because of it, and summon those who suffered its consequences to testify to what is said. Now it happened that the Hebrew people were sojourning in the desert, and Moses was summoned to Mt. Sinai to receive the Law from God there. But they took the absence of their instructor as an opportunity for thoughtlessness, and, neglecting the discipline hitherto prevailing, turned to the indulgence of unwonted cravings. "The people sat down to eat and drink," it says, "and they arose to play."[54] "Play" here means "fornicate," holy Scripture referring to it euphemistically in this way. And if you want to know the evil that came upon those who fornicated because of this, listen to what Paul says: "Neither let us fornicate, as some of them fornicated, and were killed by the snakes."[55] Consider as well the suffering they had to endure, when they came to despise the manna, the heavenly food, and, remembering the food in Egypt, said, "Would that we had been struck by the Lord and died in Egypt, when we sat by the fleshpots and ate our fill!"[56] I am sure, there-

---

50. Cf. Dn 1.8–16.
52. Cf. Dn 6.17–25.
54. Ex 32.6.
56. Ex 16.3.

51. Cf. Dn 3.
53. Jon 3.3.
55. 1 Cor 10.8–9.

fore, that the benefit of fasting has been clearly shown to you by these examples as well.

But someone may say: I know that fasting is not without its benefits, but the effort is not without its cost, and in fact is opposed to nature.[57] Now what a shameful thing it is, and quite absurd, to love what is better and value highly the acquisition of what is beneficial, but when it comes to gaining the advantage from it in the right way, either to make no start at all, or to go about it half-heartedly, and to admit that fasting has its benefits, but to avoid the effort by which its profits are secured! For in the same way that shoots sprouting from the ground make their beginning from a root, and cannot do otherwise, so also the origin of cheerfulness is found through toil, and through it rises and appears. So we have to choose one of two things: either, in deciding that we do not want to make the effort to fast at all, we will be deprived of all renown and honor, and will be like the dead, taking no thought for our own salvation; or else, in embracing the effort entailed by fasting, we will rightly gain what we will lose by not doing so. But it will be evident to all that we will choose what is best for us, thus preferring what is superior to what can be of no benefit, if we decide to be reasonable. If, then, no harm comes to those who avoid doing what is best in human affairs because of the slight effort entailed, and those who choose not to do so are safe from any loss or danger, I would still consider them the most senseless of people. If, however, in avoiding slight pains we find ourselves suffering greater and more grievous ones, then it only makes sense to choose to suffer that which means less effort and greater fruit. I should like to ask those thus inclined, whether they would call fasting or eternal punishment irksome? I think they would agree, however reluctantly, that it would be worse to be sent off for punishment. Now since it will necessarily be one or the other for us, why not grasp what is better, and make the best choice for ourselves? For we must either undertake the toil and be freed from evil, or in declining to do so be condemned to fire unquenchable.[58]

57. Although Cyril's philosophical training was limited, this may be a reference to Stoicism, which emphasized being in accord with nature. Cf. "the disciples of the Greeks," at the beginning of section 5 below.

58. Cyril may be borrowing from Basil of Caesarea here: see SC 372, 168, n.1.

It is well to add that the experience of pleasures is more enjoyable for those who have been experiencing something quite different. The blessing of health, for instance, is more obvious to those who are sick. Those laboring under poverty and the lack of necessities are for that reason more eager for gain. They are compelled to seek to enjoy what they do not have, and, in a word, the longing for these things increases when one does not have the pleasures they bring. And thus did God, the best of artificers of all things, arrange the universe, allowing the sun to appear after the night, and the night after it, in order that, by succeeding each other, they might make their presence more enjoyable, since the human mind always thinks little of what is present; it is surfeited by what it already has, and yearns rather for what it expects in the future. This holds as well for fasting and self-indulgence. Fasting is not without benefit, therefore, since your enjoyment will be more intense at the proper time.

5. Let us, then, welcome fasting as the mother of everything good and of all good cheer. The disciples of the Greeks, apparently so wise, belittle it; the Jews, who surpass all people in the novelty of their impieties, while they do not deny knowing of it, yet perform it so shamefully, that they are perhaps better when they do not practice it. For being full of all malice, so to speak, and bringing forth in themselves every sort of impurity, they pride themselves upon the bare name of fasting, and often enough make their virtue an excuse for boasting. What, for instance, can one say when one considers that most unlearned and uneducated Pharisee whom Christ our Lord portrays in the Gospels as praying in the Temple, and crying, "God, I thank you that I am not like other people, extortioners, unjust, adulterers, or even like this tax collector. I fast twice a week; I give tithes of all that I get."[59] What are you saying, you idiot, in thus boasting of your fasting? Have you no sense of how sick you are with such arrogance when you attend so carefully to these trivialities? Do you not see the enormity of your boasting? Will you not cease straining out gnats and swallowing camels, as the Savior says?[60]

59. Lk 18.11–12.
60. Mt 23.24.

You call yourself learned in the Law,[61] and yet you are quite unaware of the words: "Let your neighbor praise you, and not your own mouth; a stranger, and not your own lips."[62] "Woe to you, scribes and Pharisees, hypocrites! For you are like whitewashed tombs, which appear beautiful to people, but within are full of dead people's bones and all uncleanness."[63] For the mentality of the Jews is really quite full of every uncleanness, nor is there any wickedness which is not held by them in high esteem. They do not want to know the divine Law, and they even reject the commandment given them, and so they continue disobedient and unbelieving. It is for these reasons that God accuses them, crying out through the prophet, "To whom shall I speak and make my declaration? Who will listen? Behold, their ears are uncircumcised, and they cannot hear; behold, the word of the Lord has become a reproach for them, and they wish to hear none of it."[64] For habitual sinners find it wearisome to be admonished about what is for their benefit; nor is temperance pleasant to those who have chosen licentiousness. Just as those drunk on wine have drowned their wits and taken from them the power to think aright, because they do not sense the harm incurred from association with what is worst for them, so also those overcome by the love of pleasure, who have fallen into the swamp of sin and fastened their continent mind to impure passions, render unshakeable the evil among them, fixing their gaze and their choice wholly upon it, fastened as they are to this sickness.

6. And the Jews, those most senseless of all people, in their eagerness to outdo their fathers' impiety by the excesses of their transgressions, considered it a matter of shame and ridicule to concede victory to them in the contest of sin. For they thought the only way they could show an attitude worthy of their forebears would be if they committed the same offenses as they, or even worse. Annoyed and understandably vexed at this, God, the Master of all, spoke as follows: "From the day your fathers left the land of Egypt until the present day, I have sent you all my servants the prophets, day after day. I sent them, and they did not

61. Cf. Jn 3.10.                    62. Prv 27.2.
63. Mt 23.27.                       64. Jer 6.10.

listen to me or attend. And they stiffened their necks more than
their fathers."[65] O you who alone prove your ancestry by the kinship of your impieties, and reveal whose children you are by your
identical mentality! O you who have beaten your parents in the
contest of impiety, and by your bold wantonness against the Law
have condemned their weakness! Yours alone it was to conquer
where defeat would have done you more good. O you who have
won a victory more irksome than all ill repute! O you who had a
chance for victory—and God, the Judge of all, condemns those
who do not have it and who dare to take pride in deeds doubtless less evil—God condemns you when he says, "They have stiffened their necks."[66] For this reason he bids the prophet mourn
for them, saying, "Cut off your hair and throw it away, and take
up a dirge on your lips, for the Lord has rejected you and will
thrust you away, the generation which has done these things. For
the sons of Judah have done evil in my sight, says the Lord."[67]
Then he explains what sort of impiety they had done, saying,
"They have erected their abominations in the house upon which
my name has been invoked, to defile it, and they have built the
altar of Topheth."[68] Their ignorance had advanced so far that
they denied their very Benefactor and considered it profitable
to worship idols. Indeed, they invented names of gods for themselves, and sacrificed to them. Others, dragged off by their own
passions, divided their minds into unwonted cravings, made their
way to the fairest mountain groves, and there sacrificed to the demons, whom they invoked as nymphs, Hamadryads, and Oreads,
following the Greek poets, apparently. And in thus giving themselves impudently to every desire, and boasting of what should
have been matter for shame, they clearly caused the Legislator
great grief. For that reason he says to Jeremiah the prophet, "You
have seen what the house of Israel has done to me? It has gone
to every high mountain, and beneath every shady tree, and has
prostituted itself there. And after it committed all that prostitu-
tion, I said, 'Return to me,' and it did not return."[69]

For those who do not like being saved hate what is to their ad-

65. Jer 7.25–26.
66. Jer 7.26.
67. Jer 7.29–30.
68. Jer 7.30–31.
69. Jer 3.6–7.

vantage, and they do not avoid the chance for pleasure who do not refuse to be hedonists.[70] They are always bent on what is worse who do not know how to be temperate. The harsh, obdurate propensity of the Jews bears this out; they never, from the outset, have tried to avoid such lapses, and have disdained the honor due their Master. When they have the chance to repent and be saved, but make light of what would be to their advantage and take no account of such great kindness, do they not justly confirm that they should be shown no mercy? Have they not surpassed all effrontery when, being given the chance to escape punishment by absenting themselves from sin, they call down upon themselves a heavier penalty by adding yet greater transgressions to those already committed? To characters such as these, being punished more severely is more fitting than not suffering badly at all. One would not go wrong in advising that they be shown no mercy. This is not my idea; the Master of all says as much when he rebuffs the prophet who prays for them: "And you, do not intercede for this people, and do not ask for mercy for them, and do not pray, and do not approach me about them, for I will not listen. Do you not see what they do in the cities of Judah and in the streets of Jerusalem? Their sons gather wood, and their fathers kindle fire, and their women knead dough to make cakes for the host of heaven, and they have poured libations to strange gods, to anger me."[71] The sons gather the wood, the fathers light the fire, and the women knead the dough, so that nothing may be found without sin. But having given themselves wholly to sinning, they will hear the words justly spoken, "Because you have rejected knowledge, I in turn will reject you from my priesthood. You have forgotten the Law of your God, and I will forget your children."[72] For the kind of punishment is always in proportion to the greatness of the sins, and an appropriate penalty must be visited upon those who have lapsed.

Now how could those convicted of such enormities suffer anything fitting that would be greater or more grievous than banishment from the divine priesthood and loss of their remembrance in God's presence, through which they had attained their well-

---

70. In other words, hedonists seek pleasure.
71. Jer 7.16–18 (LXX).          72. Hos 4.6.

being and continually enjoyed what one might call complete happiness? But welfare is a formidable thing, hardly to be borne by fools. And when they enjoy it who least deserve it, then an opportunity for folly is provided them. This is what happened to the children of Israel: despising their Master's love for humanity, and unwilling to learn to keep the divine law properly, they hastened to embrace unwonted cravings in their eagerness for every indulgence. Not wanting to do what the Legislator had thought good, they made their own will their law, learning to keep only their own ordinances. No wonder the saints mourned over those with such an attitude and disposition, saying, "Hear the word of the Lord, the lamentation which I take up for you: the house of Israel has fallen, never again to rise."[73] And again, "Summon the mourners, and let them come; send for the wise women, and let them give utterance and take up a lamentation for you,"[74] for the flock of the Lord has been destroyed. And the prophet Jeremiah, as though seeing them already afflicted and their punishment drawing near, presents them as grieving for themselves and saying, "Our time has drawn near, our days have been fulfilled, our end is at hand. Our pursuers are swifter than the eagles of heaven."[75]

With such grievous error having spread everywhere, therefore, and the whole earth under heaven having fallen into the devil's power, the prophet speaks as follows: "Hell has enlarged its soul, and has opened its mouth so as not to cease."[76] Now the Greeks, for their part, slipped into polytheism out of complete thoughtlessness, and, exchanging "the glory of the immortal God for images resembling mortal man or birds or animals or reptiles,"[77] they hastened to the realm of death as though sailing there under the urging of a fair wind. The Jews, however, not only disregarded the commandment given them, but even descended to such a degree of stupidity as to think it almost a matter of dishonor to be seen practicing the things according to which they would have had to be judged to enjoy the best way of life, and hastened instead to walk the same path as the others.

---

73. Am 5.12.
74. Jer 9.17–18.
75. Lam 4.18–19.
76. Is 5.14.
77. Rom 1.23.

But with earth and sea wrapped, as it were, in night and darkness, the Lord God of all, not enduring to overlook how human beings, the fairest of his own creatures on earth, were perishing, but seeing how human nature had fallen victim to an incurable disease, sent his own Word to us, the only one able to overthrow the devil's tyranny and free us from the evils holding us fast. In assuming our likeness,[78] and becoming a human being, and being born of the holy Virgin Mary, he did not discard what he was, but took on what he was not, and so achieved our salvation.[79] "And he remains," as Paul says, "yesterday and today the same, and forever,"[80] not suffering any change or alteration in his divinity by reason of his Incarnation, but being what he was and will be forever. As for the devil—who cried of old, "I will seize the earth like a nest in my hand, and will pick it up like eggs abandoned, and there is no one who can escape or gainsay me"[81]—the Word, when he dwelt in the world, bestowed him upon those who believe as a plaything for their laughter. He has overthrown, by the "bath of rebirth,"[82] the sin which had tyrannized over us, and thus has made the earth clean. He has taught us the way of salvation, and, scattering folly like a mist or cloud, has revealed to us the bright knowledge of divine doctrine. He has made us equal citizens with the angels in heaven.[83] He has joined the terrestrial to the celestial, and given the human race a common dwelling with the spirits living there, that race sundered of old by sin and become fugitive, but now joined together by faith, and by piety in his regard.

Him the wretched Jews refused to acknowledge as Savior and Lord; on the contrary, as though they had been most seriously wronged because he came to benefit their race and to save us from such final perdition, for which they should have shown

78. Cf. Phil 2.7.

79. Cyril's Christological language is quite imprecise at this stage of his career. He would seem to imply that the Logos took a body to himself rather than a complete human being. This language is reminiscent of Athanasius's discourse in *On the Incarnation,* but is inadequate when judged by the standards of Ephesus and Chalcedon. Charges of being a secret Apollinarian would follow Cyril for decades.

80. Heb 13.8.

81. Is 10.14.

82. Cf. Ti 3.5.

83. Cf. Heb 2.5–17.

themselves grateful and acknowledged how well they had been treated, they handed him over death by crucifixion. And while watching him hang on the tree, the Jews again reviled and reproached him with the words, "If you are the Son of God, come down from the cross now, and we will believe in you."[84]

The Savior, then, underwent death for all of us, and, descending into hell, stripped the devil of his riches, saying to those in bonds, "Come out!" and to those in darkness, "Show yourselves!" as the prophet says.[85] And raising up his three-day temple, the first-fruits of those fallen asleep,[86] he freed nature from the bonds of death, and, once victorious, taught it to say, "O death, where is your victory? Hell, where is your sting?"[87] And having made heaven accessible to it through the economy of the Incarnation, he was taken up, presenting himself to the Father as the first-fruits of the human race. And as a sort of pledge to us of the future hope, he bestowed the Spirit, saying, "Receive the Holy Spirit."[88]

These are the tokens of our Savior's Advent; in their presence let us proclaim him Benefactor and Savior. And since our legitimacy is to be seen in our deeds themselves, and through them a fitting recompense is to be offered to our Master, let us obey Paul when he says, "Let us cleanse ourselves from every defilement of flesh and spirit, and make holiness perfect in the fear of God."[89] Let us in this way, then, in this fashion, celebrate a pure fast for the Master, beginning Holy Lent on the fifteenth of the month of Mecheir, and the week of the salvific Passover on the twentieth of Phamenoth, terminating the fast on the twenty-fifth of that month as usual, and celebrating the feast on the eve of Sunday, the twenty-sixth of Phamenoth,[90] adding thereafter the seven weeks of holy Eastertide. For thus will we inherit, with the saints, the kingdom of heaven in Christ forever. Amen.

84. Mt 27.40.
85. Is 49.9.
86. 1 Cor 15.20.
87. Hos 13.14. Cf. 1 Cor 15.55.
88. Jn 20.22.
89. 2 Cor 7.1.
90. March 22, 414.

# FESTAL LETTER TWO

A.D. 415

"EJOICE IN THE LORD always; again I say, rejoice!"[1] Our discourse hastens to this starting-point, and quite understandably, for it is a feast which is proclaimed. For when our message has as its purpose to announce that we should take delight in our Savior's deeds, one can hardly think of a better way to begin it. It is right, then, that it should begin thus; it will resolutely avoid what is not to the point, shrink from irrelevant excursions, and make every effort to present to its hearers in a timely manner what it is good and beneficial to them to say. The divine word, then, has declared that there is a moment for everything.[2] Now the present moment suits best our work of proclamation if ever one did.

Our wholly blessed feast, then, has come round in the cycle of the year, stands now at our door, and has all but stepped over the threshold to dwell in the souls of all. Now it would seem to me the height of absurdity, if the Jews, who take such pride in Law and shadow and type, were to announce their own feasts with trumpet blasts, while we, who prefer what is better than what they have, and who have rightly and justly decided to place the truth above figures, as is meet, would appear far less eager in this respect than they, by sitting tranquilly and telling each other to keep quiet, and thus relegating to silence the feast which is so famous, even though God says, "Sound the trumpet on the new moon, on the day of your feast so renowned."[3] Let our discourse, then, come before us, announcing with resounding proclamation the renowned day of the feast. For even if we

---

1. Phil 4.4.  2. Cf. Eccl 3.1.
3. Ps 81.3.

were to keep silence about all that nature has gained from our Savior's goodness, the stones would cry out, as our Savior himself says.[4]

2. Now when I consider attentively each of the things that has happened, they appear as quite a throng: about these, one who kept silence would be severely and rightly censured. For if, in our concern to have a right and just attitude, we reckon it to be most important to render thanks to God for how well we have been treated, and then pay no mind at all to doing so, obviously we will have set ourselves completely against our own decisions in not choosing to do the things which, if left undone by others, might rightly lead us to charge them with idleness. Let us, then, render thanks to our Savior. But perhaps we will make our inability to speak adequately of his deeds an excuse for our hesitation and timidity, even though it would be generally agreed, I think, that conceding the victory to one's betters leads one to be regarded not as weak, but as wise. But what could be nobler than our Savior's deeds? What speech would not be silenced by such divine things? "Glory covers our speech,"[5] as holy Scripture says. And the blessed Moses, so outstanding in virtue that he heard God say to him, "I know you beyond all others, and you have found favor with me,"[6] did not blush to call himself hesitant and slow of speech,[7] and unsuited to the ministry of proclamation. Now if the one who spoke thus is beyond censure or any imputation of guilt—one would have to admit, the prophet is worthy of all praise—then obviously we must grant that our Savior's deeds, which surpass the Law, also defy any attempt to give an account of them.

It should be added that we are unpracticed in contests of speech, and we do not undertake to mount a display of Attic style. Let others busy themselves with such things, and with the display of oratorical brilliance; for our part, beloved, our discourse is brief, and we write because we must. "Woe to me if I do not preach the Gospel! For if I do this of my own will, I have a reward; but if not of my own will, I am entrusted with a com-

---

4. Cf. Lk 19.40.                    5. Prv 25.2 (LXX).
6. Ex 33.17.                        7. Cf. Ex 4.10.

mission."[8] Hence I do not think that anyone will rightly criticize the modest style of my words. For we will present clearly to you what God's grace brings to mind, cloaking our untimely shyness in prudent reasoning.

3. Since Moses thus says, "Keep the month of the new growth, and perform the Passover for the Lord, your God,"[9] it is evident that we must announce the time of the feast, which is already here. For the sullen threat of winter is gone, the unwholesome air and darkness have been driven off, and the rains and blasts of wild winds have finally been banished from us. Springtime has come again, releasing the planter from idleness and inaction, and almost crying out to tillers that it is time to set to work. The meadows are bursting with a variety of flowers. The vegetation on the mountains and in gardens is budding forth the offspring it has been carrying, as though disgorging the energy from the loins of its own nature. The fields have already turned green,[10] a reminder of God's beneficence, "making grass spring up for the cattle."[11]

Now, we have not spoken thus to no purpose, nor should it be thought that we have discoursed about these things pointlessly; the point was to show how useful the commandment is. It was not in vain that the Law has bidden us to observe the month of the new growth. For it was necessary, quite necessary, that the human race should rival the earth in bearing fresh growth, and should, if I may say so, run riot with fresh blossoms of piety. Let us then consider carefully if our discourse, in transforming the meaning of these things to apply them to ourselves, and in shifting the purpose of these reflections to something useful, will fail of what is fitting when it calls the month of the new growth the time of the arrival of our Savior Jesus Christ, when all should hold festival. For that demon who is the author of evil, who fell upon the souls of everyone like winter, and drenched us with foul desires like heavy rain, is already heading for perdition. The power of the unclean spirits has been driven away, and the sullen cloud of sin has been dispelled by grace. A light as of springtime

---

8. 1 Cor 9.16–17.                    9. Dt 16.1.
10. Wis 19.7.                          11. Ps 104.14.

has spread over us; and now the first-fruits of the Spirit which are given[12] blow around the souls of all like a zephyr or light breeze, giving those in whom they dwell, in different ways, a scent no less pleasing than those of flowers. "For we are the aroma of Christ to God,"[13] as Paul says, and we have put off the oldness of our past life like a leaf, and are being renewed for another way of life which has just budded and sprung forth. Thus the blessed Paul says, "Therefore anyone who is in Christ is a new creation; the old has passed away; behold, the new has come."[14] But those who may wish to see, through holy Scripture, that our discourse has not ventured from the truth, should listen to the bridegroom explaining to the bride the true month of the new growth: "Arise, come, my beloved, my beautiful dove, because, behold, winter has gone; the rain has departed and is far away, flowers appear in the land, and the time for pruning is here."[15] For just as expert husbandmen cut off the useless branches of the vine while allowing all those which seem ready to bear fruit to remain on it, guided in each case toward what will be beneficial by their particular art, so also our all-wise God, who searches the mind of each person, severs those resolves which cannot lead to piety and, one might say, are wholly withered, while letting temperate reason spring up, be preserved, and remain.

Hence we are already dismissing the passions of the flesh, directed as we are towards salvation, and, in settling within ourselves the pure grace of the Spirit, we are being refashioned into a better way of life.[16] We remember what Paul said: "Our old self has been crucified, so that the sinful body might be destroyed, and we might no longer be enslaved to sin. For they who have died are freed from sin. But if we have died in Christ, we believe that we shall also live with him."[17] For we will truly live with him, and will reign with him,[18] rejecting the defilement that comes from the body; "hating," as one of the saints says, "the garment spotted by the flesh";[19] honoring the continence which is dear

---

12. Cf. Rom 8.23.

13. 2 Cor 2.15.

14. 2 Cor 5.17.

15. Song 2.10–12.

16. See the introduction for a discussion of the influence of the ascetical movement on Cyril.

17. Rom 6.6–8.

18. Cf. 2 Tm 2.11–12.

19. Jude 23.

to God; and rendering a life lived in virtue as a gift in return to Christ, who died for us. For thus indeed the Psalmist says, "All those around him will bring gifts."[20] It is, then, worthwhile inquiring about, and learning from holy Scripture, what kind of gift we will give to the Lord, in what way it will be presented, and further how it will be acceptable.

4. What, then, does it say? "If some soul offers a sacrifice as a gift to the Lord, his gift shall be fine flour; he shall pour oil upon it, and put frankincense on it; it is a sacrifice."[21] The particles of fine flour stuck together into one loaf, then, signify the manifold abundance of the virtues resulting in one piety, which is offered by us to God by way of sacrifice and gift. He also bids oil to be poured upon it; it is the symbol of cheer. For the just man should not be downcast at the labors required to attain piety, but should conquer sin while rejoicing in hope. As for the frankincense, that means the fragrance arising from deeds. For the one who desires to boast of his chastity must keep clear of all impurity and reject every wicked pleasure. Thus will he have his fill of praise, and his offering will be acceptable.

Now let us see what underlies the words, gauging the divine realities from what is to hand. That is, if one wished to offer a gift to someone regarded as illustrious by the standards of this life, would he dare to approach him while smeared with bodily filth? Would he not be revolting and offensive? Rightly regarded with complete disgust? And if we admit that, in our own affairs, those who go about their business in the best possible way are not deprived of good sense, then how can one fail to see how grave an offense it is to decide to approach God without first washing off the dirt of sin, even though the divine Law says clearly, "Whatever sacrifice you offer to God you will make without leaven. For you will offer as a gift to the Lord no leaven or honey. You will offer them as first-fruits. But they will not ascend upon the altar as a sweet fragrance to the Lord. And every gift of your sacrifices will be salted with salt. The salt of the covenant of the Lord will not be missing from your sacrifices, and upon each of your gifts you will offer salt to the Lord, your God."[22]

20. Ps 76.11.                    21. Lv 2.1.
22. Lv 2.11–13.

Now you can discover what the "leaven" means by listening to Paul: "Cleanse out the old leaven that you may be a new lump, as you really are unleavened."[23] For how can vice which is inveterate be accepted as a sweet fragrance to the Lord, when he seeks from us a new and guileless life? He also forbids honey to be presented. For it too stands for pleasure, since the pleasure which accompanies every sin seems sweet, and in the end is more bitter than gall. But if pleasing God is of value to us, we must not be found leading a life devoted to what is shameful and to pleasures, nor taking our ease in the most deplorable manner, but eager rather to make much of what the Legislator would approve.

He also bids the sacrifices be salted with salt, however, thus introducing this symbol of reasoning and good sense. For I think it may be said that the minds of God's ministers must be sprinkled with divine fear as with salt, lest they become dissipated and waste themselves in languid cravings, and thus become easily seduced by what is worse, once they have disdained what is better. Paul is worthy of all praise when he cries, "Let your speech be gracious, seasoned with salt!"[24] But I do not think that such speech can appear before our attitude is what it should be. For it is from the fullness of the heart that the mouth speaks.[25]

Let the mind of the pious be salted, therefore. Let it cast away sin like something superfluous. Let it not grow lax, roving toward unwonted pleasures. For this is why Paul says, "Be steadfast, immovable, always abounding in the work of the Lord."[26] For when he says, "Be steadfast," he excludes from all praise those whose minds are not yet fixed and sure. The very Master of us all denounces them when he speaks through the prophet thus: "They have loved to move their feet, and have not refrained, and God was not pleased with them."[27] Now "feet" here signifies some motion involving change of place, and the inclination of thought both ways: toward evil, and toward all that will win them admiration, quite as though their feet were fixed, and habitually steady, and shrinking from the path to evil. Such is the blessed Psalmist, who says, "He has placed my feet upon a

23. 1 Cor 5.7.             24. Col 4.6.
25. Cf. Lk 6.45.           26. 1 Cor 15.58.
27. Jer 14.10.

rock,"[28] meaning thereby the solidity and immutability of his frame of mind. Such also is the Apostle Paul, who counsels us that man should abound in the Lord's work as far as is possible to his nature, and that he should be found to be inseparable from God's friendship through good works.[29] For it is hardly the work of a sensible mind, it seems to me, to stand aloof at times from the divine laws, and then at other times, as though waking from sleep, to adhere to them again. Those who do so seem to me to be affected in the same way as those who fall from ships into the waves of the high seas, and who might have spared themselves their fear if they had not yielded to indolence; when they find themselves plunged into the misfortune itself, then, barely able to see what will help them, they swim back to the ship and seek their safety in the place from which they fell. And yet it would have been better not to wait until the danger became something actual, but to hate it before it arrived; such would have been the sounder advice. And if someone who sets out to imitate such people, and who is amazed at well-founded accusations, appears quite foolish to everyone else, then obviously one should bend every effort to hold fast to the divine laws, and to offer a spotless way of life as an unceasing sacrifice.

Listen again to what the divine Law tells us about this: "And the Lord spoke, saying, 'Command Aaron and his sons: This is the law of the holocaust: this holocaust will remain on the altar the whole night until dawn, and the fire of the altar will burn upon it, and will not be quenched.'"[30] But how can I, dearly beloved, in my weakness and insignificance, explain logically what this commandment means? What words can give us the exact meaning of the idea behind it? But since it is written, "Open your mouth, and I will fill it,"[31] let us draw courage from our Savior's grace and hold fast to what it so clearly means.

5. The kindness of God's word draws everyone to the life of piety, and rouses to the practice of virtue all those who are convinced that they ought to lend an obedient ear to his divine laws. But not everyone is equally eager for this, nor is each person led

---

28. Ps 40.2.                          29. Cf. 2 Cor 9.8.
30. Lv 6.1–2 (LXX).                   31. Ps 81.10.

by the same zeal. For some are more earnest in approaching God, and, preferring nothing to piety in his regard, present themselves as an entire sacred and undivided sacrifice to the Lord in a sweet fragrance. To them the name of "holocaust" is most fitting. For this is really a holocaust, when one offers oneself wholly to God, doing nothing evil at any time. But see what the law of holocaust says about such a one: "This holocaust will remain on the altar the whole night until dawn, and the fire of the altar will burn upon it, and will not be quenched."[32] But what kind of fire is that of the altar, if not, evidently, the possession of the Holy Spirit in us? This is what the Savior himself indicated to us when he said, "I have come to cast fire upon the earth."[33] They therefore who as holocausts offer themselves wholly to God must keep the fire unquenched upon themselves, and that holy flame must burn at full strength in them continuously. For it says "the whole night," which will be understood as the present life. For one must not at one time cool off by inclining toward evil, and then at another time rekindle one's mind; one must be constant, and always aglow with the Spirit, as Paul says. This will become clearer to us through other examples, if we investigate carefully the intent of the Law.

For the next words which God speaks to Moses, the teacher of divine truths, are thus: "And these are the offerings which you shall offer upon the altar: two lambs of a year old daily on the altar continually, a constant offering. One lamb you shall offer in the morning, and the second lamb you shall offer in the evening. And a tenth measure of fine flour mingled with the fourth part of a hin of beaten oil, and a drink-offering the fourth part of a hin of wine for one lamb."[34] Now we can see clearly from these words that we should let no moment pass by in which God is not honored fittingly and does not receive from us the sweet odor from good works as a continual sacrifice. For the command to slaughter the one lamb at the beginning of the day, and the second at its end, may be taken to mean the whole time, its middle being included in the extremes.

He also wants the fine flour to be mixed with wine and oil, or-

---

32. Lv 6.2 (LXX).    33. Lk 12.19.
34. Ex 29.38–40.

dering not that the full measure should be poured on it, but the fourth part of a hin, teaching by means of this riddle that those who continuously offer God honor, or rather who are offered to the Legislator as a most pleasing sacrifice, will find joy in receiving mercy. In the present life they bring a small part of the gift (for he orders the fourth part of a hin to be poured out), while in the future age grace will be given them in fullest measure, when, as the prophet says, "Everlasting joy shall be over their head, and sorrow and pain and groaning have fled away."[35] Since, therefore, the Law says clearly that one must never allow one's evil tendencies to turn the mind toward sin, is it not evident that we will be liable to every sort of punishment for having neglected such good teachings?

Now it may be that, when you consider the weakness of human nature, the strenuousness of this sort of conduct appears disagreeable (perhaps you will say that it is impossible to keep up such efforts unceasingly, unyieldingly, and obstinately, like an anvil), and you may declare that to live this manner of life is difficult. If so, then the Law will remove your excuse by showing you a way of life which, while inferior, and lacking by comparison to the one spoken of, is yet far superior to the others and quite beyond them. What sort of life do I mean? I will try to give you a clear picture of it by borrowing again from sacred Scripture. When God appeared to the children of Israel in fire and darkness and storm, and prescribed the laws about what was to be done, the all-wise Moses, deeming it necessary to show the children of Israel the sort of conduct that would be pleasing to the Legislator by means of something which would be clear to them, as far as their disposition and understanding would allow, for they were not yet capable of taking in what was deeper, went about it as follows. "Rising up early in the morning, he built an altar beneath the mountain, and set up twelve stones for the twelve tribes of Israel. And he sent forth the young men of the children of Israel, and they offered whole-burnt-offerings and sacrificed young calves as a peace-offering to God. And Moses took half the blood and poured it into the bowl, and half the blood he poured out upon the altar."[36] Now let us see, when

---

35. Is 35.10.                              36. Ex 24.4–6.

once again we explain in detail each of the things written, what sort of profit we derive therefrom.

6. Moses, then, rises early and erects the altar, teaching us thereby that one ought first to wake as though from sleep and rise to temperance, dispelling the mist of sin like a dark night, and then run toward the light of knowledge, in order to erect our own thought as a beautiful altar to God, so as to be able to minister to him. This is, I think, what the prophet Isaiah said too: "My spirit rises toward you very early in the morning, O God, for your commandments are a light on the earth."[37] This, then, is what Moses' early rising means, but so that we may hold to what follows from this idea, we will proceed with our investigation in due order.

He sets up the altar, not on the mountain, but beneath the mountain, which shows how low in their way of thinking were those lacking perfection, since they were unable to ascend the mountain, as it were, to the summit of the perfect commandments. Near to them they might have been, but they did not come up to them; they approached God not on the mountain, but beneath it. Then he supposed that there should be twelve stones lying around the altar, for the twelve tribes of Israel, in order that we might learn thereby, that we ought always to attend upon God, never falling into irremediable sin. This is what the Psalmist announces to us more clearly: "And I will go around your altar, Lord."[38]

After that it continues, "He sent forth the young men of the children of Israel, and they offered whole-burnt-offerings, and they sacrificed young calves as a peace-offering to God."[39] We will say that the ability to offer sacrifices to God is not the work of a mind that is idle or otherwise weak, but of a youthful and noble intelligence. It is for this reason that it says that those sent are young men, and yet they sacrifice young calves as a peace-offering. One can see in this too, however, once the subject-matter has been transposed from the realm of type and figure,

---

37. Is 26.9, although Cyril's text says "out of night" rather than "in the morning."

38. Ps 26.6.                        39. Ex 24.5.

as it were, to a different kind of discourse, that while the choice
of those making the offering is praiseworthy, it is yet not of such
consequence, and is wanting in comparison to what is greater
and more perfect. For what is offered is not a calf, but a young
calf, inferior to the grown calf in size and strength. And taking
the blood, he poured half of it into a bowl, and half onto the altar. One can see here, then, the symbolic representation of the
divided life of the worshiper. The blood is understood as a figure
of the soul, whose life God divides in equal parts with us, so that
we may not live for ourselves alone,[40] but may also guard that
part that belongs to the altar. For this is the sort of life which is
moderate and reasonable, marked neither by the severity of an
exceeding strictness, nor by the lapses into sin occasioned by an
over-indulgence in the propensity to license. It rises above laxity
through a reverent fear, but, due to its lack of zeal, it cannot be
compared to what is more perfect. Its character is a sort of mixture of both, the qualities just described being combined into a
manner of life both dignified and attractive, since their mutual
relationship does away with what is distressful in either: the rigor
of strictness will be relieved by the gentleness of license, while
excessive license will be severed as by a sickle by the redoubtable
interventions of the mind, the result being a manner of behavior
both right and unobjectionable.

7. It is good, then, beloved, to long for what is better, and to
exult rather in the way that leads more surely to virtue. As Paul
says, however, "Each of us has a particular gift from God, one of
one kind and one of another."[41] For since the Creator of us all is
good, he gives even the weaker the means to be saved; he awards
higher praise to those eager to distinguish themselves by a more
perfect manner of life, but does not deprive of his kindness even
those who do not attain to such virtue. For "as faces are not like
[other] faces," as Solomon says, "so neither are the thoughts
of men."[42] For the body has one nature made up of the same
members, but it is the difference in the character of each [mem-
ber] that produces the variety. We will find this to be true of the

---

40. Cf. 2 Cor 5.15.                    41. 1 Cor 7.7.
42. Cf. Prv 27.19.

mental faculty as well: it is equal in everyone due to the same operations, but, divided by the qualities of its states of mind, it becomes dissimilar. This, I think, is the meaning of the gospel parable. "The sower," it says, "went out to sow his seed. While he was sowing it, some fell on the roads, some on rocky ground, some among thorns, and some on good soil and produced fruit, some a hundred-fold, some sixty-fold, and some thirty-fold."[43] You see that it says that all the earth is good; it is with the difference in the yield that the variety appears. The number hundred refers to those perfect in virtue, and those who have risen to the summit of piety. The number sixty means those who do not quite come up to the preceding, but who are of no inconsiderable virtue. The number thirty is those who are still more inferior, but not outside of the best earth, nor deprived of bearing fruit, even if they fall short of what is perfect and what is slightly less so; they are, as it were, in the third rank of the virtuous. For there are many rooms with the Father,[44] as the Savior says, and they determine the amount of honor due to each person. It was the same way with the distribution of the talents to the slaves. "To one he gave five," it says, "to another two, and to another one."[45] And this even though they all enjoyed equality of nature, a nature within its own measure suited to perfection, and there should have been no determination of difference among them, but the five talents should have been distributed among them all equally. But now the disparity in the gift introduces a certain dissimilarity in the dispositions, which do not receive piety in the same degree.

But the one who got the five talents heard the words, "Well done, good and faithful servant; you have been faithful over a little, I will set you over much; enter into the joy of your master."[46] And the one who had made a profit from the two talents was commended equally, and was honored by the same declaration. But God did not appear unjust in this, but rather good and generous. For the kindness shown to those inferior does not lessen the honors given to those who are better, nor does he add to those of lesser merit by taking anything away from what is

43. Cf. Mt 13.3–8.
45. Mt 25.15.
44. Cf. Jn 14.2.
46. Mt 25.21.

due to the others; the latter will rejoice to receive what is due them in proportion to their toil, while grace will make up the remainder of the pay.

But those whose minds are so enslaved as to envy others' success do not realize that they are criticizing God's kindness. They say: those who lack the virtue of their betters are never ranked equally with them, if they are judged fairly; the amount of grace is, like a counter-weight, in equal balance to the way each person has lived. But let them hear what our Savior Christ says: "Friend, I am doing you no wrong; did I not agree with you for a denarius? Take what belongs to you and go; I choose to give to this last as I give to you."[47] May Paul, then, rouse each person to choose every good work, and may he put an end to the ineffectual hesitation of the mind when he cries, "Sleeper, wake up! Rise from the dead, and Christ will shine on you!"[48] For even if you have fallen asleep as a human being, one who has drunk deeply of sin like untempered wine, and become drunk on dark thoughts, now the time has come for you to sober up to salvation, and to lift your eyes to the sun of justice.[49] The Master will receive you in his kindness, will have mercy on you even if you have run away, will not turn you away in your tears, will render you pure when you repent, and will re-establish you in piety. But we shall now once again continue this subject by means of examples, since great benefit may be derived from lingering in discussion of these topics.

8. When God decided to rescue the people of Israel from slavery in Egypt, he ordered Moses, the teacher of sacred truths, to run to them to explain the Master's kindly intention. And since a demonstration by means of signs had to follow this, in order to win the belief of his listeners, he said to him, "'What is that in your hand?' He said, 'A staff.' He said, 'Throw it on the ground.' And it became a snake. And Moses fled from its face. And the Lord said to Moses, 'Stretch out your hand and take hold of its tail.' And it became a staff in his hand."[50]

Now the blessed Moses, I think, taught thereby that those in-

47. Mt 20.13–14.                    48. Eph 5.14.
49. Mal 4.2.                    50. Ex 4.2–4.

volved in the error of Egypt and far advanced along the way of
sin, will be refashioned for piety by the honor they render to
God. For [the human being] sprouted from the ground like a
staff,[51] but when, turning aside to carnal passions, he in a way
falls from the Legislator's hand, he then puts off his mild and
gentle manner and turns out to be a poisonous snake, vicious in
sin, fearsome in anger. But when the Legislator picks him up
again, he will be good, transformed into the original state of that
best of dispositions. For we will assign Moses the role of the Legislator. That God, then, changes and raises up those who have
lapsed through indolence into what does not befit them, should,
I think, be evident to all from what has been said. The voices of
the prophets testify to this no less clearly, when they urge sinners
ceaselessly to turn to God.

For our benevolent Master has neglected no opportunity to
call everyone to salvation. One may certainly hear him striking
out at stubbornness and pigheadedness, and denouncing the
immutable attitude of sinners. As he once said, "Will you not be
afraid of me? says the Lord, and will you not fear before me, who
have set a boundary to the sea, a perpetual ordinance, and it
shall not pass it? But this people has a disobedient and rebellious heart. They have turned aside and gone back, and they
have not said to their heart, Let us fear now the Lord our
God."[52] And once in rebuking even more severely those who
were quite unashamed about being runaways, he said, "Will the
Ethiopian change his skin, or the leopardess her spots? And will
you be able to do good, having learned evil?"[53] For the father of
all sin had such control over the people that those who feared
God, and who realized that the Legislator was to be remembered, were quite rare. But we need make no special effort now
to show this, since the Psalmist cries out plainly, "They have all
gone out of the way; they have together become good for nothing; there is none that does good; no, not one."[54]

With sin thus holding everyone in subjection, and having
spread out over the whole world like a mist, the saints besought

51. In Greek, *rhabdos* can mean either "staff" or "shoot."
52. Jer 5.22–24.          53. Jer 13.23.
54. Ps 14.3; cf. Rom 3.12.

the Word of God to come to us to illumine the minds of all with his saving light. Indeed, they cried aloud, "Send forth your light and your truth!"[55] There was sent forth to us, therefore, "the true light that enlightens every human being coming into the world,"[56] meaning God, the Word of God. Having assumed our likeness, he is born by means of the holy Virgin and saves the human race, bringing nature back to its primitive incorruption, and, as Paul says, by opening for us an unknown way,[57] he has joined earthly things to heavenly, having broken down the dividing wall, and abolished the hostility of the commandments and ordinances,[58] so that even the blessed angels, astonished at this, said, "Glory to God in the highest, and peace on earth, good will to men."[59] For since Christ our Savior has shown us good will, and has endured the cross for us, the tangled bonds of death have been loosed, and every tear has been wiped from every face,[60] as the prophet says: Grief has changed to joy.[61] Thus we too can opportunely say, "You have turned my mourning into joy for me; you have rent off my sackcloth, and girded me with gladness."[62] For what reason, that is, will we still be gloomy? What occasion will we still have for weeping? On the contrary, will not what has happened to us, thanks to the Savior, cause us boundless rejoicing? He it was who showed the way of salvation not only to us, but who also went as herald to the once disobedient spirits in the underworld, as Peter says.[63] For it would not have done for this loving-kindness to be shown only to some; the manifestation of the gift had to be extended to all of nature.[64] For he spoke opportunely through the prophets, "One part shall be rained upon, and the part on which I shall not rain shall be dried up."[65] But the word which befits the Savior is: "Come to me, all you who labor and are weary, and I will give you rest."[66]

---

55. Ps 43.3.                            56. Jn 1.9.
57. Cf. Heb 10.20.                      58. Cf. Eph 2.14–15.
59. Lk 2.14.                            60. Is 25.8; cf. Rv 21.4.
61. Cf. Jer 31.13.                      62. Ps 30.11–12.
63. 1 Pt 3.19–20.

64. Following Irenaeus and Athanasius, Cyril understood salvation as more than the redemption of the human person from the guilt of sin: salvation included the redemption of the whole created order.

65. Am 4.7.                             66. Mt 11.28.

Having proclaimed his message, then, to the spirits in the underworld, and having said to those in fetters, "Come forth!" and to those in darkness, "Show yourselves!"[67] he raised up the temple of himself in three days,[68] and renewed for nature even the ascent into heaven, presenting himself to the Father as a kind of first-fruits of humanity, having endowed those on earth with a share in the Spirit as a pledge of grace.[69]

9. Let us celebrate such great events, beloved, not with the leaven of old nor with the leaven of vice and wickedness, but with the unleavened bread of purity and truth, honoring our King with thanksgiving of every sort, and welcoming fasting, the mother of all good things, with the zeal befitting us. And let us hold to love for each other,[70] showing ourselves more intent upon hospitality, distinguishing ourselves in concern for the poor, remembering those who are in prison, as though in prison with them, and those who are ill-treated, since we ourselves also are in the body.[71] In a word, let us cherish every virtue. It is thus that we shall perform the genuine fast, beginning holy Lent on the fifth of the month of Phamenoth, and the week of the salvific Paschal feast on the tenth of Pharmuthi, breaking the fast on the fifteenth of this month, the eve of Saturday, as usual, and celebrating the feast on the next day, the eve of Sunday, the sixteenth of Pharmuthi, as the law prescribes,[72] adding thereafter the seven weeks of holy Eastertide. Thus will we inherit with the saints the kingdom of heaven in Christ Jesus our Lord, through whom and with whom be the glory and power to the Father, with the Holy Spirit, for ever and ever. Amen.

67. Cf. Is 49.9.
69. Cf. 2 Cor 5.5.
71. Cf. Heb 13.1–3.

68. Cf. Jn 2.19.
70. Eph 4.2.
72. April 11, 415.

# FESTAL LETTER THREE

N THE SOURCES CHRÉTIENNES edition of the letters, Évieux notes the following:

The manuscript tradition has made us aware of a series of 29 festal letters of Cyril, numbered 1–30. They announce the Paschal feast from 414 to 442. Since Cyril was bishop from October 17, 412, until June 27, 444, we are only missing letters from 413, 443, and 444. . . . It is evident in the dates of the letters that there is no gap in the series 414–442. The absence of the number 3 in the series is the result of a scribal error that has been maintained in successive editions. Since it is customary to cite the *Festal Letters* according to the erroneous numeration, we will not change it in this one.[1]

1. SC 372, 113.

# FESTAL LETTER FOUR

## A.D. 416

NCE AGAIN THE season for the holy feast shines upon us, with the contest of endurance getting under way shortly before and commanding us to display holiness of life and every other virtue as a sort of payment of a yearly debt to God, the Lord of all. But there is no exhortation to obedience that is unsuitable to those well-disposed, who seek to gain profit from the subject. For the fruit of good labors is glorious, while there is nothing more grievous than hesitation and idleness; the refusal to endure whatever is necessary to gain what will be of benefit will carry a heavy penalty, and this not in the sense of what concerns ordinary affairs, but what concerns nothing less than the loss of the soul.

Now since this is the situation as it really is, I think it behooves me above all to address you at this time especially about what is to your benefit, and almost to cry out with the prophet, "Prepare the way of the Lord!"[1] I have come before you again, therefore, in the conviction that I would not be an annoyance to the wise, if I should urge that it behooved them to value more highly what they were about, especially at the present time. But if there should be some who think that my discourse is not of the highest quality, even with the great pains I have taken with it, let them beware lest, with their malicious criticism of us, they rank themselves with those who esteem evil, and find themselves unwittingly excluded from the company of the wise. For it can only be a symptom of the worst kind of vice, when one enjoys things which might reasonably provoke rebuke, and considers it bad to be reputed for better things, or even finds it painful to

1. Is 40.3; Mk 1.3; Jn 1.23.

hear them spoken of. As for me, I believe that those who have decided to be serious about living a better life need the consolation and encouragement provided by discourse of the best quality, which can sharpen their eagerness for just this thing.[2] Those, by contrast, whose attitude is not what it should be, need to be provided with the medicine suited to correction, and efforts need to be made to see that they become better later on. Our instruction, then, will prove of the greatest profit in both cases, furnishing both kinds of persons with what is due them.

2. It is, then, the choir of prophets that draws us to this proclamation, and persuades us that we must announce the brilliant festival in advance, the prophets who rejoice in the Savior's achievements and bid us reject completely all thought of silence about them. Indeed, they cry out, one of them as follows: "Cry aloud, and spare not; lift up your voice as a trumpet!"[3] while another, whose thought and teaching are like the first, says, "Go up on a high mountain, you that bring glad tidings to Zion; lift up your voice with strength, you that bring glad tidings to Jerusalem; lift it up, fear not!"[4] With the removal of anything which could possibly impede our enthusiasm for these matters, therefore, I will proceed to speak of my subject with all due frankness, and, seeing as I do the season of continence hurrying toward us as though from a mountain far off, I will all but signal with my hand to the athletes of piety when I say, "Strip yourselves, lads! Take off the old self!"[5]

The time of fasting has come to us again, requiring the demonstration of every virtue. In this contest, though, the decision is not given to bodily strength, nor to the leaps on the wrestling floor, and it is not even the one judged superior in these matters who is regarded as capable of victory. "For we are not contending against flesh and blood, but against the principalities, against the powers, against the world rulers of this present darkness, against

---

2. Statements like this one extolling the value of rhetorical persuasion are common throughout these letters. See G. Kennedy, *Greek Rhetoric Under Christian Emperors* (Princeton: Princeton University Press, 1983).

3. Is 58.1.                                    4. Is 40.9.

5. Eph 4.22.

the spiritual hosts of wickedness in the heavenly places."[6] Now anyone who has decided to do battle against their attacks ought, I think, to be the kind of fighter who can be adjudged the more courageous. Otherwise, the danger to those not of that sort will be all too clear, and their boasting will be mere pretense. For to be ranked among those inferior, while thinking ourselves greater than we are, causes us to be laughed at with good reason, and to be placed at risk also. And it is advisable to avoid that situation (and anyone properly endowed with caution will say so), and if it is not profitless to rebuff, with all one's might, the shame that comes from wicked deeds, then obviously we must seek what is better, and achieve together with great zeal the victory over our opponents.

And if the evil spirits drive upon us in battle, then those who make bold to take up arms against them must have an ardor of spirit that can be seen. And if bodily skill and power are of no avail to us here, then it follows that, as Paul says, the soldier should "put on the weaponry of God, and strap on tightly the whole armor of piety toward him,"[7] that thus the fiery shafts of the evil one may be quenched.[8] Those who act with courage will succeed in escaping every wound. But let me return to language taken from contests in the theaters,[9] since those who are anxious to be of help must gather what they need from every side, as I am sure you yourselves will readily agree.

I understand, that is, that those who preside at gymnastic contests, and who doubtless find the expenses to be paid for the glory of their position no heavy burden, sound a trumpet to announce the contest when they are about to begin it, summoning to it all that it may be useful to see, and those with a good reputation in such events, but dismissing from the combats those whose technique does not appear as vigorous. For they judge it improper, and quite rightly so, that those with a name for bravery, or those in a position to have acquired experience deserving more respect in some other field of endeavor, should be

---

6. Eph 6.12.          7. Cf. Eph 6.11–14.

8. Cf. Eph 6.16.

9. See Christopher Haas, *Alexandria in Late Antiquity* (Baltimore: The Johns Hopkins University Press, 1997), 45–90.

grouped with those who are less honorable; nor should those of understandably higher repute be tarnished by the loathsome manners of the others.

Now if these folk strive with such noble intent for payments so small and unremarkable, and one can see their enthusiasm tuned to the highest pitch by the fear that their strength may appear less than others', then it is surely worth our while to ponder how we may prove better than they, and that indeed to the extent that the crowns are different. For if it is discovered that one has avoided a minor challenge, and shrunk from making the effort, an excuse may perhaps be found. One may say that it was not worthwhile running risks so great for prizes so small. But if that excuse is not available to us, since the crown so far excels the effort required, then what else is there to prevent us from competing eagerly? Nothing. We can only be accused of hesitancy, laziness, and the inclination to baseness which cools our enthusiasm for what has been praised. In my opinion, though, all of those of whom we have been speaking have been called to the efforts of the contests not because they were overcome by the desire for wealth so much as by that for honors and fame. For that has a certain attraction for them, and not getting what they want is regarded by each of them as an impeachment of his glory, that glory, I repeat, which is held in honor among them.

Such, I believe, is the attitude they seem to have, and they are of such high spirits that, if one were to approach any of them and ask: Given that there are so many occupations in life, why is it, dear sir, that you have adopted this role and attitude, for the sake of which you have abandoned everything else to show such esteem for the games on the wrestling-floor? What do you hope to gain here? Honors or wealth? Which would you prefer as the result of such efforts at the contests? I believe that any of them would reply at once: Away with wealth! I would be pleased to give an abundance of it in exchange for victory, and would offer my very life, if the occasion demanded, to avoid being laughed at. Now if these folk are thus disposed, it can only be the height of absurdity if we ourselves, before whom greater prizes are set, are not seen to rival their zeal, nor to strive to gain the upper hand, but hesitate and are worn down by our lack of resources, when we have from God such an abundance of aids which will render us victorious. For these others have the ability to defeat their opponents from their own experience and from their bodily strength, so that if any of them lacks these, he will be quite deprived of the joy of victory. But for us, the contest is not decided in this way; the situation is quite the reverse. If you lack strength, ask the contest judge, and you will receive it readily. And if your skill at wrestling is not what it should be, then the trainer is at hand who is an expert in sports. That is to say that God will supply the ability. And as for how to counter your opponents, that you will learn by examining holy Scripture. There you will find Paul's words: "I can do all things in Christ who strengthens me."[10] There you will hear with wondering ear the Psalmist singing and crying out to God, "In you will we push down our enemies, and in your name will we bring to naught them that rise up against us."[11]

It might be as well, though, to have recourse to other ways of speaking to you that may whet your courage, in addition to what has been said. That is to say, in contests in the present life, anyone who succeeds in defeating everyone else, whether surpassing them by his expertness in the particular skill, or attaining his ambition by bodily strength, will also certainly win the bitter hostility of the provider of the crowns. For the more highly the victors are praised, the higher are the costs facing the contest sponsors, and the more popular the former become, the more their ambitions will grow, the rewards, that is, being reckoned in proportion to the greatness of the achievements.

But the competition of piety is not run along those lines. The sponsor is rich; if he has any human emotions, he rejoices over those who do bravely as much as he grieves over the vanquished. For he says through one of the prophets, "Woe is me! for my soul faints because of the slain."[12] It is indeed for this reason that he raises even those who have fallen, even though the rules of the other kind of contest exclude from renown those condemned once for this, and banish them from the honor of victory. And God certainly rebukes those who, when they have fall-

10. Phil 4.13.                         11. Ps 43.6 (LXX).
12. Jer 4.31.

en, remain a long time where they are; he says through the prophet, "Can it be that the fallen do not arise?"[13]

3. This means that every effort should be made to avoid what has been said, and there is no one who will not declare how wicked it is to be negligent about what is good. But if something of the disagreeable sort occurs when nature, human nature I mean, looks too closely at sin, then there will be, I think, something like a second way to achieve good repute, and that is to long wholeheartedly to join one's betters, and to return eagerly to the resolution which one ought to have shown from the outset and preserved throughout. And let no one think, from what has been said, that the victory is too harshly demanding and difficult to achieve; let Paul, rather, anoint such a one with the cry, "God is faithful, and he will not let you be tempted beyond your strength, but with the temptation will also provide the way of escape, that you may be able to endure it."[14] That he will give this, as Paul says, I present in evidence Christ himself, when he says, "Behold, I have allowed you to tread upon serpents and scorpions, and over all the power of the enemy; and nothing shall hurt you."[15] Christ, that is, does really provide us generously, through the action of the Holy Spirit and the salvific cross, with the ability to achieve everything having to do with virtue. The cross is ridiculed by the Greeks, who are wise as far as speech goes, and whose finery consists of bare words, but who are so slow when it comes to finding the truth, that the very thing they seem to resemble is nothing other than pack-asses, who waggle their ears at those accustomed to making the loveliest music, but who understand nothing of the art of playing the lyre. They ought to be ashamed of their own thoughtlessness and seek to be benefited by the instruction of those who could teach them the truth, but instead they laugh at those they should envy, and flee from those whom it behooved them to imitate thoroughly, were they wise.

But those who import into the world however many gods each person wants, apart from him who "is" by nature, and who reject our words, would do well to listen to what in fact they say

---

13. Ps 40.9 (LXX).                    14. 1 Cor 10.13.
15. Lk 10.19.

one of their poets said: "The rule of many is not good; let there be one lord, one king,"[16] the One who is in all and through all and over all.[17] But I shall pass over what may be urged against them for now, and move on to what it seems fitting to speak of as closely connected to the present season.

4. The Jews, that is, who practice impiety to the last degree, are scandalized at the cross of Christ our Savior, and exceed the madness of the pagans to such an extent, that I believe that if anyone were to sit as judge of the two peoples, he would, I think, condemn the former and declare the practices of the latter less evil. For since they have not yet read the holy Scriptures, he would doubtless say, it is hardly surprising if they have failed to attain to true doctrine. The others, although they are instructed in piety by the Law and the prophets, have outdone the pagans in unreasonableness to the same degree that the excuse for the others' ignorance may be thought reasonable; they are without any defense which might present their stupidity as an unavoidable illness. You may, if you wish, see Christ himself supporting what I say, since he speaks about them as follows: "If I had not come and spoken to them, they would not have sin; but now they have no excuse for their sin."[18] And they have by now reached the sort of state, where one could not really be thought of as reviling them, if one insisted that they should be ranked with the pagans, and with those who do not know God at all. And there is nothing to prevent us from proving this from the very facts; on the contrary, this now seems what we are bound to do. For thus we shall rid ourselves easily of the charge of abuse, and shall make it clear to our listeners how determined we are to tell the truth. I will go back, then, to the beginning of this people, the Hebrew people that is, whence the matter to be explained may be made clear.

The blessed Abraham, of Chaldaean stock, was reared by a father who did not know the true God, was governed for a time by his parents' laws, was reckoned with the ignorant, and counted at that time among the idolaters. For youth is usually guided by

16. Homer, *Iliad* 2.204.    17. Cf. Eph 4.6.
18. Jn 15.22.

the wishes of others, and that it is not readily aware of what is to its advantage, is the fault of the time, not its own.

But when God decided to plant the Hebrew nation, he called him to an acquaintance with himself, extracted him as though he were a root of good stock from the midst of thorns, and transplanted him to true religion, and he became what he now is, changed as though into another person by the circumstance of his acquaintance with God, and simply by his decision to serve God, superior to all of those who were before him. If, then, the way of life of piety and the power of God's service were what refashioned the man, then it will be the loss of these things that will reduce to his former state the one who suffers it. It is good, that is, to redirect our discourse away from the person of the just man, and toward the fruit from his root. In this way it will be shown to be true that they quite deserted piety through their disbelief in Christ. Listen to what the Savior says through one of the prophets: "Woe to them! For they have turned aside from me: they are cowards, for they have sinned against me."[19] For this is the first and the main charge to be laid against the Hebrews. But anyone who wished to add to the list of their transgressions would find such a heap that he would be unable to tell their tale, no, not even were he an orator of the highest accomplishment, and of an eloquence so practiced that he yielded to none of the others who consider brilliance in this art better than any other happiness. So as not to remain quite silent, however, as though stupefied at the number of accusations, I shall do my best to subjoin just a few of them, which will show us how they have turned aside.

5. God, the Master of us all, speaks, then, in his annoyance at their impiety: "All of their rulers are disobedient. Ephraim put forth his roots, and they are dried up. He shall in no wise any more bear fruit: wherefore, even if they should beget children, I will kill the desired fruit of their womb. God shall reject them, because they have not hearkened to him: and they shall be wanderers among the nations."[20] Now does not experience itself

19. Hos 7.13.
20. Hos 9.15–17.

shout this more loudly than my words? And does not the outcome of events testify to the truth of what has been said? Since
they had shaken off their spirit of reverence for him in disobedience and contradiction, they were driven toward a condition of
sterility, and in a fair way to drying up, like plants removed from
water; deeply distressed in their roots at the time when the
words of the prophets reached them, they finally dried up completely through disbelief in Christ.

Thus it is that, shut out from his friendship, they hear what is
rightly said: "I hate, I reject your feasts, and I will not smell the
odor of your general assemblies. Wherefore, even if you should
bring me whole-burnt-offerings and sacrifices, I will not accept
them; neither will I have respect to your grand peace-offerings.
Remove from me the sound of your songs, and I will not hear
the melody of your instruments."[21] For God, in his love for the
truth, did not deem that one ought to enjoy figurative honors,
but made known that the time of worship in the Spirit had not
yet been proclaimed, announcing that it was to be the overthrow
of the ancient customs, in place of which he would grant better
ones. As indeed he proclaims clearly through one of the prophets: "And it shall come to pass in those days that they shall say no
more, 'The ark of the covenant of the Holy One of Israel'; it
shall not come to mind, nor shall it be named; neither shall it
be visited; nor shall this be done any more."[22]

Now if one wants to learn which time the prophet meant in
which, he affirmed, the ark would not come to mind or be
named any more, then let him look at the present state of affairs
in which he lives, and let him consider the Christian mysteries.
Clearly God did not intend that we too should employ the Hebrew customs in worship; nor have we an ark bright with gold
outside, and holding Moses' books within.[23] Each believer in
Christ, rather, is made a temple of the Spirit,[24] receiving the entire source of sanctification, if I may so speak. And let none of
our listeners think that our words either are directed against
Moses or are criticisms of the laws established through him. May
I never become so insane as to adopt this purpose, since holy

21. Am 5.21–23.     22. Jer 3.16.
23. Cf. Heb 9.4.     24. Cf. 1 Cor 3.16 and 6.19.

Scripture speaks otherwise: "For the Law, and the command-ment, is holy and just and good,"[25] as Paul says. It was in place until the time of correction, but did not yet introduce true wor-ship. For this reason God promised through one of the proph-ets that he would remake it into something better, with the words, "Behold, the days are coming, says the Lord, when I will make a new covenant with the house of Israel and house of Judah."[26] Paul understands this quite well when he says, "In speaking of a new covenant he treats the first as obsolete. And what is becoming obsolete and old is ready to vanish away."[27] And again, "For if that first one had been faultless, there would have been no occasion for a second."[28] Since, then, he has said that the first one was not free of fault, "for the Law made noth-ing perfect,"[29] he affirms that the second was perforce brought in in its stead for the world's salvation.

6. How long, then, will you disobey, O Jew? When will you come to agreement with the voices of the saints? But you may say, "Paul is yours, not mine, dear sir! I should be quite mad to ac-cept what is said by those with whom I am in no way related. It would be as if someone in battle were to accept happily his adver-sary's blows!" Do your words seem fair and right to me? For you are incorrect in your denial, and you banish from equal kinship Paul, who is Hebrew. For I hear him saying: For I too "am an Is-raelite, a Hebrew born of Hebrews; as to the Law a Pharisee."[30]

But since it seems in a way unpleasant for you when we men-tion the apostle's words, and attempt to convict you of ill-will, I will pass over this now. While I could cite countless passages from Moses and the prophets, I shall ask just one additional short question, and then leave the topic. Come then, dear sir, let us leave aside the deeper matters of the inquiries, and tell me clearly: if you do not expect the Law to be transformed into the truth, and think that it will remain always as it is without the least change, what is it that prevents you from remaining in the same situation? For what reason do you so neglect the worship of God,

25. Rom 7.12.
27. Heb 8.13.
29. Heb 7.19.

26. Jer 31.31 (LXX 38.31).
28. Heb 8.7.
30. Phil 3.5.

as to depart from the customs of your ancestors, and consider of no account what was held by them in the highest honor? Where, I mean, has your Temple gone? Where are the altars in it, and the sacrificial offerings? Where should one look for the inspectors of sacred victims, the swarms of them, that is, in the priestly registers, and the levitical colleges? Where, for that matter, to ask further, have your high priest's vestments gone, and his variegated garb? And the bells fastened to the fringes: for what reason have they fallen silent, and there is no "indicator"?[31] For the stone was called such from its function: the alterations of its colors forecast the future according to God's will.

And tell me why it is that you do not offer the sacrifices according to the Law. If you say that your negligence is deliberate, you stand convicted as a law-breaker, and thus, having used you as a witness in your own indictment, I will need no others. But if you hold that your inactivity in these matters is involuntary, and yourself agree that you are hindered by the bond of some necessity, then beware lest you be charged with lack of consideration, when your disobedience has lasted so long. Who is it, I mean, that is strong enough to make subject to necessity someone who is helped by God (for I know that you pride yourself highly on this point)? There is no one. It is, then, God's wrath—that is all that remains—which has fallen upon those from Israel and deprived the nation of all joy, not allowing it to boast any more of the Law, and exacting satisfaction for the impiety shown to Christ from those who mistreated him. And God has, with grace, transformed the fashion of worship into something better.

And now I will show you that this time of your inactivity was also proclaimed by the prophets. For I suppose that you are ashamed of your misfortunes, and try to hide what you must know, but pretend ignorance of, out of embarrassment lest you appear to have been cast far off by God. The blessed prophet Hosea speaks of such matters when he says, "The children of Israel shall abide many days without a king or a prince, and with-

31. The word "indicator" here translates the Greek *dēlos,* which appears in the LXX translation of Ex 28.30 and Lv 8.8. This in turn translates the Hebrew *urim.* The meaning of this term was as much a puzzle to ancient commentators as it is to modern ones. Cf. Gregory of Nyssa, *Life of Moses* 189.

out a sacrifice, and without an altar, and without a priesthood, and without indicators."[32] Who will deny that your books say this, and be so shameless as to dare to say that what everyone has seen would never happen? For the fulfillment of the words is evident to the most casual observer. But you will doubtless refuse again to accept this, and in cherishing your habitual disobedience, can you not see that you are no different from lifeless stones? The prophet speaks truly when he says, "All the house of Israel are stubborn and hard-hearted."[33] And God speaks the complete truth when he expounds your shamelessness through one of the saints in the words, "For I know that you are stubborn, and your neck is an iron sinew, and your forehead brazen."[34] The Savior himself denounces the enormity of your disobedience when he says, "All day long I have held out my hands to a disobedient and contrary people."[35]

And what, tell me, is the reason for the disobedience that has lasted so long? Did you not know, you who have been taught by holy Scripture, what was owed you from the promise? Did you not realize that the Word of God was to come to stay? Did you not hear what the prophet Zechariah said: "Rejoice and be glad, O daughter of Zion: for behold, I come, and I will dwell in the midst of you, says the Lord"?[36] How should you not have rejoiced, and been quite enveloped in gladness, when the arrival of our Savior Christ in all its brightness was announced by the saints? For the devil, falling like a hurricane upon all of humankind, if I may so speak, had enslaved it, and from then on there was no one left untouched by his arrogance, but all were in sin, no one being restrained by shame, but aspiring to do every frightful deed as though achieving the greatest renown thereby (for everyone's goal was to outdo in malice both those who had gone before and those to come after, and our glory was in our shame, as Paul says);[37] and so the Creator of all, searching for the needed ways of remedy, sought out all means to save the hu-

---

32. Hos 3.4. This particular passage was sometimes cited in patristic literature as a proof that God now favored the Church over the Jews. Cf. Origen, *On First Principles* 4.1.3.

33. Ezek 3.7.                    34. Is 48.4.

35. Is 65.2; cf. Rom 10.21.      36. Zec 2.10.

37. Cf. Phil 3.19.

man race. Prophets appeared when opportune, presenting the means of salvation to all. But since no one obeyed them, they called from heaven the very King of all, the Word of God, sometimes saying, "Lord, lower your heavens, and come down,"[38] and sometimes crying, "Send forth your light and your truth!"[39] The Only-Begotten Word of God came to stay, therefore, he who is the exact impress of the Father's substance,[40] who put on our likeness,[41] and, having become a human being, "appeared on earth and lived among human beings,"[42] as one of the wise has said. Seeing human nature running toward complete destruction and unable to accomplish anything good, he did not give the grace of justification to works, but, granting it to the believer, he called everyone to salvation. Then, when he should have been recognized by reason of such great kindness and of everything else, and the Word of God should have been adored who became a human being for us, quite the contrary happened: the all-daring Jewish people nailed him to a cross, inflicted upon him every kind of pain together with dishonor, and handed him over to death. But since, as holy Scripture says, "it was not possible for him to be held"[43] by death, he rose again on the third day, having said, "Come forth!"[44] to the spirits in the underworld, and despoiled the devil of all his wealth. He also destroyed the power of death, having placed in us the Holy Spirit as our earnest of future hope, the pledge of the good things we expect, offering himself for us to the Father like the first-fruits from paradise, appearing as he did in human form. For he stayed among us that he might make the human being a citizen of heaven, and join him to the choirs there.

For all of these things, beloved, even if the Jews do not wish it, it is obviously necessary for us to render deepest thanks, and to offer to God, as a sort of just return for having cherished us and loved us so, holiness in our works, mutual affection, hospitality, charity, familial love, and, the greatest remedy for sin among them, pity for the needy. For we must remember those in

---

38. Ps 144.5.  
39. Ps 43.3.  
40. Heb 1.3.  
41. Phil 2.7.  
42. Bar 3.37.  
43. Acts 2.24.  
44. Cf. Is 49.9.

prison as though we were imprisoned with them, and those mistreated, since we too are in the body.[45] Then indeed will we keep
festival in purity, and will achieve the fast that is the mother of all
good things in the proper way. We begin holy Lent on the twenty-sixth of the month of Mechir, and the week of the salvific Passover feast on the first of Pharmuthi; we break the fast, as the Gospel prescribes, on the eve of Saturday, the sixth of Pharmuthi,
celebrating the feast on the following day, the eve of Sunday, the
seventh of Pharmuthi.[46] We add subsequently the seven weeks of
holy Eastertide, believing that we will receive with the saints the
promises in the heavens, in Christ Jesus our Lord for ever.
Amen.

45. Heb 13.3.
46. April 2, 416.

# FESTAL LETTER FIVE

## A.D. 417

"HERE IS A TIME for everything,"[1] says holy Scripture, and that seems to me an excellent view of the nature of things, for nothing can be more harmful to it than missing the proper time. Since, then, no one will deny that to do this is bad, and those of sound mind will certainly agree, it behooves one, by contrast, to prefer the better idea, meaning the time suitable to everything, and fitting to each thing.

The present time, then, is that of festival, and we must once again obey holy Scripture when it says, "Blow the trumpet at the new moon, in the glorious day of your feast."[2] What season, then, will shine upon us more gloriously than the present? What is so conspicuous as our all-praised feast, which proclaims the truly genuine new moon, the new age for us of the Savior's sojourn, "in which everything has become new, and the old has passed away,"[3] as Paul says? Let the Church's trumpet sound, therefore, and let it send forth to us in joy once again its annual proclamation.

Will it, though, sound like an army bugle? Does it signal to us that the ranks of the enemy are now upon us? Does it announce the combat that looms, and fear of death, and tell us to take up our weapons as quickly as we can against our attackers? Not at all. I know that the sound of my trumpet is different, announcing nothing of the sort; its music is one of victory, sounding most joyously to those who hear it. "Come," it will say, according to the holy Psalmist, "let us exult in the Lord; let us make a joyful noise to God our Savior."[4]

What is it, then, on account of which one knows that the joy-

---

1. Eccl 3.1.  2. Ps 81.3.
3. 2 Cor 5.17.  4. Ps 95.1.

ful noise comes at the right time and decides that one must exult and lift up to the Savior his death as something sacred? I
know that you know, but I will explain it anyway. Death has been
conquered, which refused to be conquered. Corruption has
been made new.[5] Invincible suffering has been destroyed. Hell,
stricken with insatiable greed, and never satisfied with those who
had died, has learned, all unwillingly, what it could not bear to
learn earlier. For it does not strive to get hold of those who are
still falling, but has disgorged those already taken, having suffered a wonderful desolation by the Savior's power. For he paid
it a visit with the words, "You in prison, come out! You in the
darkness, show yourselves!"[6] And having made his proclamation
to the spirits in hell,[7] who had once disobeyed, he ascended victorious, having raised up his own temple[8] as a kind of first-fruits
of our hope,[9] made resurrection from the dead a way on which
revived nature can travel, and performed for us other good
things as well.

2. It is in these things, beloved, that we have the radiant signal
for the feast, and for these reasons that I think we must leap for
joy as we say, "The right hand of the Lord has wrought mightily;
the right hand of the Lord has exalted me."[10] All others, wher-
ever they may be, honor the custom of festivals, doing their utmost to dress in their finest, and it is regarded as the worst kind
of negligence or wickedness to fail to appear dressed in whatever item of value each has. When city-wide feasts are celebrated,
accordingly, one may see the common people participating in
them arrayed splendidly in flowers, making their way eagerly to
a still more splendid table and delighting in the digestive penalties rather than being pained by them. For us, though, the festivals are not conducted in this way, nor do we care to follow
the public customs or make efforts to do so. But the garment

5. The Pauline idea that salvation includes deliverance from decay is highly
developed in Cyril's theology and is a common theme in Greek patristics reaching back to Irenaeus. See Norman Russell, *The Doctrine of Deification in the Greek
Patristic Tradition* (Oxford: Oxford University Press, 2004).

6. Is 49.4.                          7. Cf. 1 Pt 3.19.
8. Cf. Jn 2.19–21.                    9. Cf. 1 Cor 15.20.
10. Ps 117.16 (LXX).

which is purest of all is Christ: "Put on the Lord Jesus Christ,"[11] Paul says. The table is not weighed down under a lavish outlay of dishes giving rise to profligate ostentation; that table rather is preferred to which Wisdom calls us when it cries, "Come, eat my bread, and drink the wine that I have mixed for you."[12]

For to fill the stomach with earthly food—and that not because one is yielding to the necessities of nature, nor because one is giving way to the unavoidable needs of the body to the extent that that is well done, but rather because one is overcome by pleasure at the mere sight of it—is simply to emulate the nature of irrational animals, which rejoice simply at the abundance of what they get to eat, and are happier when they overturn satiety itself in their insatiable desires, and go far beyond what is sufficient. To love the divine teachings, by contrast, and to consider the words of wisdom a splendid banquet, is, as everyone of good sense will say, something most remarkable and admirable, befitting one who is truly a rational human being made in the image of the Creator.[13]

I realize, though, that I have passed over in silence the thing which is the favorite of those at festivals. What is it? They arm themselves with torches against the darkness of the night, and do not let the evening darken their hearth, but surround the entire house with lamps, thus expelling the gloom of darkness with their gleaming. But we, again, do not have an artificial light, so to speak, nor is it lamps merry with modest flames that drives away the darkness, but Christ himself who says, "I am the light of the world."[14] That he would come to us is what the blessed Isaiah promised when he cried, "Be enlightened, be enlightened, O Jerusalem, for your light has come."[15] For the Savior's grace has visited us, dazzling everything as light does, and dispersing the gloomy cloud of ignorance.

This cloud the devil spread over us like a roof, and so took possession of the whole earth under the sun, so to speak, allowing no one to lift up in purity the eye of his heart or to measure

11. Rom 13.14.                    12. Prv 9.5.

13. Like most ancient theologians Cyril understood humanity's creation in the image of God as a reference to rational capability.

14. Jn 8.12.                    15. Is 60.1.

the power of the Creator by proportion to the beauty of things created; for that would have been of no small benefit to those in error. But lest they should gain something of the various things which could contribute to their salvation, and they should recover the freedom due to their nature, he blinded their thoughts, as Paul says, to keep them from seeing the light of the glory of the Gospel of Christ.[16] But the wretch failed in his hope. For the One who called to salvation was greater. The great multitude of the nations has, then, been saved, and, even though belatedly, has nonetheless recognized the Creator.

The Jews, however, taught by the Law to recognize Christ our Savior, and instructed by Moses' teachings, "have forsaken," as it is written, "the ways of their own vineyard, and have caused the axles of their own husbandry to go astray."[17] For they did not recognize the Word of God who became a human being for us, "who became poor for us," as Paul says, "that we might become rich in him."[18] It is indeed for this reason that the prophet Jeremiah rebuked them strongly, crying, "How will you say, We are wise, and the law of the Lord is with us? In vain have the scribes used a false pen, the poor are ashamed, and alarmed, and taken. What wisdom is there in them, that they have rejected the Word of the Lord?"[19] For they really have rejected the Only-Begotten Word of God, but he became the cornerstone,[20] however they may resist this. It is for this reason that the prophet says rightly of them somewhere, "The children are foolish and unwise."[21] And what is said of them must appear true to everyone. They are obviously foolish and senseless when, having at hand the readings from the prophets to teach them the mystery of piety, and being able likewise to learn sufficiently about it from the writings of Moses, they are shown to be so negligent of their own salvation as not to care as much about it as even the gentiles do! Indeed, God speaks to them somewhere as follows: "I have set watchmen over you, and I said, Listen to the sound of the trumpet. And they said, We will not listen. Therefore, the gentiles have heard, and they that feed the flocks among them. Hear, O earth: be-

---

16. Cf. 2 Cor 4.4.                    17. Prv 9.12b (LXX).
18. 2 Cor 8.9.                        19. Jer 8.8–9.
20. Ps 118.22; Mt 21.42; cf. 1 Pt 2.7.    21. Jer 4.22.

hold, I will bring evils upon this people, the fruit of their rebellions; for they have not heeded my law, and they have rejected my word."[22]

For they really have rejected the Word of God, neither understanding that it behooved them to follow the preaching of the holy apostles, nor thinking that they had to pay attention to the older books. For one may suppose that it behooved them, if they were really concerned for what was to their advantage, not to let their mind be deceived by being puffed up by a reputation for knowledge of the Law, but to let the fear of not appearing exact in its observance, and of being punished as a result, lead them rather to examine what has been said about the Savior by the saints, or what has been expressed otherwise in figurative language. For one may see many images of the realities in the words of the Spirit, images which present the clearest possible picture of our Savior's sojourn.

But now there springs to mind a variety of ways of looking at these topics, since I am moved to remember holy Scripture, and a whole swarm of thoughts vies for my attention. I think, however, that I must begin what I say with the older realities, and proceed now by way of those things which will make them readier to believe us.

Let us examine, then, if you will, blessed Abraham's very way of life, how and in what circumstances he lived; I will, in addition, look into the birth, so dearly desired, and the descendants of Isaac. For in these things, O Jew, you will see into the very root of your people, if I may so speak: the mystery concerning our Savior beautifully and skillfully molded as if in bronze. Lest I appear deceitfully glib, however, with nothing true in what I say, I shall add Moses' own exposition, and reveal the history clearly; thus you will understand more easily what we say.

3. Sarah, then, was joined lawfully to the forefather of the people. He had also a slave, the Egyptian that is, Hagar by name.[23] But the free woman, of free stock, had not known childbirth or

22. Jer 6.17–19.

23. Cyril's interpretation of Paul's allegory resembles that of Philo and was probably mediated through Clement of Alexandria: see SC 372, 294, n. 1.

its pains, and had seen no fruit of her own womb. Drawn, then, toward the love of children by the strongest of natural desires, she fell into a deep unhappiness. And what chiefly elicits one's sympathy is the following. Abraham had reached the age of eighty, in which, it was reasonable to suppose, the warm impulse of nature for procreation had now cooled. She herself, grieving over her lack of children, and bewailing deeply the sterility of her womb, had arrived at extreme old age. Cleverly managing her longing, therefore, she countered the natural sting that accompanies it by urging her spouse to enter into marriage with the slave, and thereby to become the father at least of illegitimate children, since he had not been granted legitimate offspring. This is how holy Scripture has it: "Sarah the wife of Abraham had borne him no children; and he had an Egyptian slave, whose name was Hagar. And Sarah said to Abraham, Behold, the Lord has restrained me from bearing; go therefore in to your slave, that I may get children for myself through her."[24] Let it not be thought that the patriarch was being goaded unreasonably by Sarah's words to the enjoyment of pleasure, or was somehow being instigated to incontinence![25] That was not her purpose; far from it! It was rather, as I said, that she blamed her own inability to bear children, and thought it cruelly hard, if that just man of such stature should not have offspring at least from another woman. Such then was Sarah in her relationship with her spouse, and in fact the plan was carried out by the patriarch, and an illegitimate child, Ishmael, was born to him from the Egyptian.

At his birth the yearning of the free woman was frustrated, for she had looked forward to being overjoyed at a legitimate childbirth, and now she drank off a keener grief at not being able to bear, and was cast down in the drunkenness of her suffering. But God, the provider of every good hope, who has power over all, pitied her in her deep distress over what had happened. Her who had long been sterile and childless, and deprived by length of time of the ability to give birth, he at once rendered fruitful and able to bear a child. And he said to Abra-

24. Gn 16.1–2.

25. Cyril, like many early Christian authors, struggled with Old Testament passages that appeared to cast the patriarchs in an "immoral" light.

ham, "Sarai your wife—her name shall not be called Sarai; Sarah shall be her name. And I will bless her, and give you a son of her, and I will bless him, and he shall become nations, and kings of nations shall come forth from him. And Abraham fell upon his face, and laughed, and spoke in his heart, saying, Shall there be a child to one who is a hundred years old? And shall Sarah, who is ninety years old, bear? But God said to Abraham, Yes, behold, Sarah your wife shall bear you a son, and you shall call his name Isaac; and I will establish my covenant with him for an everlasting covenant, and with his seed after him."[26]

This promise to Abraham was true. And when what had been announced came to fulfillment, and the sterile woman experienced the giving of birth, the little child was then before their eyes, and appeared as the heir of his father's property. The slave, who had the illegitimate Ishmael from Abraham, was then driven from her master's house as redundant. While she was fleeing, and had already come far from the house, an angel spoke to her from heaven, saying, "Hagar, slave of Sarah, where are you going?" She answered, "I am fleeing from the face of my mistress Sarah." The angel replied to her, "Return to your mistress, and submit yourself under her hands."[27]

The story needs a longer telling, but we may conclude it here. It remains now for us to show the image of our Savior in it. For this was the very reason for our extended discourse to you. The divinely inspired Paul, then, summing up briefly the history, and gathering into one reflection a series of extended narratives, transformed the charmless character of what was written into a most appealing image of the realities. He writes to certain people: "You do not read the Law. For it is written that Abraham had two sons, one by a slave and one by a free woman. But the son of the slave was born according to the flesh, the son of the free woman through promise. The women are allegorical; they are two covenants. One is from Mount Sinai, bearing children for slavery; she is Hagar. Now Sinai is a mountain in Arabia; it corresponds to the present Jerusalem, for she is in slavery with her children. But the Jerusalem above is free, and she is our mother."[28]

26. Gn 17.15–19.    27. Gn 16.8–9.
28. Gal 4.22–26.

Now I must say, beloved, that while I deeply admire the force of the allegory, and with every reason, I still think that, since holy Scripture is so extensive, one must come up with other ideas about it in addition to what has rightly been said. Not that one can say anything fairer (let me not be so foolish as to imagine that I can think of anything greater or better than what has been communicated by the herald of truth!); but since there is no reason not to take some practice, let us add some more natural ideas to these considerations, decorate the image with something like a variety of colors, and thus, using the same figures, arrive by a different way at an equivalent form of the allegory.[29]

4. Let us, then, regard Abraham as the ancient age and, so to speak, time grown old, and the woman living with him as human nature. The feminine character represents fertility, and the antique character represents old age. For human nature is quite ancient and quite fertile, and, while living together with long age, has yet been enclosed, as it were, in one bridal chamber under this firmament.

This free human nature, then—for so it was made by God—having inherited authority over all things, ran together, all but hand-in-hand with time as it pushed on, and, having no legitimate, God-given offspring, gloried in children which were, so to speak, foreign and illegitimate, those from the Egyptian I mean, that is, from the darkened one. For "Egypt" means "darkening." And whom will we reckon to be the one being darkened? Why, none other than the falsely named wisdom of the world, of whom the wise men of old were born, so to speak, they who engender as it were from the womb of the error which bears them; they were children of the age,[30] for so the Savior calls them. They are spurious nonetheless, and, reared for slavery, they served those not gods by nature.

But when the Son of the promise was given to time now grown old and in decline toward its end, free human nature, consider-

---

29. Unlike many modern interpreters, ancient exegetes believed that texts could generate any number of interpretations as long as they were doctrinally sound. Even Paul's allegory can be "tweaked," as it were.

30. Cf. Lk 16.8.

ing to be as good as nothing what was idle and useless in abundance of offspring, and for that reason called sterile and childless, brought forth the noble infant, the one chosen, I mean, out from myriads.[31] There appeared at last the heir, our Lord Jesus Christ, and the slave was expelled together with her children. "For where is the wise man? Where is the scribe? Where is the debater of this age? For God has made foolish the wisdom of the world,"[32] as Paul says.

It is the one from the free woman, though, who inherits. For "Ask of me," the Father who is in heaven says somewhere to the Son, "and I will give you the nations for your inheritance, and the ends of the earth for your possession."[33] The divine goodness, though, did not let the slave who was expelled perish with her own children. It brought her back, and bade her submit herself under the hands of the free woman. "Return," it says, "to your mistress, and submit yourself under her hands."[34] For the falsely named wisdom of the world, which long ago laughed at the marriage of the free, now is a slave to the nobility of God's children, serving the consideration of divine things through the most judicious articulation of language.

The birth of Isaac, therefore, who is from the promise, signifies nothing other than Christ born at the completion of the ages. And no one should complain if not all the parts of the story adapt themselves to the truth. Allegorical figures, after all, function to the extent possible.[35] The just man, for instance, is often compared to a sheep, because of the animal's natural gentleness, but to speak of him as having horns, or even as walking around on hooves, is completely absurd. Let us proceed, then, to demonstrate the matter at hand. For I believe that Christ appears of necessity in Isaac's birth, expressed there as in figure. Lest I seem, though, to be using superfluous and overwrought language, and to be making every effort to play tricks with the truth, or even to declaim and to fashion sorry images of empty ideas, let us, once again, prove from holy Scripture itself that I am telling the truth.

---

31. Cf. Song 5.10.       32. Cf. 1 Cor 1.20; Is 19.12.

33. Ps 2.8.       34. Gn 16.9.

35. That is, allegories never correspond exactly to the realities they point to.

5. It was for no other reason that God made the promise to Abraham, I mean the one concerning Isaac, than simply on account of our Savior's sojourn, in whom the blessing as well was fulfilled. Let me give you the divine words themselves: "I will bless her," God said of Sarah, "and give you a son of her, and I will bless him, and he shall become nations, and kings of nations shall come from him."[36] And again: "I will establish my covenant with him for an everlasting covenant, and with his seed after him."[37]

It will be clear to all, though, that Isaac became the father of one son, and the blessed Jacob alone sprang from him. To him were born twelve boys, but only one nation came from them, that of the Jews, of course. How, then, will the words "he shall become nations" be fulfilled? For even if the nation from Israel is divided into twelve tribes, yet it is one people, consisting indeed of something like many members, but still forming one body from them all. And that, further, the covenant established through Moses will not be an eternal covenant from God to those from Isaac's seed, we know from what the prophet Jeremiah says: "Behold, the days are coming, says the Lord, when I will make a new covenant with the house of Israel, and with the house of Judah."[38] Paul understood this very well when he says, "In speaking of a new covenant he treats the first as obsolete. And what is becoming obsolete and growing old is ready to vanish away."[39] There is, therefore, a setting aside of a former commandment,[40] as he says further, and "a better hope is introduced, through which we draw near to God."[41]

Since, therefore, it has been proven clearly in every way that Abraham's descendant became the father of one people, and since, further, there is an additional reason which compels us to display the truth of what is written of him (namely, that God cannot lie), then we cannot but refer to Christ himself the fulfillment of the promise. For he was the one who, as I said before, was portrayed in the other. He became the father of many nations, drawing everyone to himself through faith,[42] and greatly

36. Gn 17.16.                          37. Gn 17.19.
38. Jer 31.31 (LXX 38.31).             39. Heb 8.13.
40. Heb 7.18.                          41. Heb 7.19.
42. Cf. Jn 12.32.

rejoicing at the multitude of the nations with the words, "Here I am, and my children, which God has given."[43]

That will be enough from us on this matter. But let us hear from the witness to the truth himself; let Paul in his supreme wisdom support what has been said when he cries out with me, "Does he who supplies the Spirit to you and works miracles among you do so by works of the Law, or by hearing with faith? Thus Abraham 'believed God, and it was reckoned to him as righteousness.' So you see that it is those of faith who are children of Abraham."[44] The force of the promise therefore extends by no means to the children according to the flesh, but to those of course, whoever they may be, who claim Abraham as their father through faith in Christ.

This is the very thing which the blessed Baptist seems to me to be saying so clearly to those born from Israel when, in boasting of their relationship simply according to the flesh, they claimed Abraham as the founder of their nation: "Bear fruit, then," he said, "that befits repentance, and do not presume to say to yourselves, 'We have Abraham as our father.' For God is able from these stones to raise up children to Abraham."[45] He calls "stones" here those whose minds are dried up, who are weighed down by their unfeeling hearts, as it were.

But if one considers carefully those from the nations, one will find that they are none other than those who have been raised up by faith, and have been born as children to Abraham, and constituted co-heirs with Isaac, and become sharers in the blessing given him. Paul bears witness to this when he cries, "The Scripture, foreseeing that God would justify the gentiles by faith, preached the Gospel beforehand to Abraham, saying, 'In you shall all the nations be blessed.' So then, those who are of faith are blessed with Abraham, who had faith."[46]

That therefore Abraham's offspring Isaac represents our Lord Jesus Christ himself, may be shown in all sorts of ways, and quite easily. I think that even the dullest person will be persuaded by

43. Is 8.18; cf. Gn 48.9.
44. Gal 3.5–7; cf. Gn 15.6, Rom 4.3, Jas 2.23.
45. Mt 3.8–9; cf. Jn 8.33–40, Rom 9.7–8, Gal 4.21–31.
46. Gal 3.8–10.

what blessed Paul writes to the Galatians: "To give a human example, brethren: no one annuls even a human being's will, or adds to it, once it has been ratified. Now the promises were made to Abraham and to his offspring. It does not say, 'and to offsprings,' referring to many; but, referring to one, 'and to your offspring,' which is Christ."[47] And that, further, the promise to Abraham has been fulfilled in those who believe in Christ, and that we are not forced to transfer the promise to the nation which is according to the flesh (thus expelling grace), Paul himself assures us when he says, "For all of you who were baptized into Christ have put on Christ. There is neither Jew nor Greek, there is neither slave nor free, there is neither male nor female; for you all belong to Christ Jesus. And if you are Christ's, then you are Abraham's heirs according to the promise."[48]

I trust, then, that my discourse has reached a length sufficient to prove what was intended. But if my words seem trivial to you, O Jew, and you consider a correct view of things to be of no consequence, and, once again, you by no means agree with us that this is the way these things are, the fault, dear sir, is not mine, but is rather your lack of belief. For those who have applied themselves to say what is best can in no way be blamed for being wholly unable to persuade their listeners. For when they have applied great zeal to doing what they could, they are rightly free of all blame. For the very unwillingness to accept what is excellently said is itself a mark of the most disgraceful character on the part of the listeners, when one has spoken well to them, just as one who has received a loan from someone, and then turns out to be ungrateful and forgetful of it, surely demonstrates his own malice, and not that of the lender.

When I look at the experiences of physicians, however, I am aware of how wisely they practice their profession, and of the way in which what they devise for the sick accords with prudent reason. Let us then emulate their ways, and apply the same medicines, so to speak, to the dull Jew. Physicians, that is, in fortifying the diet of those whose strength is failing, if they see that the sickness has deprived them of their appetite, provide them with a variety of food in abundance, prescribing quite wisely that what

47. Gal 3.15–16.　　　　48. Gal 3.27–29.

will suffice should be sought from every possible quarter. Since we intend to imitate them, let us, likewise, add some other considerations to what we have already said; let the Jew, whose wits have wandered so far, be called by all possible means to willing obedience. Let him see once more our Lord Jesus Christ represented by Isaac even of old.

6. Let the all-praiseworthy Abraham enter once again, therefore (for I will begin now to speak of him); Abraham, to whom God said, "Take your son, the beloved one, whom you have loved—Isaac; and go into the high land, and offer him for a whole-burnt-offering on one of the mountains which I will tell you of."[49] The order may well seem strange to some and understandably difficult. For if he was an only child, and beloved, and late-born, the son barely able to be given to him, and that in his old age, how is it that God advises him that he must sacrifice him? And tell me: is it not the height of absurdity for the just one to kill the child? Who would be so cruel, hardened by the savagery of beasts, as to arm himself against his own child, and to treat his own offspring like an enemy? What it was, then, that the patriarch was being taught, and that, precisely by means of this sort of command, is what it is now necessary to explain, as far as may be. For it is certainly obvious to all that, if we passed over in silence the providential arrangement linked to the order given, it would be like condemning as inhuman that nature which is the gentlest of all.

Since, then, the promise made with respect to Isaac could not otherwise be kept by God, except through the cross of Christ who sends the blessing to all the nations, God, in wanting to show him the nature and magnitude of the grace imparted for the salvation of his seed when he handed over his own Son to death, said to him in words of the deepest significance, "Take your son." And, as though to kindle in him the affection suiting a parent for a one and only child, he adds and repeats: "the beloved one, whom you have loved—Isaac; and offer him on one of the mountains which I will tell you of," all but saying, "that in your suffering you may learn what it is that the Father of all will

49. Gn 22.2.

later undergo when he offers as the supernatural sacrifice the Son he has loved." The Savior himself in fact expressed his complete astonishment at it when he said, "For God so loved the world, that he gave his only Son, that everyone who believes in him might not perish, but might have eternal life."[50]

The patriarch therefore obeyed God unhesitatingly when he gave these orders, since he held the divine commandment in higher regard than he did his affection for his son. "Rising up in the morning," as it is written, "he saddled his ass, and he took with him two servants, and Isaac his son. And having split wood for a whole-burnt-offering, he arose and departed, and came to the place of which God spoke to him, on the third day. And Abraham, lifting up his eyes, saw the place far off. And he said to his servants, Sit here with the ass, and I and the lad will proceed thus far, and having worshiped we will return to you. And Abraham took the wood of the whole-burnt-offering, and laid it on Isaac his son, and he took into his hands both the fire and the knife, and the two went together. And having gone, they came to the place which God spoke of to him. And there Abraham built an altar, and laid the wood on it, and having bound together the feet of Isaac his son, he laid him on the altar upon the wood. And Abraham stretched forth his hand to take the knife to slay his son. And an angel of the Lord called him, and said, Abraham, Abraham. And he said, Behold, I am here. And he said, Lay not your hand upon the child, neither do anything to him, for now I know that you fear God, and for my sake you have not spared your beloved son. And Abraham lifted up his eyes and beheld, and—lo!—a ram caught by his horns in a plant of Sabec; and Abraham went and took the ram, and offered him up for a whole-burnt-offering in the place of Isaac his son."[51]

7. So runs the passage from holy Scripture, representing in its entirety the mystery concerning the Savior. But what we must do is relate the beauty of the truth to what is presented figuratively, and explain clearly each of the things said. For thus the deep mystery of piety will be easily taken in by our listeners. The thrice-

50. Jn 3.16.
51. Gn 22.3–13.

blessed Abraham, therefore, takes the lad, and hastens off to the place that God had shown him. He just manages to arrive on the third day itself, having bidden two servants to follow as well. That the lad, then, is offered in sacrifice by the father, signifies, symbolically and figuratively, that it was no human power, nor the arrogance of those plotting against him, that brought our Lord Jesus, the Christ, to the cross, but the Father's will, if I may so speak, which allowed him to undergo death for all providentially. This is just what the Savior said when he was speaking once to Pilate: "You would have no power over me, if it had not been given you from above."[52] And again, once when speaking to the Father in heaven himself, he said, "Father, if it be possible, let this cup pass from me; nevertheless, not as I will, but as you will."[53] The lad does not oppose his father. "For the Son, God though he was, humbled himself, becoming obedient unto death to the Father, death on the cross."[54] It was for this reason that he spoke as well through the prophet Isaiah: "I do not disobey, nor do I resist."[55]

And that he just manages to reach the place on the third day signifies the final time, the time when the Savior came to sojourn. For with the first and middle times gone by, the third will certainly be the one at the end. And the pair of servants bidden to follow signifies further, in symbol, that the two peoples were to follow Christ when he went up to his salvific Passion. But that the blessed Abraham saw the place from afar signifies the Father's eternal foreknowledge, with which he watches his own offspring, Christ. For thus Peter speaks of the Savior as "foreknown before the foundation of the world, but made manifest at the end."[56]

Then comes, "Sit here," says the blessed Abraham to the servants, and also, "with the ass, and I and the lad will proceed thus far."[57] What this passage means to us, I will explain as best I can.

---

52. Jn 19.11.

53. Mt 26.39.

54. Phil 2.8. This passage, which describes Christ's *kenosis,* appears in 13 of the 29 letters (SC 372, 318, n.1). It, along with Jn 1.14 and Heb 2.14–17, heavily influenced Cyril's Christological thinking.

55. Is 50.5.          56. 1 Pt 1.20; cf. Jn 17.24, Eph 1.4.

57. Gn 22.5.

Those who have just been called to believe, and have decided to follow Christ the Savior, but remain still in servile subjection to their sins, and are not yet called to the freedom of justice through holy baptism, but are still in a state of irrationality and ignorance, which is signified by the ass: they will not see clearly the saving Passion, nor share immediately in the sacrifice of the true Lamb. They will remain below, and persevere in the humble instruction of catechesis, until by God's mercy they can shake off the weight of sin and ascend to the highest grasp of the divine mystery as though to some radiant mountain summit, just as some have said: "Come, let us go up to the mountain of the Lord, and to the house of the God of Jacob; and he will tell us his way, and we will walk in it."[58]

But I wonder deeply at what the blessed Abraham says to the servants, as I mentioned earlier: "Sit here, and I and the lad will proceed thus far, and having worshiped we will return to you." Now he prophesies as a just man, for they were to return. As a wise man, though, he keeps silence, not revealing the mystery to those yet uninitiated; and in this too he presents himself as a figure to us, to whom the Savior himself says, "Do not give what is holy to the dogs, nor throw your pearls before swine,"[59] by "pearls" meaning the clear and shining words of the Spirit.

Then it continues: "Abraham laid the wood of the whole-burnt-offering on the boy."[60] It was with the Father's providential permission, and well nigh even his cooperation, that the Jews placed the cross on the Savior; they did not force the divine power against his will. The prophet Isaiah will be found to be a truthful witness to this when he says of him, "The chastisement of our peace was upon him; by his bruises we were healed. All we as sheep have gone astray; everyone has gone astray in his way; and the Lord gave him up for our sins."[61] And when he had reached the places of which he had been told, the patriarch built the altar admirably and wonderfully well, in order again that we might realize thereby that, while what was upon our Savior appeared to human eyes to be a cross of wood, in the eyes of the Father of all

---

58. Is 2.3.
60. Gn 22.6.

59. Mt 7.6.
61. Is 53.5–6.

it was really an altar great and lofty, raised up for the salvation of the world and smoking from a sacrifice sacred and all-holy.

And that Isaac was placed upon the wood, but that the ram underwent the immolation in his place, shows most clearly that, while it was God the Word who went up upon the cross, and who was in the temple which was suspended there, it was not the Lord himself, passionless by nature, who suffered. For the knife was not brought to Isaac, that is, to the Word who came forth from the Father's substance; but in his place, as though it was he, the temple from the holy Virgin, which is signified by the sheep, was brought to the slaughter. The Word, however, made the suffering his own, and quite rightly. For the body was his, and none other's.[62] The reason again is that when his body was scourged, and even spat upon by the all-daring Jews, he himself spoke through the prophet Isaiah: "I gave my back to scourges, and my cheeks to blows."[63] "For there is one God, the Father, and one Lord, Jesus Christ,"[64] "who is blessed forever, Amen."[65] Who for our salvation "despised the shame,"[66] as it is written, and "becoming obedient to the Father, humbled himself unto death,"[67] in order that, in dying because of us and for us, he might raise us again with himself from the dead, after giving us life through the Holy Spirit, open to us the gates of heaven, lead human nature there which of old had been made fugitive by sin, and present it before the Father.

In the presence of such mighty deeds of our Savior, dearly beloved, let every mouth open in acclamation, let every tongue busy itself with songs of praise for him, let it cry aloud as in clear melody, "God has gone up with a shout, the Lord with the sound of a trumpet."[68] For he has gone up after fulfilling the economy in our regard, and he has not simply ascended, but has done so "after taking captivity captive, and giving gifts among men."[69] For

---

62. See the introduction for a discussion of Cyril's efforts to articulate conflict between the Son's passionless nature as God and the Son's engagement with flesh in Christ.

63. Is 50.6.             64. 1 Cor 8.6.

65. Rom 9.5.             66. Heb 12.2.

67. Phil 2.8.             68. Ps 47.5.

69. Cf. Ps 68.18, Eph 4.8.

after snatching all of us who had remained captives from the devil's hands, he redeemed us, and filled us with good gifts. For various are the gifts which have come to us through the Spirit.

8. Filled by Christ with every blessing, let us therefore keep festival, beloved, without being distressed at the beneficial labor it takes, nor considering burdensome the effort required to fast, but betaking ourselves to the contest with cheerful mind, "rejoicing in hope,"[70] as Paul says, and exulting henceforth in the good things we await. But before all else, let us hold to love for each other; let the bitter demon of detraction be driven out; let jealousy be banished from our souls; let malice and deceit take flight; let falsehood be absent, and that most chief of evils, perjury. But let us not swear at all; let our "yes" be "yes," as the Savior says, and our "no," "no."[71] Let us visit those who struggle with that cruelest of beasts, meaning those in poverty. Let us refresh the orphan and the widow. Let us offer respite with the appropriate remedies to those mistreated.[72] Let us be found kindly and compassionate to prisoners. For it is then, yes then, that we will achieve a true and perfectly pure fast for Christ.

We begin holy Lent on the sixteenth of the month of Phamenoth, and the week of the salvific Paschal feast on the twenty-first of Pharmuthi, completing the fast on the twenty-sixth of Pharmuthi, the eve of Saturday. We celebrate the feast the next day, the eve of Sunday, the twenty-seventh of Pharmuthi.[73] Next we add the seven weeks of holy Eastertide. Thus will we inherit the kingdom of heaven in Christ Jesus our Lord, through whom and with whom be glory and power to the Father with the Holy Spirit, now and forever and for endless ages. Amen.

70. Rom 12.12.                    71. Cf. Mt 5.37.
72. Jas 1.27.                     73. April 22, 417.

# FESTAL LETTER SIX

## A.D. 418

ITH OUR HOLY FEAST shining forth and appointing the renowned contest of endurance for those accustomed to a reputation for good works, I think it fitting for everyone to be gathered to the spiritual theater, saying, "Come, let us go up to the mountain of the Lord, and to the house of the God of Jacob."[1] Thus when we form an all-hallowed company in it, and through our unity with one another in the Spirit are joined together as though to form a single lyre, let us praise in song our chorus-master with the words, "All nations, clap your hands; shout to God with joyful cries."[2]

For one might be rightly accused of hesitation and delay in pursuing the better course, if one declined to render, in payment of debt, thank-offerings to the Savior who has adorned human nature with an untold multitude of good things, transformed it wholly by his ineffable power to restore its ancient glory, destroyed the hideous appearance inflicted on it by sin, and restored to their original image and to the features of their proper nature all those who acknowledge him in the words of that wisest of disciples, "My Lord and my God."[3]

To the blessed prophet Isaiah, then, were spoken the following words through the Spirit: "Cry out loudly and unsparingly; lift up your voice like a trumpet."[4] And since the law of the priesthood that we inherited from of old, and custom descending from ancient times, make us realize that we too must execute this with great zeal, let us again call out more melodiously than a trumpet this announcement: that, as is written in the

1. Is 2.3.                    2. Ps 47.1.
3. Jn 20.28.                  4. Is 58.1.

101

Psalms, "It is time to act for the Lord."[5] Now, that the time is here to act for the Lord, I suppose no one will deny. But what one ought to do is something which the studious might rightly ask us. And in my deep admiration for those who ask, and who think it necessary to inquire about these things, I think it well to use the words of the holy prophets. Let them listen to Isaiah when he says, "Let us make peace with him; let us who are coming make peace."[6] But since these words are not altogether clear, as one might judge, let us practice something like what those persons do who make it their business to reveal things from of old which are now hidden, and let us make clear the meaning of the passage.

2. There is innate in the members of our flesh a certain law which is natural and, so to speak, akin, and which musters us in arms against the Creator God, and sets our own thoughts in opposition to the desires of the Spirit. Hence arise arguments in us, and a countless swarm of disorderly desires opposed to the inclinations which draw us in the better direction, as though they had ranged themselves like a crowd of enemy troops against our impulses toward what is beneficial. This law of the flesh, so arrogant and tyrannous in us, is manifested as well by the blessed Paul when he cries, "For I delight in the law of God, in my inmost self, but I see another law at war with the law of my mind and making me captive to the law of sin which dwells in my members."[7]

As long, then, as this law prevails in us and acts boldly against the desires of the Spirit, marshals against them its own will, and even in fact forces us to act as it likes, it renders completely hostile to God those in whom it appears in control, banishing peace from those who are just, and shuts them out from the affection of their Maker. But when it grows weary, and is overcome by the energy devoted to piety, and becomes like someone who is defeated in battle and throws away his shield and flees, then it

5. Ps 119.126. This translation tries to render the ambiguity of the LXX; the original Hebrew certainly means: "it is time for the Lord to act," and that must be what the LXX translator probably meant.

6. Is 27.5.                              7. Rom 7.22–23.

makes the road to friendship with God a highway for those who choose to live rightly and according to the divine law. And then, once the base of operations of the intervening forces has been destroyed in this way, we will agree with whatever the Spirit bids us do. And having nothing remaining to put up a resistance, we who are coming to salvation through faith in him will regard "peace with God"[8] as something to be loved. "Let us therefore make peace with him, let us who are coming make peace."[9] "Let us put to death what is earthly in us: fornication, impurity, passion, evil desire, and, above all, covetousness."[10] Let the law of the flesh die to the desires for what is good, as though it had been pierced with sharp iron. Let the earthly and unclean mentality in us fall. Let God's law dominate. Let it be the pursuer, rather than the one seen to be fleeing. For when it prevails, and shows itself superior to its opponent's power, it causes every virtue to take root in us, makes those who were once runaways to be the closest friends of their Master, and procures for those not having it the hope of the saints which is so deeply desired.

But if it is pushed back by carnal movements, as by contrary winds, then, and then indeed, all of our security proceeds to be undone, once sin is strengthened in us from our own will. And, as is written, "We will become portions for foxes,"[11] bestowing our own adornment upon wicked and unclean demons. And like a vineyard without a wall or sober guards, we will be left wide open to those who want to seize us as fodder.[12]

But it is agreeable to everyone to avoid such an experience; let each give a warm welcome to fasting, the mother of all sanctification, mortify and subject the body,[13] and by choosing to undergo this labor, "hedge his own possession about with thorns,"[14] as one of our wise men has said.

This will, then, suffice, I think, for those with a more perfect attitude, those able to partake of more solid doctrine,[15] to enable them to proceed quite easily to hunt for what they need, and to collect from everywhere whatever seems to them of ben-

---

8. Is 27.5.
9. Ibid.
10. Col 3.5.
11. Ps 63.10.
12. Cf. Is 5.5; Mt 21.33–41.
13. Cf. 1 Cor 9.27.
14. Sir 28.24.
15. Cf. 1 Cor 3.2; Heb 5.12.

efit. And I doubt they will need to make great efforts. For what will suffice for their success is the eagerness which incessantly undermines obstacles as a river current does to its banks, and sweeps away resistance with its irresistible impetus.

But now it is necessary to add what is of chief importance in this topic, and that is that the all-conquering God comes to the aid of those who are disposed in this way,[16] and his supreme strength and power become a staff and bowstring. The all-wise Psalmist testifies to this when he says, "Your rod and your staff, these have comforted me."[17] That the fruits of peace with God are luminous and admirable, all those of good sense will then, I think, agree.

3. Now when I pause to consider, and, like those who spring to the top of a hill in an attempt to look as far as the eye may see, I look around me with the eye of my mind, considering closely the natures of things as far as may be, it seems to me that it is not only those just mentioned in this discourse who ought to be advised to concern themselves with being at peace with God; but another multitude of men comes into my view as well.[18] They are like suckers recently sprouted and just growing up which have scarcely appeared above ground when the gardeners' skills and the supplies of water urge them to grow. In the same way, those others, who have just barely taken root in the gardens of the Church, summon to themselves the skill of the instructors as though it were a spring. It is to them that I believe those beautiful words of the prophet are especially fitting: "Let us make peace with him, let us who are coming make peace."[19] But it is worth asking from where they are coming, and where they are to lodge.

It is quite clear, though, that the nations are walking, through

16. As with most Eastern fathers, Cyril shows no sensitivity to the theological issues of the Pelagian controversy, which was already underway in the west. Cyril is much closer to Origen on this. See Peter Gorday, *Principles of Patristic Exegesis: Romans 9–11 in Origen, John Chrysostom, and Augustine* (New York: Edwin Mellen, 1983).

17. Ps 23.4.

18. A likely reference to the newly baptized.

19. Is 27.5.

faith, from ignorance to learning, from thoughtlessness to sound reasoning, from great and inveterate error to a truer understanding of reality, to a knowledge of God, to reverence, to a life quite different from the earlier one, to freedom, to renewal, and, in a word, to the virtue and manner of life befitting a human being; a human being, that is, who is of course rational and made in the image of the Creator. For those whose minds are frightened by the devil's tricks, and who are terrified by the deceits involving the idols, and "who say to the stock, you are my God," as the prophet says, "and to the stone, you begot me,"[20] are plainly full of complete nonsense and summon this disapproval upon themselves, as anyone who is interested in judging rightly would say of them. And it appears to me (if I may speak more truly) that, as far as the nature of the body goes, they still retain their humanity, and that it is only from the features and forms found there that one may recognize that they are in fact rational animals; but as far as the mind and its contents go, their ambition seems to be to rival the senselessness of irrational beings. A contest in which one may admit they prevail, if one looks carefully at the results.

Lest I seem, however, to be railing at them rather than trying to prove that they are far from behaving as they ought, and are at the furthest remove from such behavior, I will now present God himself, the Master of all, as he speaks through one of the prophets: "Behold how their heart is ashes, and they err."[21] For they really do err, having abandoned that understanding of the knowledge of God which is, so to speak, straightforward, and being swept away into complete senselessness by absurd aberrations and the deceits of perverted arguments, so that they squander upon stocks and stones the glory of the ineffable and all-surpassing essence, and consider superior to human nature the things it has brought into being, and address as masters the things they themselves own. Now what could seem more ridiculous to anyone of good sense?

20. Jer 2.27.
21. Is 44.20; cf. Wis 15.10.

4. In speaking of these things, however, I have not overlooked something additional: there are those who do abandon this lowly cult, but then, as though involving themselves in a higher error, think that they must flee to the more distinguished beings in creation. And raising their brows to their temples, expectorating widely and generously, and combing their long beards with their hands, they stare in wonder at the sky, speaking of how it encircles all of the earth under the sun, and how it holds everything as though in its bosom, enveloping what is inside like a tent. Then they busy themselves with the positions of the stars in it, and are astonished at the courses of the sun and moon.[22] They present fire, water, air, and earth as the principles of reality, and fancy that they have found in the conjunction of the elements the root of things which come to be. Then, when they should seek the Commander and Governor of the things mentioned and should go back from the beauty of created things to God, the Giver of their beauty,[23] they bestow all of their admiration upon the things made. How could they have been more greatly mistaken? How could anyone examine the nature of reality more senselessly?

And yet it must be most evident to all of reality, that if one saw a house or ship or something similar which was constructed with the greatest skill, one would not squander all one's admiration upon it, but after praising the location, construction, and beauty of what was to be seen, one would straightaway form a picture of the master Artificer, and realize who and how intelligent was the Creator of such surpassingly lovely things.

But these people—their eloquence being a matter only of turns of speech founded in a variety of their so-called disciplines—stay their thought at what is visible alone, and cut short the impulse of the mind to go to what is beyond, and thus do not see God, the Creator and Artificer of all. Nor, rendering to him

22. Critiquing astrological practices was a common trope in ancient Christian literature. For a discussion of astrology in ancient Egypt, see David Frankfurter, *Religion in Roman Egypt: Assimilation and Resistance* (Princeton: Princeton University Press, 1998).

23. Cf. Wis 13.5. Cyril often turns to this text, sometimes in conjunction with Rom 1.20, to urge his flock to use the creation to ascend to God; see SC 372, 350, n. 1.

the glory as Lord and Maker of all, do they accept the order among created things, that they may in fact be ranked among those who are understanding and truly wise.

As it is, though, they do not perceive that they have fallen so far into folly that, even if they applied every effort to fling themselves into the deepest thoughtlessness, they could not, I think, better achieve their absurd desire. Let Paul, however, come to my assistance, and support what I say about this when he declares, "The wisdom of this world is folly with God."[24] And that what the saint says is true we learn from an examination of the facts.

In the first place, they attribute life to a crowd of deities who are unknown even to their worshipers, and for some of whom they do not reserve even this common form of humanity; combining it with part of a pig or dog, they present us with what amounts to an adulterous nature, and break apart the fairest image of the things upon earth with their spurious modifications of its features.

But why should I extend my remarks about things which are so laughable? Let us proceed rather to what is essential. And that, I say, is as follows. The pagans are wrapped in a deep darkness of ignorance, which, mist-like, covers the understanding of all of them, and thus not only does not allow them to direct their sight toward what would benefit them, but banishes them rather from the doctrines of truth by means of unexamined and deceitful arguments. For what do these senseless people do? They deprive man of what is loveliest, and in their foolishness they destroy what is the great gift of his nature. I mean that they neither say, nor wish to hold, that he possesses the power of choice, nor that he makes a free choice about what is to be done, so that the inclination connected with each of his acts does not lie in his own will, but is assigned to the decisions of others. For a certain fate and natal situation, they say, weighs each one's life as it likes. It assigns to some the fairest things with which one might justly hope to be familiar, while to others again it dispenses things which one would never choose to experience. Thus in no situation does he proceed of his own accord, having neither the power to do good, nor indeed the contrary, but is summoned both

24. 1 Cor 3.19.

ways as though by chains and by the cords of necessity, so to speak. Thus he who was given from on high the governance over all things, comes at last to differ in no way from the irrational animals. And those who assent to such doctrines seem to me to behave as though they were to make someone a charioteer, and have him mount the chariot, and then bid someone else drive. That person will not receive the glory in the event of victory, nor, if he falls and gets smashed up, will he be held responsible for his own injury. Either will result from what others have done; the outcome will be due to those holding the reins, and not to him mounted upon the chariot to no purpose. For how could one be fairly called to account for things over which one had no control? Where someone can choose how to act, however, that person, obviously, and not others, is responsible for the results of the action, and even for whether it is performed.

But that we may show more plainly to our audience that the teaching of these people is full of extraordinary ignorance, and that the supposition that man does not use his own will in making decisions, nor proceed as he wants in autonomy of choice, must be judged quite absurd, and that we may do so by gathering evidence of their foolishness from the facts of the life of those against whom they declaim, and from the fables they recite, I will make mention of a few of the people to whom I just alluded.

Their discourses mention one Tantalus, and Tityus, and Ixion, and the hardship borne by Sisyphus, and they affirm that the punishments they suffered in perfect justice were those which they themselves probably wanted. For they say that Tantalus was punished by having an immensely heavy rock suspended above his head and by the fear of ever-imminent danger. If one asks the reason for this evil, one will hear them clamor that it was because he had an unbridled tongue, and in their writings they call this affection the most hideous kind of illness. As for him called Tityus, they stretch him out over an entire nine plethra, and they say that his liver is torn by a pair of savage vultures, and they affirm that the reason for his irremediable misfortune was some kind of intemperance. And as for Ixion and Sisyphus, the one they say is subject to the ever-rotating revolutions and turnings of a wheel, while the other is punished by labor hard and long.

And then, that their penalties may seem to be fair, they charge them with various misdeeds. But if in fact we follow their concept and idea, and consider that man is subject to the constraints of fate, then, at least it seems to me, the misdeeds resulting in suffering would not be of those persons just mentioned, but of the fate which calls them to them, and this by reason of its power to dominate each person's mind and bring it under its own control.

Either let these persons be released, therefore, from their incurable punishments, and from undying hardship, and let their natal situation, which has had the better of them, be the one rather to be accused and subjected to the tortures, whoever they may be who understand how to do this, or else, if someone claims that these persons are punished justly, let him present us with man stripped of necessity, and let him do away with fate's control, in order that the accusations may appear to pertain to Tantalus and Sisyphus.

For if even with us the law of justice considers it quite absurd to demand satisfaction, not from those who have done wrong, but from others instead, then it must be clear to everyone that one would probably concede that there is nothing more wretched than those whom these people acknowledge as gods, if in fact those who are the distributors and stewards of all things, who are believed to have the power to judge, cannot do so rightly. It is evident that those we have with us who pronounce a correct judgment on each person are better, since they honor the just as is fitting, while they reckon that those proven liable to the more serious charges are to be hated, and they punish them in proportion to the misdeeds of which they are convicted.

Now this, dear sir, is just what your own poets and leading writers think as well on these points. But listen to what one of our own wise men says: "The folly of a man spoils his way: and he blames God in his heart."[25] Thus if one were free from folly, one would not have one's way spoiled, nor would one accuse the divine nature at all, as though it called toward that which it also

25. Prv 19.3.

forbade by law. For those who have established their own mind within themselves as guide and teacher, and as the best judge, are always eager to distinguish themselves in those matters which one would reckon to be of highest value, while avoiding with the greatest firmness whatever one would exclude from the best sort of intention and action. It is not true, therefore, that fate and one's natal situation control each person, as they think, and make man a doer of evil or a doer of good; on the contrary, everyone proceeds voluntarily to either, and whichever way anyone decides to go, there is nothing from necessity to prevent one from directing oneself. But if we ought to add something to what has been said, and indicate the originator of the pagans' ignorance, and how it happened that they fell so far into thoughtlessness, I will be most happy to explain.

5. The demon, that author of evil, the father of sin, who displayed man as transgressor of the divine commandment, made him submit to him like some captive, and showed himself tyrant over us by means of his deception, feared that the free nature might return to what it had been. For he knew, he knew well, that man, when convicted by his conscience, is always driven to return to what is better, hates sin as something intrusive, and always grows unhappy when he transgresses, even if he is cheated into this by some slight pleasure. Lest he make use of his autonomy, however, destroy the tyranny of pleasure by the tension pulling him toward freedom, return to the superiority he had originally after loudly bewailing his sins, and, in employing himself in deeds of justice, be found then to be invincible by the assistance already rendered him from on high, the demon thought up another method of deception, having always used this as the weapon of his malice: he stole away, as it were, most of the grief attendant upon sin in his incessant battle, waged by means of trickery, against the conviction arising from conscience. It is not you yourselves, he says, who are responsible for your own inability to do better, nor has God put self-control among your powers. He has forced upon you a yoke you must bear; fate and your natal situation control you, and you must needs do as they decide. With such deceptions the evil one dominates man, and, leading him

astray from the doctrines of truth, renders him readier for any sin. For when he attributes to fate the outcome of his affairs, and says that he is subject to the inescapable bonds of his natal situation, he assumes that he will undergo no punishment for his apparent transgressions. Such, then, is the position of these people, in their rejection of temperance.

But let the heralds of the Church, "who have put on Christ,"[26] and whose minds are instilled with the truth, speak out. "For we are not ignorant of his designs."[27] Lest, however, those who have fallen for the deceptions just described, suffering as they do from the illness of their inveterate thoughtlessness and mustering their thoughts against the Legislator's will, should wage war against the One they ought least of all to oppose, let them listen to what we said originally: "Let us make peace with him."[28] Let us dismiss enmity; let fighting and war depart; let us offer our right hand to the Savior. Let us ask for peace through faith; let us too say with the prophet, "Lord, our God, give us peace. Lord, take possession of us; we know not any other beside you; we name your name."[29]

6. For the pagans, then, and those who have just entered the doors of the Church, I think that that will be of sufficient benefit. But since I find myself looking at another people as well, one equipped with the weapons of ignorance to be a completely thoughtless soldier, one which thinks it must battle against the truth of the facts by mustering against the Savior a mentality formed by shadow and figure and letter, while "having in the Law the embodiment of knowledge,"[30] as it is written, let us, then, please, cry out to them as well from our mutual affection, "Let us make peace with him."[31]

How long, O Jew, will you remain sunk in the figures deriving from the letter, and pass by the power of truth? When will there come an end to your ignorance? When will you remove your mind from the shadow in the Law? At what time will we find you with more sense? When will you offer to God, the universal King,

---

26. Cf. Gal 3.27.
27. 2 Cor 2.11.
28. Is 27.5.
29. Is 26.12–13.
30. Rom 2.20.
31. Is 27.5.

the worship which is in the Spirit? "God is spirit," as it is written, "and those who worship him must worship in spirit and truth."[32] But you neglect to worship in the spirit, and find the tendency to what is worse more agreeable than the one to what is better, and so take pride in the thick-headedness of the letter. Then you think thereby to honor God, and, rejecting that understanding of the Law which is most accurate, as though you had a complete knowledge of what is written, you do not perceive how foolish you are. Let us, then, please, discuss a little with you each of the things held in honor among you. For you will realize quite easily thereby, I think, if in fact you have any desire to come to your senses, that you are spending a long time in error.

7. You accept, for instance, the circumcision of the flesh as something important, and as the principal item in your worship. You also hold in the greatest admiration the Sabbath repose, and you gladly sacrifice sheep. And you think that God is overjoyed with you when you sacrifice cattle, and your doctrine concerning foods and their differences is a model of exactitude. This is what you take pride in; your exercises to attain the highest virtue have this as their result; here have you fixed for yourself the description of a good reputation. As for me, though, I say that the wisdom and understanding of the Legislator are above all discourse and wonder, and I would denounce, and quite justifiably, the Jewish absurdities. For they are reluctant to think; they avoid learning, transgressing yet again, and guided only by their own ignorance to the failure to enjoy anything that is good. But let them also listen themselves to the prophetic voice: "Awake, you drunkards, from your wine!"[33]

Let us examine, if you please, what benefit may come from being circumcised, or what advantage the Legislator offers us from it. For to apply circumcision to those members of the body which nature uses for procreation would be ridiculous, unless there were an excellent reason for it. Or rather, it would call into question the skill of the Creator, as though he had weighed down the

32. Jn 4.24.
33. Jl 1.5.

form of the body with some vain excrescences. How, then, if this is the substance of what is said, and is the way we understand it, may we avoid the inference that the divine mind fails to achieve what is fitting? For if it is rather in being circumcised that what is most fitting to the body's nature is preserved for it, then obviously this would have been in every respect the superior and better thing in the beginning. Tell me, then: is there anyone who claims that the unerring and uncontaminated nature failed to achieve what is fitting, and who does not appear delirious to everyone else? For the God who is over all fashioned countless sorts of irrational animals. But there is nothing in their constitution which seems either lacking or superfluous for a most exquisite beauty. They are quite free of either reproach, and escape both charges. How is it then possible that God, as masterful a craftsman as he is, who bestowed such forethought upon what is lesser, should have erred when it came to that which is the most valuable of all? And when he presented the one made in his image, did he contrive to have him appear uglier than the irrational animals, if indeed he made no mistakes with the latter, but did make one with the former? But I suppose that the Jews themselves will agree that if nothing good is signified by the circumcision of the flesh, it will prove to be ridiculous in itself; but since I consider that those in whom the Savior lodges, and the Holy Spirit dwells, should show themselves superior to their ignorance, let us again fit the suitable explanation to the Legislator's ordinances, and thus show how very remarkable is the meaning they contain. Why is it, then, that the law given through Moses orders the infant to be circumcised on the eighth day, and to be presented to the Lord God, once the usual sacrifice has been offered for him? And then, what object of contemplation is given us by what is suggested by carnal circumcision? This is what is now to be unfolded and explained, and the reason for circumcision to be examined carefully, as best as may be.

8. The mind, then, which is in us, is by nature the most fertile of all things, having in itself the seeds of every virtue, and furnishing continually from its own movements, as from a spring, the desires for what is best in every case. For thus has it been

made by the Creator. But forgetfulness spreads over it like a veil, creeping out as from an innate root, that forgetfulness which is the source of all impurity. It covers, mist-like, the impulse to what is better, and devours it, and, by overshadowing the memory that we ought to act well, produces in us an earthly mentality instead of a spiritual one, and thus displays man as full of every impurity.

And in fact those in whom this state of mind occurs are addressed by the prophetic words: "Remember, you who are far from the Lord, and let Jerusalem arise in your hearts."[34] For what was needed, really needed, was the memory of what was good to be poured upon the evil arising from forgetfulness like water upon a fire; and for grief to vanish because of the assistance which opposes it.

As long, then, as the mind in us is covered over by the evils arising from forgetfulness, and that which by nature engenders what is fairest of all is troubled by the ignorance thence arising, and has from no source the power to distinguish itself in what is good, we are reckoned by God as impure and quite abhorrent, not to mention other adjectives. But when we have shaken off the forgetfulness concerning what is better, and cut off the errors resulting from it like some superfluous excrescences, we will maintain within ourselves our virile and completely fertile mind free from all wickedness and stripped of the evils arising from vice. Thus at last, having banished from our own soul the agedness coming from sin, and been transformed into the infancy coming from innocence, we will stand confidently before God.

By no means, however, will we present ourselves, any more than the newborn baby brings itself to God. The one who will present us is Christ, who regenerated us by faith, offering himself as a sacrifice for us to the Father. And he will present us on the eighth day, that is, after the Sabbath observance which is in the Law.[35] For this is the time of our Savior's visitation, since Christ is also the end of the Law and the prophets.[36] It is for this reason, I think, that the eighth day has been called the Lord's

34. Jer 51.50.

35. The "eighth day," symbolized by Sunday, is the day of the Sabbath rest of the saints in the Heavenly Jerusalem.

36. That is, Christ is the fulfillment of all prophetic expectations.

Day by us; or rather, to speak more precisely, because it brings to
a close the time of the Law, and introduces to us the beginning
of the years of the Lord, in which everything is made new. Paul
of course says so: "So that if anyone is a new creation in Christ,
the old has passed away, and behold, the new has come."[37]

We must realize that the circumcision of the flesh furnishes us
with this figure of what is to be contemplated, the circumcision
which is performed on the eighth day, as I said, and which brings
the newborn into God's presence. But let these words be support-
ed by the supreme wisdom of Paul; let the steward of the Savior's mysteries enter with the cry: "For he is not a Jew who is one
outwardly, nor is circumcision something external, in the flesh.
He is a Jew who is one inwardly, and circumcision is a matter of
the heart, spiritual and not literal. His praise is not from human
beings but from God."[38] Let him write further to others about
the same things, saying, "Look out for the dogs, look out for the
evil-workers, look out for the mutilation! For we are the circumcision, who worship God in spirit, and put no confidence in the
flesh."[39] For I do not think that those who are sensible ever take
any pride in the circumcision of the flesh, if it is regarded in itself, and not as having that beauty which comes from contemplation. But when it serves as a figure of the circumcision in the Spirit, and suggests the purification of the heart, then one may well
praise it as an excellent symbol of the purification found in the
refinement of contemplation; but one will evidently leave off un-
dergoing it, when one is practicing the purification of the heart.
This is what a prophetic message advises the Jews to make haste
to do, when it says, "Thus says the Lord: Break up fresh ground
for yourselves, and sow not among thorns. Circumcise yourselves
to God, and circumcise your hardness of heart, you men of Judah
who inhabit Jerusalem."[40] Thus if one is circumcised in the flesh,
one certainly does not do this for God. The one who receives the
circumcision in the Spirit because of the gospel proclamation, by
contrast, is obviously circumcised to the Master of all, and not
to the letter of the Law, that letter which customarily represents
the truth as it were in shadows. And that the meaning of that cir-

37. 2 Cor 5.17.                    38. Rom 2.28–29.
39. Phil 3.2–3.                    40. Jer 4.3–4.

cumcision which is the true one is not fulfilled in what is done to the flesh, but in the willingness to act as God bids, is what Paul says so clearly: "Neither circumcision counts for anything, nor uncircumcision."[41]

Lest, however, he appear to be speaking mere words to us when he says that that which is held in honor by the Law counts for nothing, he explains himself more clearly, saying, "Circumcision indeed is of value if you obey the Law; but if you break the Law, your circumcision becomes uncircumcision. So, if a man who is uncircumcised keeps the precepts of the Law, will not his uncircumcision be regarded as circumcision? Then those who are physically uncircumcised but keep the Law will condemn you who have the written code and circumcision, but break the Law."[42]

Since, therefore, he says that circumcision is seen to be meaningless among those who undergo it, when they do not have in addition the good repute coming from deeds, while those who retain their physical uncircumcision turn out to be better keepers of the Law than those otherwise, I should like to ask these absolutely senseless Jews what sort of pride can still be taken in it. And we may add, if necessary, that Paul insists that circumcision was given as a different sign, and like a "seal of his faith while uncircumcised"[43] to Abraham, the ancestor of the people, "that he might be the father of many nations,"[44] "not only," as he says, "for those of the circumcision, but also for those who follow the example of the faith which our father Abraham had before he was circumcised."[45] "For he believed God, and was justified,"[46] even before he received circumcision. It was after his faith, and the justification coming from it, that circumcision became for him the sign of that reality.

9. Receive therefore, O Jew, the sword of the Spirit; put away your hardness of heart; as it is written, "Circumcise yourself to God."[47] Learn to keep the Sabbath, not in the way you yourself

---

41. 1 Cor 7.19.  
43. Rom 4.11.  
45. Rom 4.11–12.  
47. Jer 4.4.  

42. Rom 2.25–27.  
44. Gn 17.5.  
46. Gn 15.6.

think good, but as the will of the Legislator bids. For it is in fact
worthwhile seeing what the Legislator says about this too. He orders that one should refrain from work, and avoid corporal labor, on the Sabbath.[48] He does not want one to leave Jerusalem,
nor undertake long journeys.[49] Nor to make use of food cooked
at the time, but that prepared in advance. He also strictly forbids
the carrying of burdens, and being heavily laden at all, speaking
quite clearly through Jeremiah: "And you will not go out of the
gate of Jerusalem on the Sabbath day; nor will you carry burdens
out of your houses."[50] In these passages the Law defines for you
the honors due the Sabbath.

But let the one who is bent on defending the literal meaning
come forth to me again, let someone from the Jewish community tell us whether a wise explanation has ever been fitted to the
God-given precepts, or whether the meaning of the divine mysteries is available to us in the words by themselves, and in the
bare letter. If he, then, acknowledges, as is most reasonable, that
the mind-numbing grossness belonging to the letter is spread
over the matters for contemplation like a veil, let him seek what
is intended, and not remain contentedly in what is spoken by
way of symbol, thus depriving himself of what is best. If, however,
he says that one should attend to the letter alone, and not consider what more there may be to it, and he applies himself to do
so himself, and also strives to teach others, he will hear the Savior saying, "Woe to you, scribes and Pharisees, you hypocrites,
for you have taken away the key of knowledge. You do not enter
yourselves, nor do you let those entering go in."[51] Let us, that is,
examine carefully the nature of the reality in the case of the passage about the Sabbath as well, and what it may be, and, by inves-
tigating more closely the meaning of the passage, let us see
whether here once again the understanding of the Jews does not
turn out to be utterly foolish.

10. What I mean is that I should like to know what it was that
persuaded the Creator of all to make a law, in addition to all the

48. Cf. Dt 5.12–15; Ex 20.8–11.
49. Cf. Is 58.13.                          50. Jer 17.21–22.
51. Mt 23.13; cf. Lk 11.52.

others he thought good, that one should remain idle on the Sabbath, even though all the rest of creation is active in natural movements without hindrance on the Sabbath, and without ceasing to do what each being has been assigned to do because of the Sabbath. The sun rises, and does not stop in making the round of its usual course. The earth, with its mane of varied plants and adornment of different kinds of growths, is not made barren because of the Sabbath, nor has it held back its nutritive power from the things which come from it. The springs likewise, the mothers of cold waters: have they ever stopped supplying the abundance usual to them by shutting off the stream from their own breasts? But this you will not now say, O Jew, even though we believe that laws have been made by the Creator for each thing that has been made, laws which concern their movement, nature, life, and preservation.[52]

But if, as you think, it was his intention that the Sabbath be honored by the inactivity, since nothing else of use came from this legislation, why did he not make the same law for everything? What harm is there, I ask, if one of us cooks or kneads bread on the Sabbath? Or what is there to prevent the preparation of other foods for the body on the occasion? But as it is, the law, which is presented to us as something great and eagerly desired, bars us from all work. It does not allow one to carry a burden out of the house. Nor even to pass the threshold of Jerusalem's gate and travel far. And as for food, it bids one go to table for one's meal and eat, not what is made ready at that time, but what is prepared in advance, and it punishes the transgressor with death. And this, even though not one of the things mentioned, if done at another time, will bring an accusation of sin against the one who does it.

And one really could not say, if one had any sense, that these things are listed in the law under the heading of transgressions, in the same way as the other matters which it clearly says are to be avoided absolutely. The words, that is, "You shall not murder, you shall not commit adultery, you shall not steal, you shall not bear false witness,"[53] and whatever else accords with these re-

52. Cf. Acts 17.28.
53. Ex 20.13–16.

garding one and the same ordinance, are to be observed not only on the Sabbath by a man who hates to be punished; they are things to be avoided at all times. Hence I suppose I may be confident that it will be clear to my listeners that the things forbidden on the Sabbath are not sins, but rather that they yield for us a most wonderful image of the realities. This is an image which I will not hesitate to expound for your benefit to the best of my ability. I will deal first with the discourse about inactivity, which presents a double object of contemplation.

11. For when those from Israel left the land that had borne them and settled in Egypt, passing long years there, they did not retain even the memory, as is not surprising, that they were of Hebrew stock and descended from Abraham. They forgot their ancestral customs, denied the piety of their forebears, and went over to the false worship of the natives. They assumed that the immigrant people would behave, as it were, quite wrongly toward those who had received them within their own land, unless they shared with them their same error, and thus they supposed that the sun was to be worshiped, and the sky and earth and moon and stars; to which of the elements did they not think they had to render the glory proper to God? Deep within them was the darkness of ignorance, and, as Paul says, "they worshiped the creature rather than the Creator."[54]

But when the Legislator hastened to free them from the cruelty of the Egyptians and from that bitter servitude, and indeed called them to the land of promise, he bade them get rid of the Egyptian error without further concern: "Beware," he says, "lest, having looked up to the sky and having seen the sun and the moon and the stars, and all the heavenly bodies, you should go astray and worship them."[55] "The Lord your God is one Lord."[56]

But since it was in a way necessary also to force them, as it were, through some evident reality, to acknowledge, even though unwillingly, that the sky had been made, and that the sun, moon, stars, earth, and all the rest of creation, had been moved into existence by the Creator's skill, he orders them to conform them-

54. Rom 1.25.        55. Dt 4.19.
56. Dt 6.4.

selves to the Creator, and he wants those who take the Sabbath off to know the reason for the feast. "For God ceased from all of his work," it says, "on the seventh day."[57] And those who are intent on ceasing from theirs, together with the Creator who ceases, can hardly avoid acknowledging, quite clearly, that all things have been made, and there is one Fashioner and Artificer of them all. It thus came about, through the inactivity on the Sabbath, that the doctrine about the Divinity was presented to those from Israel, the nature of the Artificer and Creator of all was recognized, and the slavery of the visible elements was no longer unknown.

This was one reason for the inactivity on the Sabbath. The second reason following it is quite venerable, and most suited to those more perfect in character. For it does not do to set the more solid doctrinal food before those still in their infancy, but rather before "those who have their faculties trained by practice,"[58] as Paul says. The Sabbath inactivity, then, and the putting aside of the work itself, signifies the repose of the saints at the end. When indeed they have shaken off their labor, washed off the perspiration of the contests, and leaped up to the city above, the heavenly Jerusalem, they will pass all their time in rest and enjoyment. No longer will they take upon themselves work and labor. Having what they may boast of in their past life as waybread for salvation,[59] they will nourish their own souls unto immortal life. That, I take it, is the meaning of having to prepare in advance the Sabbath foods. And that it is not allowed to weigh oneself down with burdens or loads on the Sabbath, would seem to mean, at least as we see it, that after the resurrection of the dead, during the Sabbath observance in the city above, the burden of sin will no longer lie upon us, nor will the evil one crush us again by enticing us to wrongdoing, since he will undergo the punishment of eternal fire in hell, while the sin now active in us will have been destroyed forever.

As for staying within the gates of Jerusalem on the Sabbath,

57. Gn 2.2.

58. Heb 5.14; cf. 1 Cor 3.1.

59. A reference to the Eucharist. The term *evodion,* which originally meant provisions for a journey, evolved in liturgical usage to mean the final Eucharist before death, as in the Latin viaticum; see SC 372, 388, n. 1.

that seems to signify the same thing in the same way. For those once called into the choirs of the saints, who have entered into the church of the firstborn, will never depart from the security of what they enjoy, nor leave the gift given them; they will remain in it always, their mind protected by the grace of the Spirit. For thus it is written: "Everlasting joy shall be upon their head; for on their head shall be praise and exultation; sorrow and pain and groaning have fled away."[60] They will forget their former distress, and it will not mount upon their hearts.

But again, that the Sabbath signifies the repose that will belong to the saints at the end of the ages, let Paul enter as our witness, and let him speak to the Hebrews in his letter about the elder times: "Therefore, while the promise of entering his rest remains, let us fear lest any of you be judged to have failed to reach it. For good news came to us just as to them."[61]

But since those lacking the wits to think seemed to suppose that the "rest" mentioned here was the entry into the land of promise accomplished under Jesus' command, "Jesus" here being the son of Nun,[62] he shows more clearly that nothing of what he is saying concerns that entry, but rather the entry which is hoped for, this being the whole purpose of his reflections, and so he goes on, "For if Jesus had given them rest, God would not speak later of another day. So then, there remains a Sabbath rest for the people of God,"[63] by "Sabbath rest" here quite clearly meaning the cessation from labor of the saints at the end. And in fact he gives a clear sign of his meaning in the passage which follows, when he adds, "For whoever enters into his rest also ceases from his labors as God did from his. Let us therefore strive to enter that rest, that no one fall by the same sort of disobedience."[64]

Learn, and understand well, O Jew, through the words spoken here by the one who was "brought up at the feet of Gamaliel,"[65] who knew the Law through and through, "a Hebrew born of Hebrews, of the tribe of Benjamin, as to the Law a Pharisee,"[66] that when he speaks of the figurative inactivity observed

60. Is 35.10.                    61. Heb 4.1–2.
62. That is, Joshua: in Greek, "Jesus" and "Joshua" are the same name.
63. Cf. Heb 4.8–9.               64. Heb 4.10–11.
65. Acts 22.3.                   66. Phil 3.5.

on the Sabbath, that which is introduced by the letter of the Law, he says that it is nothing at all; or rather that it presents an image of the good things hoped for, and the respite to be given to the saints at the time when the Savior of all will come from heaven in the glory of his Father,[67] as is written, and will give the saints their gifts.

I think, then, that this will suffice for our exposition of this topic; let us proceed to matters which are familiar and more fitting.

12. Since, then, the pagans had erred, "worshiping the creature instead of the Creator,"[68] and, abandoning themselves to the deception of polytheism, had sprung into the wide gate of death, while the Jews, for their part, had sinned so badly against their own souls that they had no concern for the Law at all, but considered tiresome those who offered them the best instruction, and supposed them foolish, and spoke quite plainly to those chosen by grace from on high: "But speak and report to us another error; remove from us this path, and remove from us the oracle of Israel";[69] for this reason, the Master of all by necessity no longer used any ministers or servants to bring about our salvation, but, matching himself against the devil's tyranny, became a human being. He was born of the holy Virgin, and, working many signs and wonders along with his words of teaching, changed everything for the better; refashioning corrupt human nature into newness of life,[70] as though releasing it from bonds, he presented it free to the Father, and those who were broken by sin he called to himself by the gentlest of teachings, saying, "Come to me, all who labor and are heavily laden, and I will give you rest."[71] Such was then our situation.

But the tyrant was once again cut to the quick at our Savior's achievements. He made our salvation an occasion for mourning, and, expelled from the realm his greed had won for him, he was plunged into deep grief. For, seeing the divine proclamation shining like the sun, and the mist of ancient impiety now scat-

---

67. Cf. Mk 8.38; 1 Thes 4.16.
69. Is 30.10–11.
71. Mt 11.28.

68. Rom 1.25.
70. Cf. Rom 6.4.

tered, he felt sharp pain at this. But rekindling his anger, and consumed with the fiercest jealousy, he decided to overcome life with death. In his supreme madness, he expected to subject to the bonds of corruption the Lord who had come for the salvation of all, and so he persuaded some of the Jews of like mind to become his assistants in the deed and champions of his unholy boldness. And they, in proceeding even to hand over for crucifixion the Master of all, went beyond the devil's intention in outdoing his audacity, and, by overmatching his arrogance, relegated their own chief to a minor part in the business.

The Savior of all, then, in managing the project of the salvation of our race in the best possible way, and with the highest skill, "laid down his life for us,"[72] as it is written, because he is a good shepherd who does not refuse to run risks for the flock of sheep. But as for the instigator of the Jewish audacity, the one who set the snare in which he himself was caught, he hardly realized in his suffering that he had failed of his hopes, the enterprise having gone completely contrary to them; like a seaman who, having started with a fair wind, finds his ship right in the midst of his nets, he grieved to see quite the opposite of what he had expected. Having thought, that is, that he would be victorious, and would subject us to a harsher tyranny, the wretch now found himself deprived instead of all power. Bound fast by chains unbreakable, like a beast, and robbed of his inner strength, he made his place and city the inmost cranny of death, and, having been deceived by his fond hopes, since he had thought he would be like the Most High, and had once striven to set his own throne above heaven, he could not claim that there was anyone in hell more miserable.

For the human souls that had been caught for their perdition by his wickedness came out of the subterranean gates, and, emerging from the deeps of the abyss, fled the sunless halls of death. And swimming through that deep darkness, they were making their way to the Savior's light. For he had arrived, "saying to them that are in bonds, Go forth; and to them that are in darkness, Show yourselves!"[73] And when hell was despoiled of its

---

72. Cf. Jn 10.11, 15, 17.
73. Is 49.9.

spirits, and the power of death broken, the Savior arose victorious. He raised up the temple of himself on the third day,[74] and, in a manner, painted a most striking picture of the resurrection of the body. And, planting all of our hopes for good things, mustering his disciples, and bidding them baptize "all the nations in the name of the Father, and of the Son, and of the Holy Spirit,"[75] he ascended to heaven itself to show the Father that human nature, which had been crushed by sin, revived unto incorruption by grace, presenting himself to his Parent like some first-fruits of grain.

For these reasons, beloved, in making some modest repayment to the Savior, and gladdening our Benefactor in return with what thanks we can, let us acknowledge our poverty, saying, "What shall I render to the Lord for all the things wherein he has rewarded me? I will take the cup of salvation, and call upon the name of the Lord."[76] For thanksgiving to God is truly a cup of salvation. But while we offer thanks insofar as words and speech go, let us also bring him what we add to them from our brave deeds. This means keeping the body from any wicked pleasure, and purifying the spirit as well, and hastening to free it from all evil; visiting those who are injured, comforting those in poverty, lightening the burden of misfortune on orphans and widows,[77] suffering imprisonment together with those in prison, and assisting those who are mistreated, "since you also are in the body."[78] In keeping to this holy way of life, and acting always according to the divine law, we will win the esteem of Christ, the Savior of all. We begin holy Lent on the first of the month of Phamenoth. The week of the salvific Paschal feast begins on the sixth of Pharmuthi. We break the fast on the eleventh of Pharmuthi, the eve of Saturday, according to the gospel tradition. We celebrate the feast on the next day, the eve of Sunday, the twelfth of Pharmuthi.[79] We add the following seven weeks of holy Eastertide. This so that we may be granted fellowship with the saints in heaven in Christ Jesus our Lord, through whom and with whom be the glory and the power to the Father with the Holy Spirit, now and always, and for all ages. Amen.

74. Cf. Jn 2.19–21.          75. Mt 28.19.
76. Ps 116.12–13.            77. Cf. Jas 1.27.
78. Heb 13.3.                79. April 7, 418.

# FESTAL LETTER SEVEN

## A.D. 419

"REJOICE IN THE Lord always; again I say, rejoice!"[1] Behold, the thrice-longed-for time of our holy feast has arisen for us, coming in the course of the same cycles, like those from foreign parts putting into home port. It already appears in the harbor, and now the cables are being made fast to the shore. But since it is already here, and has all but come ashore among us, I consider it reasonable and proper, that we especially who, belonging to the divine priesthood,[2] bear the sacred trumpet in our mouth, should give the clarion signal for the festival, and gather together as for a common banquet those who are from everywhere, saying in the words of the holy Psalmist: "Come, children, listen to me; I will teach you the fear of the Lord."[3]

For to apportion to each season what befits it is something I consider quite good and wise. To try not to fail in the quest for what is of benefit, however, is the habit most suitable only for those of good character.

Therefore, since the season of glorious exertions is upon us, let us seize it eagerly when it is here. "Let us cleanse ourselves of every defilement,"[4] and through our good fast "let us put to death what is earthly in us: fornication, impurity, passion, and evil desire."[5] Thus it is, thus indeed, that we will be with God most holy, who says, "Be holy, for I am holy."[6]

The most skillful physicians devise a variety of ways to offer

---

1. Phil 4.4.

2. This is most likely a reference to the office of bishop rather than the presbyterate. See John Chrysostom's *On the Priesthood* for a similar usage.

3. Ps 34.11.                                4. 2 Cor 7.1.

5. Col 3.5.                                    6. Lv 11.44.

healing for bodies, and they provide yearly purges for those troubled by the things which usually spoil the well-ordered combination of elements in us; they cause some minor momentary discomfort to their patients, whom, however, they dismiss free from illnesses hardly minor. Thus also I think we should consider it of great importance to accumulate for ourselves a great store of the means to secure our future, accepting a moderate degree of discomfort in the course of beneficial actions, rather than refusing some slight suffering and then falling prey to the pains caused by punishment, which are greater and more grievous, or rather harsh and inexorable. Realizing this, and convinced of it, then, there is only one thing to do: to welcome to our souls, with the liveliest determination, the all-holy fast, the mother of every virtue, the guide to holiness, the ever-reliable counselor in the matter of distinguishing oneself in good deeds, to act as a purgative remedy. For it battles against the inordinate movements of the mind, does away with the law that runs riot in the members of the flesh,[7] and lulls the crowd of unruly pleasures in us, all but crying aloud with piercing voice: "Present your members as a living sacrifice, acceptable to God, which is your spiritual worship."[8]

But I do not see how one could readily excel in such a glorious contest, unless one was emboldened by high spirits on the one hand, and resolved gladly on the other to hasten to engage in frequent labors for virtue, and considered it glorious to spend oneself to good purpose. It is like those who exercise in gymnasiums, and boast of their great bodily strength, but of skill to match it as well: if even before the match begins they encounter their opponents in the wrestling-hall when they themselves are gloomy and downcast, and vanquished by fear before they touch the dust in the stadium, then they readily fall, and even before they come to grips with their adversaries, they have undone themselves by fright. Those, however, who are not at all so affected, and who often shake their opponents' confidence simply by their very posture, win the decision for themselves; and so it is, I think, and not otherwise, for those who live with the divine law, and are serious about leading a life of excellence. Those who are

7. Cf. Rom 7.23–25.
8. Rom 12.1.

eager and perfectly steadfast rejoice rather than grieve at labor, and consider contests to be their wealth and delight. The timorous and fearful, however, who suffer from the illness of hesitancy which makes them sluggish, tremble at the mere words stating that they must labor if they are to grow rich. The Wise One therefore assails them in the following terms: "For how long," he says, "will you lie, O sluggard? You sleep a little, and you rest a little, and you slumber a short time, and you fold your arms over your chest a little. Then poverty comes upon you as an evil wayfarer, and want as a swift courier."[9] Let us therefore avoid the loss incurred by hesitation, let us refuse to be impoverished of the virtues, and let us keep far from us, as the worst of all illnesses, any want of goodness. "Let us be of good courage, and let our heart be strengthened,"[10] as it is written. Now the tokens of this sort of virtue have been given to us by our Lord Jesus Christ himself, when he said, "Amen, amen, I say to you, whoever does not take his cross and follow me is not worthy of me."[11] And I think that one who decides to follow Christ ought to be superior to all timidity, or rather I say that all would agree that that is so, and that by looking haughtily down upon all fear, one all but shoulders one's own cross.

For just as a recently-born baby cannot use its tiny, tender feet, on which it can barely go a short way, to follow after swift-footed youths, so also the mind that looks only at what is cowardly is unable to follow in the footsteps of Christ, who "endured the cross, despising the shame,"[12] and tasted the bitterness of death[13] for us, even though he was God passionless and immortal, since he is the Word, the Father's Only-Begotten; this he did in order to make himself an example and model for us, and so call us to that imitation of him which is possible for us.

It was precisely on this achievement that Paul, so noted for his bravery, prided himself: "Be imitators of me," he says, "as I am of Christ."[14] With what sort of successes, then, did Christ's soldier,[15] who through his inner virtue was rightly appointed

9. Prv 6.9–11.        10. Ps 27.14.
11. Mt 10.38.        12. Heb 12.2.
13. Cf. Heb 2.9.       14. 1 Cor 4.16.
15. Cf. 2 Tm 2.3.

commander over us, strive to crown himself? It was that he so loved Christ, that he thought nothing of suffering everything, that he might become a genuine disciple of Christ. Listen to him, if you will, crying out to some of his associates, when they were anxious to keep him from his trophies: "What are you doing, weeping and breaking my heart? For I am ready not only to be imprisoned but even to die for the name of our Lord Jesus Christ."[16] Such was he in his faith; what sort of man he is seen to be in his own life, you will be amazed to learn. He who was of such great virtue took fasting as his comrade-in-arms in his battles against the body, and, in subjecting it, as though it were a tried and true soldier, to the good motions of his intellect, he prevailed over the laws of the flesh. And as for the pleasure that plays the tyrant in our members, he seized it like some prisoner of war and subjected it to the spirit's control. And that he might benefit us thereby, he wrote again, saying once that he had fasted often,[17] and another time, "I pommel my body and subdue it, lest after preaching to others I myself should be disqualified."[18] He remembered, it seems, his own Master crying, "Whoever then relaxes one of the least of these commandments and teaches others so, shall be called least in the kingdom of heaven; but whoever does them and teaches them shall be called great in the kingdom of heaven."[19]

What therefore he preached to others, he himself hastened to perform, putting fasting as a bridle to his flesh, and taking abstinence from food as a collaborator in obtaining this so admirable virtue. And it is not in these matters only that he appears as our instructor, nor does he stop his own disciple when he reaches the domain of continence. For that by itself did not suffice for approval, in the absence of every other virtue. He guides one, rather to each of the beneficial things in an orderly way, and brings us up to the chief good, which, I say, is mutual love. This the Lord defines as the clearest mark of genuine friendship with him, when he says, "By this will everyone know that you are my disciples, if you have love for one another."[20] It is worthwhile no-

16. Acts 21.13.                    17. 2 Cor 6.5 and 11.27.
18. 1 Cor 9.27.                    19. Mt 5.19.
20. Jn 13.35.

ticing by what words the inspired Paul conducts us to this virtue. He writes to the Corinthians as follows: "And I will show you a still more excellent way. If I speak in human and angelic tongues, but have not love, I am a noisy gong or a clanging cymbal. And if I have prophetic powers, and understand all mysteries and all knowledge, and if I have all faith, so as to remove mountains, but have not love, I am nothing. If I give away all I have, and deliver my body to be burned, but have not love, I gain nothing."[21] Do you see how unsightly and quite unattractive he says the enviable array of other virtues is in the absence of love for God and for one another? And how, in its presence, it renders most glorious the renown of those who possess them?

Well, one may say, he does praise love as something great and admirable, but he has not defined how it is to be practiced, nor how one may achieve it. Hold your tongue, sir! Our sober disciple has overlooked nothing that needs to be said. Not only does he take pains to teach that one must value love for God and for one another; he also shows how one may be seen to practice it. He goes on as follows: "Love is patient, love is kind, love is not jealous or boastful; it is not arrogant or rude. It does not seek its own interests; it is not irritable or resentful; it does not rejoice at wrong, but rejoices in the right; it bears all things, believes all things, hopes all things, endures all things. Love never ends."[22] Do you hear that it is not difficult for those who choose to rise to the dignity of love and mutual affection, but that the undertaking already appears attainable? Do you see that the way to the good repute which comes from it is not hidden, but shines like the sun? Proceeding therefore by way of it, and following the very high-road of the saints, so to speak, we will arrive at the city above, whose Artificer and Creator is God. If, however, we go off in the opposite direction, and fall away from a correct and straightforward attitude, and then conduct our lives down a twisted track, we will arrive at the bottom of hell, as the wise author of Proverbs says.[23]

But I think that, since we are rational human beings, made to the pure image of the Creator, we must necessarily be softened

---

21. 1 Cor 12.31–13.3.   22. 1 Cor 13.4–8.
23. Cf. Prv 9.18.

by the laws of love, and hasten the more to imitate the Lord when he says, "Learn from me, for I am gentle and lowly in heart";[24] not lapsing into the ferocity of the savage beasts, and in place of love being provoked to mutual hatred; or rather appearing as more savage than savage beasts, and less rational than irrational animals.

For wild beasts, and with them the many kinds of irrational animals, even though not guided by reason to the situation ideal for them, still habitually live together, and spend their time with each other. Cattle are glad to associate with cattle, and sheep with sheep. Not only that, but dogs, who so often rage against many other animals, and whose nature, as it were, excels in point of fury, have caused astonishment at the way they love each other as being of the same kind. And bears do not attack other bears, nor do lions other lions.

But man, who has received the rule over all of these, and who is steered in each situation by sense and reason, does not realize that he has fallen into complete senselessness. He considers savage behavior a kind of courage, and to gaze at length upon ferocity is, he thinks, conspicuous glory. He does not respect the common nature, nor does he honor the One who created it, nor does he keep in mind any of the other things which contribute to sound reasoning. But what should rather be an occasion for embarrassed grief incites him to boorish boasting, so that Paul rightly says, "They glory in their shame."[25] And the blessed prophet says in his amazement, "Did not one God create us? Have we not all one father? Why have you forsaken everyone his brother?"[26] For all of us who dwell upon the earth are recognized as having been begotten by one father. Adam, that is, is the one ancestor of our race, and one God has created us. Not so that we might be divided against each other and disagree, but rather that, since we spring from one root, and are bound by the natural attractions of love to mutual affection, we might reject the mad passions which are unnatural, and banish fratricidal anger from our minds.

---

24. Mt 11.29.                    25. Phil 3.19.
26. Mal 2.10.

2. And what we have just said applies especially to all of you who live in Egypt. For since we are your spiritual father, we simply could not leave you unadmonished; we had to lead you, our children, to what benefits you and to a lawful way of life. The reason is that terrible rumors have reached us that the most horrid and cruel deeds have been done brashly by some among you. It is said that youths emboldened by their physical prowess have perverted their youthfulness to the most senseless acts, arming themselves with cruel swords and teaching the wielding of clubs more savagely than the law customarily allows. Thus they waste their physical vigor on unholy pursuits. Either they gather motives for anger against those nearby, and rage against their neighbors without the slightest reason, or they take delight in inflicting harm by taking away what belongs to others, not realizing that they are being caught in inescapable snares, and exposing themselves to cruel dangers and death. For thus it is written: "Iniquities ensnare a man, and everyone is bound in the chains of his own sins."[27] But now, my children, I adjure you as Paul does when he cries, "Admonish the disorderly!"[28] Guide those who since their unbridled youth have been, and still are, letting their greed carry them to acts of senselessness; to them I myself say: Leave off such acts of greed; stop grieving and inciting against yourselves the King and Lord of all; drop from your hands your murderous swords, and rid your minds of your unjust desire for the things of others. Stop your attacks on each other. Control your temper. Cease your unholy undertakings. Do not be like Cain, the fratricide, the pitiless one, the teacher of bloody impiety. It was to him that the Creator of all said, "The voice of your brother's blood cries out to me from the earth!"[29] And these words extend to all of like character. For let everyone arrogant enough to do such things listen to God crying even now no less: "The voice of your brother's blood cries out to me from the earth!" But just as he said to him further, "You shall be groaning and trembling on the earth,"[30] so the God of love will speak thus to everyone of this sort. For what is more wretched than the law-breaker? Is there anything he hears spoken which

27. Prv 5.22.
28. 1 Thes 5.14.
29. Gn 4.10.
30. Gn 4.11.

does not frighten him? Is there anyone at whose glance he does
not shiver if he simply notices it turned toward him? His conscience is always cast down within, unnerved by his conviction of
having sinned. For "the righteous man is confident as a lion,"[31]
and, attested for every good deed by his free conscience, he de-
fies every accusation. There is nothing more prone to cowardice, by contrast, than a sin-loving soul. To quote the prophet,
therefore: "Awake, you drunkards, from your wine; mourn, you
that drink wine to drunkenness: for joy and gladness are removed from your mouth."[32]

Now is not the truth of these words in our regard proven by
experience itself? O peasants of Egypt, what tale is heard among
you at present? Is there anything that is said which evokes joy and
gladness? Is there anyone among you, great or small, who has become so desensitized by the recent assault of anger as to be able
to set aside grief and mourning, and not display cheeks drenched
with tears? Thus the prophet's words apply now to us as well: "O
husbandmen, mourn your property on account of the wheat and
barley; for the harvest has perished from off the field. The vine is
dried up, and the fig trees are become few; the pomegranate,
and palm tree, and apple, and all the trees of the field are dried
up: for the sons of men have cast shame upon joy."[33] For God,
who is good by nature and delights in mercy, covered the land
thickly with a joyful crop, and the stalks of grain were tall, causing the laborers to conceive abundant hopes, and filling the
peasant's soul with happiness. But the inhabitants of the land
have cast shame upon their own joy, since some of them have
turned to killing, and have made the fruitful earth drunk on human blood; they have raised the fratricidal sword against each
other, and that iron which is so good for husbandry, and for that
reason especially was created by God, they have made the instrument of the worst impiety. It is understandable that our God, in
his love for virtue, has been angered; the fertile land he has
made barren by fire, and, checking the joyous expectations as
though with a rein, has changed the joy into sorrow. And this was
just what had been said by one of the holy prophets: "Thus says

31. Prv 28.1.                          32. Jl 1.5.
33. Jl 1.11–12.

the Lord God Almighty: In all the streets shall be lamentations; and in all the ways shall it be said, Woe, woe! The husbandman shall be called to mourning and lamentation, and to them that are skilled in complaining. And there shall be lamentation in all the ways, because I will pass through the midst, says the Lord."[34]

Now see how true these words are! Is not what has happened worthy of lamentation and endless grief? Behold the savage beast of famine devouring our whole country! The land that feeds the entire earth beneath the sun,[35] so to speak, itself needs whatever bread may fall by the wayside, and food that is hardly fit for human consumption, so that the prophet Jeremiah says rightly of it in his lament, "All her people groan, seeking bread."[36] And also, "The tongue of the sucking child clove to the roof of its mouth for thirst. The little children asked for bread, and there was none to break it for them. They that feed on dainties have collapsed in the streets."[37] "For we have sown much, but brought in little,"[38] as is written, because we have angered the Spirit of the Lord.

Let us repent, therefore, and let us cease from our transgressions of old. Let us approach the merciful God, our eyes shedding tears in abundance, and let us say with one of the prophets, "Who is a God like you, canceling iniquities, and passing over injustices, and he has not kept his anger for a testimony, for he desires mercy?"[39] And again: "Our iniquities have arisen up against us, O Lord; act for us for the sake of your name; our sins are many before you; we have sinned against you. O Lord, you are the survival of Israel, and deliver us in time of troubles."[40] For it is to those whose repentance is such as this, yes, such as this, that he grants to hear those sweet words: "Behold, I send you grain, and wine, and oil, and you shall be satisfied with them. Be of good courage, O land; rejoice and be glad: for the Lord has done great things. Be of good courage, you beasts of the plain, for the plains of the wilderness have budded. For the

---

34. Am 5.16–17.
35. Cyril refers to Egypt's role in supplying the Empire with grain.
36. Lam 1.11.                              37. Lam 4.4–5.
38. Hg 1.6.                                39. Mi 7.18.
40. Jer 14.7–8.

trees have borne their fruit; the vine, and the fig tree, and the pomegranate have yielded their strength. Rejoice in the Lord your God then, and be glad, you children of Zion: for he has given you food unto justice, and he will rain on you the early and the latter rains, as before. And the floors shall be filled with grain, and the presses shall overflow with wine and oil. And I will recompense you for the years which the locust and the caterpillar and the palmerworm and the cankerworm have eaten. And you shall eat, and be satisfied, and you shall praise the name of the Lord your God for the wonders which he has wrought for you."[41]

Do not doubt, then, O man, nor think to yourself that if you approach him repentantly, he will not grant you mercy readily. You have even now a pledge of what you hope for in prayer, which is hardly negligible; you already have a surety of his benevolence. Behold, he has flooded the whole land with river waters; behold how he still grants to sinners the enjoyment of the abundance of his customary provision. Your tears have not yet appeared, and God has continued to show himself merciful. If he does not refuse to show pity to those who are not yet weeping, will he not rejoice in those who readily repent?

Let the fathers among you listen,[42] therefore, the fathers of the holy altars, the ministers and servants: "Sound the trumpet in Zion, sanctify a fast, proclaim a solemn service: gather the people, sanctify an assembly, assemble the elders, gather the infants at the breast. Let the bridegroom go forth from his bridal chamber, and the bride from her room. Between the porch and the altar let the priests that minister to the Lord weep, and say, Spare your people, O Lord, and give not your heritage to reproach, lest they should say among the heathen, Where is their God?"[43] When we approach him in this way he will receive us at once with the following words of compassion: "I, even I, am he who blots out your sins, and I will not remember them."[44]

For is there any way in which he will be severe toward us, "he

---

41. Jl 2.19, 21–26.

42. Cyril means here bishops, clerics, and heads of monastic communities: cf. SC 392, 48. n. 2.

43. Jl 2.15–17.          44. Is 43.25.

who," as Paul says, "did not spare his own Son, but gave him up for us all"?[45] For since those of old were guilty of such transgressions, the devil had control of the whole earth under the sun, so to speak, while sin thus ruled over us and corrupted our entire race, so that no one was to be seen who acted well. On the contrary, as the Psalmist says, "there was no one at all. They have all gone out of the way, they are together become unprofitable."[46]

It was necessary that the only-begotten Word of God, "though he was in the form of God the Father," as it is written, "did not count equality with God a thing to be grasped, but emptied himself, taking the form of a slave."[47] And for our sake he was counted among those in our condition, born of a woman,[48] and appearing on earth as a real human being, "so that," as Paul says, "he might become a merciful and faithful high priest in the service of God,"[49] in order that, as is further written, "by bearing" all of "our sins in his body on the tree,"[50] he might cancel the bond which stood against us.[51] This was so that by appropriating the weaknesses of our flesh, he might put to death the pleasure which plays the tyrant in our members, and might say to the passions in us, as to a raging sea, "Peace! Be still!"[52] and, having brought everything in us into a better order and stability, he might reshape as virtue all of nature, even according to the original image in which it was made. And the Only-Begotten did not restrict his generosity to us through his Incarnation even to these good things. For since by nature he is life, as is also the One who begot him, he rendered the flesh in which he dwelt superior to death.

For the wretched Jews, full as they are of every impiety, handed him over to the cross and death,[53] obeying in everything the devil's plans. But he conquered by suffering, and showed us the death of his own flesh as the basis of our salvation. For he despoiled all of hell at once, opened the inescapable gates to the spirits of those asleep, left the devil there solitary and alone, and

---

45. Rom 8.32.

47. Phil 2.6–7.

49. Heb 2.17.

51. Col 2.14.

53. Cf. Mt 26.2; 27.26.

46. Ps 14.3; 53.3.

48. Cf. Gal 4.4.

50. 1 Pt. 2.24.

52. Mk 4.39.

then rose on the third day, "having loosed the pangs of death," as is written, "because it was not possible for him to be held by it."[54] And having blazed the new path of resurrection from the dead for human nature, he ascended into heaven itself, "now to appear in the presence of God on our behalf,"[55] as Paul says, that he might render the bright dwelling-places of the angels accessible to those upon earth. For he "is our peace, who has made us both one,"[56] and joined men to angels in friendship, while bringing down to us the affection held by the angels, in order therefore that we might reign with Christ, that we might be found to be sharers and participants in immortal glory,[57] having dismissed all hesitation and laziness in doing good, putting it, as it were, out of our minds, and embracing with the greatest delight the labors performed for virtue. "As we have opportunity, let us do good to all";[58] let us not spend our time in reveling and drunkenness, nor in debauchery and licentiousness,[59] but let us put on the Lord Jesus, let us assume the attitude of compassion and pity,[60] let us practice mutual love, gentleness, humility, continence, and mercy toward the poor. In a word, let us hold fast to piety toward God, practicing an entire reverence for him.

For thus it is, yes, thus, that we will celebrate the all-holy feast with a clear conscience and joyful outlook, beginning holy Lent on the twenty-third of the month of Mechir, and the week of the salvific Paschal festival on the twenty-eighth of Phamenoth, breaking the fast on the third of Pharmuthi, the eve of Saturday, according to the apostolic tradition. We celebrate the feast on the next day, the eve of Sunday, the fourth of Pharmuthi.[61] We add the following seven weeks of holy Eastertide. For thus will we inherit even the kingdom of heaven in Christ Jesus our Lord, through whom and with whom be glory and power to the Father, with the Holy Spirit, now and forever, and for endless ages. Amen.

54. Acts 2.24.
55. Heb 9.24.
56. Eph 2.14.
57. Cf. 2 Pt 1.4.
58. Gal 6.10.
59. Cf. Rom 13.13–14.
60. Cf. Col 3.12.
61. March 30, 419.

# FESTAL LETTER EIGHT

## A.D. 420

"OUND THE TRUMPET in Zion,"[1] says the sacred law some place, rousing the Church to its yearly call to the customary acts of zeal, and compelling those who have chosen a life of excellence to rally to the signal for the divine contests. For behold, behold, once again the season of the holy feast arises upon us as though from some circle or circuit, preceded of course by a fast, and by the contest of perseverance which rises before it like the day-star. For that body all but speaks aloud in announcing to the industrious the radiance of the sun, and, so to speak, enters within doors to display the light of day and advise that it is now time to dismiss sleep from one's eyes and to refuse to do what suits the night. This fast most holy and pure, on the other hand, which springs up shining before our holy feast, reminds those who love virtue of what Paul proclaimed in the Spirit: "The night is far gone, the day is at hand. Let us then cast off the works of darkness and put on the works of light; let us conduct ourselves becomingly as in the day, not in reveling and drunkenness, not in debauchery and licentiousness, not in quarreling and jealousy. But put on our Lord Jesus Christ,"[2] the truly bright robe of the pious.

Those who take pleasure in sailing, and who choose usually to travel by ship, are encouraged by light and fair breezes to leave harbor as soon as possible, and to have no fear of casting off. Then too, the grape darkening on the vine, whose skin is already splitting and brimming, calls in a way for the vintage-songs to begin. And the ear of grain bristling in the field, bright upon its stalk already golden and weighed down with well-grown seed,

1. Jl 2.1.
2. Rom 13.12–14.

137

feels annoyance perhaps at the reaper's delay. For everyone, I think, welcomes the arrival of that time which suits each thing that is useful.

Since all this is well known, it is obviously quite shameful, and fully abhorrent, if we err in the reckoning that matters, and find ourselves ridiculous in God's sight. And quite rightly so, if we do not eagerly seize the time which is already upon us, and which offers a chance to distinguish themselves in the virtues to those who drive for them at the gallop. For if we shrink back, and continually neglect the opportunity to stir ourselves to search for what is better, and foolishly bring upon ourselves the loss of what is good, we may rightly find spoken to us the words which apply to the indolent: "The slothful come to want."[3]

I, at any rate, would say, then, that always to do good, and to take pride in behaving in the best possible way, is most fitting to those who are devout, for it seems to me that to stop acting justly would be the beginning of evil. But it accords with the present season to exert even more than the usual generosity, the season that demands that we pay down our liberality in these matters as against a debt. It is the same as with those who value bodily strength, and who prefer to all else the approval of their trainers: what suits them is constant exercise, and acquiring the skills of the arena helps them attain their goal. And when the contest judge calls them to demonstrate their valor, and they realize that it is then or never that they must show the results of their lengthy exertions in a way that will provoke admiration, they apply all of their strength to their desire to appear most distinguished. In this way also I think that those who keep in view the divine law as though they were in a contest or exercise, must practice piety constantly, and attach great importance to the Legislator's will; and with the season of fasting calling one to a more magnificent exhibition, must reject that hesitation which is the source of cowardice, and cultivate an attitude which will outdo in valor even that courage which has been honed by practice.

Come, therefore, and let us once again gird[4] on the zeal to do good, prefer what is by nature beneficial to the charms of loath-

3. Prv 11.16 (LXX).
4. Cf. Eph 6.14.

some pleasure, and, in our desire for what will profit us, have the good sense to reject out of hand the company of the unjust, and thus present ourselves to Christ as genuine worshipers,[5] keeping a faith in him which is unbroken and unfeigned, and guarding a confession which is unbending and undeviating, the one we make in the presence of many witnesses, by which I mean the holy angels. For many there are who, in putting on the semblance of piety like a mask "while denying its power,"[6] as Paul says, plunder the minds of simpler folk, seducing them with deceitful language and persuading them to slip with them into death's trap and into hell's snare,[7] as is written. For they have decided that they should speak to those who approach them not about what accords with holy Scripture; rather, what their disreputable minds have dreamed up on their own is what they persuade them to think, knowing neither what they are saying nor the matters about which they make their affirmations. "But as for you, continue in what you have learned,"[8] as Paul says, abandoning vain disputes about words, spitting from your mouth the silly chatter[9] of the heretics,[10] turning away from aimless myths, keeping your faith within simple arguments, and placing the tradition of the Church in the storerooms of your heart like a treasure; thus hold fast to those pursuits which are pleasing to God, so that you may be not only notable for your faith, but henceforth fully conspicuous as well for your achievements in piety.

2. For while the path that leads to the ability to accomplish virtuous deeds has many a fork, and one may arrive with difficulty "at the prize of the upward call"[11] by way of a road that is complex, yet our entire good is nonetheless bound together in one thing: "You shall love your neighbor as yourself."[12] And there is

---

5. Cf. Jn 4.23.  
6. 2 Tm 3.5.  
7. Cf. Prv 9.18.  
8. 2 Tm 3.14.  
9. Cf. 1 Tm 4.7; 6.4.  

10. The theological discussion that follows has anti-Arian overtones. In much of his early writing Cyril rehearses anti-Arian arguments as a way of presenting Nicene theology. The originality of Cyril's thinking becomes more evident after 428 and the beginning of the Christological controversy. See Norman Russell, *Cyril of Alexandria* (London and New York: Routledge, 2000), 21–30.

11. Phil 3.14.  
12. Mt 19.19.

no difficulty in showing that these words have become true for us. For Paul in his supreme wisdom provides excellent support for what we have said on these matters when he writes, "Owe no one anything, except to love one another; for he who loves the other has fulfilled the Law. The commandments, 'You shall not commit adultery, You shall not kill, You shall not steal, You shall not covet,' and any other commandment, are summed up in this sentence: 'You shall love your neighbor as yourself.' Love does no wrong to a neighbor; therefore, love is the fulfilling of the Law."[13] You hear how all that is said is bounded about by love. For whatever it is that clearly oversteps the divine law has certainly lapsed from the circles of love. Those, on the other hand, who happen with good reason to be admired may be seen to have the quality of being visibly within love by their deeds. For while those who act unjustly do not love their neighbors, those who hate injustice certainly do love, fulfilling the whole Law thereby. For the effort to honor love brings about the fulfillment of the contents of the Law, while the neglect of it gives rise to what the Law condemns. For who is it, please tell me, who would approach someone else's wife, and would attack another's marriage, when he is ashamed to grieve someone out of love? And I think I may ask if there is anyone who would not refuse with the utmost vigor to commit murder, from the reverence and respect which he bears toward the one who would be the victim and which reins him in the direction of gentleness? And is there anyone existing who would not regard the acquisition of what belongs to others as detestable and abominable, when he realizes what a bitter thing it is to harm one's brother, something regarded as among the worst evils?

The Law, therefore, which steers us toward all virtue, has its fulfillment in love. But once one has examined carefully the constitutive parts of the virtue just named by us, one should, I think, state the result. I will, therefore, use here again what Paul says: "Love," he says, "is patient and kind; love is not jealous; love is not boastful; it is not arrogant or rude. Love does not seek its own interests; it is not irritable or resentful; it does not rejoice at

---

13. Rom 13.8–10.

wrong, but rejoices in the right. Love bears all things, believes all things, hopes all things, endures all things. Love never fails."[14] Do you see the great quantity of good things which the power of love produces for us? "Love," he says, "is patient"; that is, it does not weaken at a neighbor's pettiness. For those who are completely patient are certainly so even with the offenses committed against them by others, and they conquer the things that usually vex one. The prudent do not yield to the anger which leads to retribution. For injustice is really hard to bear, with the power to kindle terrible rage. And the experience of suffering anything first at the hands of anyone furnishes arms and encouragement to one's passion, however evil it may by nature be. One may even be persuaded by it that one is not acting unjustly in one's counter-move when one hastens to strike back at the wrongdoer. Those, however, whose vigorous intelligence keeps in view the law of love, and who realize that it befits them to be patient, bring their anger back under control when it flares up, as though they were applying the reins of forbearance to a colt leaping wildly about. And afterwards, since they have been seen to be better than those who did them wrong, they win the approval of all good people.

But what the most wonderful aspect of love is has nearly passed by unnoticed. Let us look further at what the champion of virtue says about love, and what he commands in addition as a marvelous way of putting it into practice. "Love," he says, "does not seek its own interests; it is not irritable."[15] The exposition of this topic that is accurate and in tune with the law, then, is the one which would show that those who do not seek their own interests are those who have no concern for what is their own, as long as the many benefit. What do I mean? Let me proceed by way of examples. The leaders of the Jewish communities once ordered the holy apostles to speak to no one in Christ's name.[16] But they, paying no mind to this nonsense of theirs, even though it meant running the gravest risk, once again taught the crowds they met, judging rightly that they should help those in error, and disregarding completely the threat that arose therefrom.

14. 1 Cor 13.4–8.    15. 1 Cor 13.5.
16. Cf. Acts 4.5, 18.

For they were not seeking their own interests, but those of others, not overstepping love's boundary, so dear to God. But even though the subject at hand requires of us some observation of this kind, still, for the sake of those who are accustomed to think about it in simpler terms, let us turn to it once again and bring it into relationship with what the Savior says.

In raising us, therefore, to the highest kind of gentleness and brotherly love, and clipping from our soul, like a thorn, contention and quarrelsomeness and the desire for what simply does not belong to us, he says, "Give to everyone who begs from you; and of those who take away what is yours do not ask for it back."[17] Do you hear how he orders you to shy away from what belongs to others? He does not want us to resist even if someone takes what is rightly ours, but to show ourselves superior to the provocations arising from injury, rather than always flying into an unseemly rage when we fail to control the pain caused by our losses to whoever it may be.

3. But then, what will the robber say to me in reply? He crouches like a beast at the crossroads, lying in wait for passersby who have done him no wrong, as though they were enemies, and casting his pirate's net into the river waters, and if he catches someone, he springs upon him at once, on fire with a recklessness that is unnatural.[18] What have you done with the Savior's law, please tell me, in defiance of your claim to be a Christian? For you transgress the commandment of love; you no longer realize that you have been, as it were, transformed into an untamable beast, and have fallen into a monstrous savagery. In treating as of no account one who was made in the divine image, you do what is not to be endured. You dare to do what is unholy in striking with your iron. But are there not times when, seeing the still-quivering corpse upon the earth as your fellow human being, you long for this earth to gape open beneath you, and does it not strike you when you rush to do these brutal acts of arrogance, that you have been used to plowing the earth, to cleaving

17. Lk 6.30.
18. As in the previous letter, Cyril describes problems related to violent crime in his diocese.

the fields with the plow, and then to hiding in them what you choose, and reaping with the iron again what God has made to ripen? You marvel then at the earth as the mother of good crops, as the one who supplies you so excellently with the provision of what you need. And you doubtless praise the use of the iron. How can you then not blush to treat unjustly the things that have given you life's necessities? Down goes your murder victim, and you empurple the earth with innocent blood. How can you still entreat her to become the mother of your crops, when you wrong her so mercilessly? And how will you apply to a mother the bright iron which you have perverted from its rightful function and made into a murderer? Or how, please tell me, will you be able at all to ask God to flood your field with the yearly waters, if you have any sense, when you sit among the reeds with no good intent, rowing your skiff about not because you are hunting for what is in the water but because greediness is your enterprise? You defile the God-given inundation with bloodshed, and give your fellow human being to the aquatic beasts. And then, tell me, what kind of hands will you lift up to God? What kind of prayer will you be able to say at all, or how will you ask for good things from the God who says through one of the prophets, "When you stretch out your hands to me, I will turn away my eyes from you; and though you make many supplications, I will not listen to you, for your hands are full of blood."[19] But what further concern will be bestowed upon one who takes no account of the laws coming from him? "I will honor them that honor me," says the Savior, "and the one who sets me at naught will be set at naught."[20] Either bow your neck to him, then, and demand in return your penalty, and the generous benefaction of all that you need, or else, if you cannot bear the yoke, put up with your punishment!

If there is anything to be added to the foregoing, it is that to be immersed in good things, and to have poured out upon one what one has prayed for, has sometimes been the occasion of this great impiety of yours. The Lord God of all says something of the sort: "And they were completely filled; and their hearts

19. Is 1.15.
20. 1 Sm 2.30.

were exalted. Therefore, they forgot me."[21] And indeed, luxury, which leads to lapses, is really dangerous, and it can also lead to conceit, the parent of madness. And the bitter offspring of madness is contempt of God, while the fruit of the contempt in this offspring is transgressions of every sort. And so? When we see you suffering from this, we will be understandably grieved, and in our mutual affection, distressed by your impieties, we will speak to you the prophet's words: "Alas my soul! For the devout has perished from the earth; and there is none among human beings that acts rightly. They all quarrel even to blood: they all afflict their neighbors: in oppression they lift up their hands to mischief."[22] At these our transgressions God is understandably provoked, and, as you see, indignant. For see now, see, how the words of the prophets have been fulfilled for us, not once, but often already: "Consider your ways, says the Lord almighty. You have sown much, but brought in little. You have eaten, and are not satisfied; you have drunk, but not to intoxication; you have clothed yourselves, and have not become warm thereby; and the wage-earner has gathered his pay into a bag full of holes."[23] And he adds, "You looked for much, and there came little; and it was brought into the house, and I blew it away, says the Lord almighty."[24] Let us see, then, if this has not truly happened. Let someone come forward and show me a happy person, and I am defeated; let the eye be sought that is without tears, and, if it is found, I will say no more!

My dear Egyptian peasants,[25] you are at present contesting for only one thing: to see which of you suffers more severely than the next, with the victor among you more wretched than those seemingly defeated. For he wins the contest by means of what pains him, and has a more abundant misfortune than his neighbor's troubles. But as for the things of which you used to boast, they have been absent now for long years. Is not your tale replete with tears and distress? Why is it, please tell me, that we see the

---

21. Hos 13.6.                    22. Mi 7.2–3.
23. Hg 1.6.                       24. Hg 1.9.

25. While the primary audience for these letters was monks and clerics, this passage clearly indicates that the content was intended for the general population, perhaps mediated through homilies delivered locally in Coptic.

villages in the condition in which they are? Here is one that has been struck by hail, is wasting away from famine and grief, and is receiving no help at all from anywhere, not even to moderate his pain. The grain, now at its prime and standing tall, was all but crying out, "Harvest me!" and the one who had plowed the soil now took his sickle from the hearth, girded himself, and proceeded to work, perhaps repeating to himself over and over again that the threshing-floor would not be wide enough. But it was all a dream or a shadow: it was the hail that did the work, not the harvester. He had expected to be inundated with good things, and suddenly he was bereft of everything. He abounded not in grain but in hail, and far and wide stretched the ruin of his hopes. As for the neighboring village bordering upon the other, which was less afflicted by the wrath, it bewails the labor spent upon plowing, but, having cultivated a crop of great extent, it considers itself wealthy if it has enough to satisfy its present need for food, or rather far less even than what would satisfy.

4. Let us look, then, for what may be the reason for this, and let us find it in sacred Scripture. The One therefore who possesses all power will say to us again, "Your ways and your devices have brought these things upon you; this is the wickedness for it is bitter, for it has reached to your heart."[26] For it follows that those who transgress excessively must be punished justly, and it is necessary that the penalty equal our imbecilities. Let us therefore cease from all unholy audacity. Let us, as is written, "beat our swords into plowshares, and our spears into sickles,"[27] and, as the Psalmist says, "Come, let us worship and fall down before him,"[28] and weeping let us say, "We have sinned, we have transgressed, we have done iniquity."[29] For it is then, then indeed, that God will be gracious, and put away his anger, and the earth will again bear bountifully, and will cheer us with its usual gifts.[30] "For we have not a high priest who is unable to sympathize with our weaknesses," as Paul says, "but one who has been tempted as we are, yet without sin."[31]

---

26. Jer 4.18.
27. Is 2.4 (and, in contrast, Jl 3.10).
28. Ps 95.6.
29. Dn 9.5.
30. See *Letter* 6, n. 16.
31. Heb 4.15.

For I do not think any effort will be required of me to persuade you that the Only-Begotten is inherently willing to show mercy readily; I suppose that you too are quite prepared to agree, since you have considered carefully the extent of his affection for us, and have reflected on how much it is that he has undergone for us. For when all of us who dwell upon this earth had been netted like fish by the irresistible greed of the tyrant demon and faced destruction and perdition, the Only-Begotten became a human being, that he might rescue everyone, "and might proclaim release to the captives and recovery of sight to the blind," as he himself says somewhere, and might in addition call for "an acceptable year of the Lord."[32]

The Only-Begotten is therefore merciful, even if the Jews, not understanding the mode of the economy, were so far from even wanting to accept him that once they even insulted him by calling him a "Samaritan," and another time, after vexing him unendurably, and bursting into a monstrous fury, they then attempted in their arrogance to stone him.[33] And when, in confuting these adversaries of God, the Lord asked them the reason for their reckless madness with the words, "I have shown you many good works from my Father; for which of these do you stone me?"[34] they spoke nonsense, saying, "It is not for a good work that we stone you but for blasphemy; because you, being a man, make yourself God."[35] What does the Savior say to them then? "If I am not doing the works of my Father, then do not believe me; but if I do them, even though you do not believe me, believe my works."[36] For he did not ask that what concerned him be assessed from the way he appeared as man to those who saw him, but from the works he performed as God, since he did not possess the dignity of divinity as something acquired as we do, when holy Scripture speaks of us as gods;[37] it was rather present in him substantially, as being by nature God, and heir to the property of the One who begot him. He also has the power to do everything, not having received it from someone else, but as being the Lord of the powers and from the substance of God the

---

32. Is 61.1–2; Lk 4.19.
33. Cf. Jn 8.48–49; 10.31.
34. Jn 10.32.
35. Jn 10.33.
36. Jn 10.37–38.
37. Ps 82.6; Jn 10.34.

Father.[38] For even if he became a human being out of love for us, we will not for that reason fail to recognize the Lord of all, nor will we exclude Immanuel from being by nature God, nor will we adopt the same attitude as the Jews and reproach him for his humanity which is for us. Nor will we, in an unholy way, accuse the One who for us became like us, yet without sin,[39] saying, "We would not worship you, since, being a man, you make yourself God." For he was, is, and will be God by nature, before the flesh and with the flesh. Paul supports this when he writes, "Jesus Christ is the same yesterday and today and forever."[40] You see that he is not to be found chopping Immanuel into a duality of Sons, nor does he attribute his being the same way perpetually to the unclothed Word by himself, resplendent from God the Father; rather, knowing that there is only one Son by nature, the One who became a human being, he names him both Christ and Jesus. For when could one show that the Word is named Jesus or Christ, except when he became a human being? He is called "Jesus" because he saves the people, and "Christ" because he was anointed for us. It is not, therefore, the Word from God the Father, unclothed still before the Incarnation,[41] whom he calls Jesus and Christ, but he who came to be in the flesh, and about him he says, with no uncertainty, that "he was the same yesterday and today and forever."[42]

5. But perhaps someone imbued with heresy will come up and disgorge the venom of his habitual impiety as he shouts, "Tell me, sir: was not Christ born in the last times? How then was he always, even before being born?" Against this sort of stuff we muster the words in defense of the truth with the cry, "What you say agrees with what we have said, my man!" For how is it that

38. Cyril's language here and in the following discussion is thoroughly Nicene. He, like many involved in the Christological controversy, was slow to realize that the language of Nicaea alone could not bring clarity to the new Christological questions.

39. Cf. Heb 4.15.

40. Heb 13.8.

41. The word used here is *enanthrōpēsis* rather than *ensarkōsis*, which is more typical of Cyril.

42. Heb 13.8.

the Spirit-bearer, the steward of the Savior's mysteries, bestowed upon the temple[43] born in the final times those things which belong to the Word, who lives and is always, unless he considered it impious to make a severance, and shrank from dividing in two, after the Incarnation, the one and only true Son? The things which belong peculiarly and naturally to the Word, even before the flesh, are what he applies to him again even when he has come into the flesh, knowing that he has not become other on account of the flesh, but preserving intact for him the dignity of divinity even when he became a human being. And do not wonder, my man, at Paul's words. For he was not having his own way with the doctrines of orthodoxy and simply straining them to fit his views when he said this; rather, he had been taught by the Savior's own words. For what he said to Nicodemus may be seen in the Gospels, if you want to find out. But I will quote the words, so that everyone may be helped: "If I have told you earthly things," he says, "and you do not believe, how will you believe if I tell you heavenly things?"[44] And: "No one has ascended into heaven but he who descended from heaven, the Son of man."[45] Another time when he was speaking to the Jews he contended, and showed clearly, that they would remain without any share whatever in eternal life, since they had not tasted the mystical blessing.[46] When they took this badly and drew back, as is written, he said further, teaching beforehand his departure from there into heaven, "Do you take offense at this? Then what if you were to see the Son of man ascending where he was before?"[47]

If I may sum up the general issue once again: even though he was born upon earth through the holy Virgin according to the flesh, God the Word still came down from heaven. How, then, does he say that the Son of man came down from heaven to us? How, further, does he say that he will go back up where he was

43. As the Christological controversy developed, Cyril would retreat more and more from this language. Cf. SC 392, 95, n. 4.

44. Jn 3.12.                              45. Jn 3.13.

46. Perhaps a reference to the power of the Eucharist in the process of divinization. Cf. H. Chadwick, "Eucharist and Christology in the Nestorian Controversy," *JTS N.S.* 2 (1951): 145–64.

47. Jn 6.62.

before? Do you see how, when he constricts the Word in the inseparable and indefinable unity of the ineffable conjunction,[48] he intends that Christ be confessed by us as one both before the flesh and with the flesh? That is precisely why he says that the flesh, even though it is by nature from earth, came down from above, even from heaven, and that it will ascend into heaven where it was before.[49] For what is in him by nature he bestows upon his own flesh, as not being other than it as far as the unity from the dispensation is concerned. And we will not destroy, through that which unifies them as completely as possible, the things which are by nature dissimilar: the existence as the Father's unique radiance on the one hand, while yet as something other, that which is carnal, from earth, or fully man. No; even when we have distinguished them in this way, and separated by thought alone[50] what may be said of each of them, we will constrict them again in an inseparable unity. For "the Word became flesh,"[51] as the holy evangelist says; not that he changed into flesh—that is not what he says—but rather, he uses the word "flesh" instead of speaking of "man" as a whole.[52]

6. Surely, then, as our all-praiseworthy father and bishop Athanasius,[53] the undistorted rule of the orthodox faith, has said as well in his own writings, what has happened is a conjunction

48. Greek: *synodou.*

49. Statements like this one left Cyril open to the charge that he was an Apollinarian. He would later have to make special efforts to refute this charge.

50. Cyril will develop this idea that the natures are separable in thought alone into a more formal theology of hypostatic union, one of the pillars of his mature Christology. See J. A. McGuckin, *St. Cyril of Alexandria: The Christological Controversy: Its History, Theology, and Texts* (Leiden and New York: Brill, 1994).

51. Jn 1.14.

52. That is, the word "flesh" signifies a complete human being. This qualification suggests that Cyril was already becoming aware of the need for greater precision in his language.

53. Cyril always saw himself as a disciple of Athanasius. Indeed, he attributed many of his early Christological formulations to him, such as the controversial "one incarnate nature of the word made flesh." Cyril would eventually have to develop his own vocabulary. Since Athanasius had been primarily concerned with Trinitarian questions, he did not always foresee the implications of his thought for later Christological orthodoxy.

in the same place of two realities by nature dissimilar, divinity and humanity. But there is one Christ from the two.[54] And the manner of the mixture is for us ineffable, and wholly incomprehensible; but the depth of the mystery is accepted by faith. For what surpasses the mind and understanding that we have, is admired not by a meddlesome curiosity, but by faith alone. Since, therefore, he did not consider the flesh alien to him, but made of it rather his own temple, and, having become a human being, is worshiped even by the holy angels (for it says, "When he brings the firstborn into the world, he says, 'Let all God's angels worship him'"),[55] I should be very glad to learn from the mindlessly arrogant exponents of a different doctrine, if indeed there are any, who divide "what God has joined,"[56] as the Savior himself somewhere says, and think that there are two Christs and two Sons: in what way may the title "firstborn" be well suited to the One who was the Word from God the Father before the Incarnation? For how is he still Only-Begotten, if he is firstborn? For if he is Only-Begotten, he would not be firstborn. Christ, however, is both at once, and one will not be able, in dividing in two the one and only Son, to attribute to one the title of "firstborn," and to the other that of "Only-Begotten." For one will find all of the divinely inspired Scripture against one; indeed, we will find both titles applied properly to Christ because he is "firstborn," on the one hand, as human being "among many brothers and sisters,"[57] while he is also "Only-Begotten," as Word from God the Father. Thus, as Paul says, "there is one God, and there is one Mediator between God and human beings, the human being Christ Jesus."[58] Knowing, that is, that Christ is one and the same, even if he is presented sometimes as Word and sometimes as human being because of the economy of the Incarnation,[59] he writes further about him: "In whom we have redemption, the forgiveness of sins. He is the image of the invisible God, the firstborn of all creation; for in him all things were created, in heaven and on earth, visible and invisible, whether

54. While greater precision may have been evolving, this phrasing could easily be construed as overtly monophysite.

55. Heb 1.6.                              56. Mt 19.6.

57. Rom 8.29.                             58. 1 Tm 2.5.

59. Literally, "the economy with flesh."

Thrones or Dominions or Principalities or Authorities—all things were created through him and for him. He is before all things, and in him all things hold together. He is the head of the body, the Church; he is in the beginning the firstborn from the dead."[60] You can see again how, after combining what is proper to humanity with the dignities suited to God, he tells us that he is one and the same, and the image of the invisible Father. For he is the radiance and stamp of his subsistence.[61] He also calls him the firstborn of creation, and acknowledges him to be the Artificer of Thrones and Dominions and, in a word, of all things. He says also that the same One is the firstborn from the dead. And yet, inasmuch as he appeared as a human being in the final age, how can he be before everything? And how will he bear the dignity of Creator? Or in what way will he be the image of the invisible God? And furthermore, before he has become a human being, what reason is there to apply to him the words, "he is the firstborn of all creation, and the firstborn from the dead"? For in the same way as it is not thought suitable to a human being to create, which does suit God, so also is it foreign to God to die. But apparently Paul applies both to the same One. For he does not know of one Son and another, but One and the same. Just as the blessed prophet Isaiah may certainly be found thinking and speaking in much the same way about Christ: "And they shall follow after you bound in fetters, and shall be slaves, and shall worship you. And in you shall they pray, because God is in you, and there is no God beside you. For you are God, yet we knew it not, the God of Israel, the Savior."[62] Do you hear how he says, "You shall they worship, and in you shall they pray," and "God is in you, and there is no God beside you"? They will say this, and, because they know the temple in which he has settled, and are not ignorant of the Word dwelling in it, they do indeed worship not only him who dwells therein, separating him from the garment of flesh, but him who is the one result of the ineffably accomplished mixture of the two.[63]

---

60. Col 1.14–18.  61. Heb 1.3.
62. Is 45.14–15.

63. Although reminiscent of the language used by Athanasius in *On the Incarnation*, such images would later require much qualification.

For God the Word did indeed dwell as in his own temple, the body assumed from a woman, which has the rational soul. But he transformed what was assumed into his own glory. It is for this reason that, even though our holy Scripture tells us that worship is due only to the One who is really God by nature, Paul once again makes bold to say, "At the name of Jesus Christ every knee will bend, in heaven and on earth and under the earth, and every tongue will confess that Jesus Christ is Lord, to the glory of God the Father."[64]

And what, furthermore, will we say, when in reading the writings of the holy evangelists, we find our Lord Jesus, the Christ, breathing bodily upon his disciples and saying, "Receive the Holy Spirit"?[65] And Paul also writes, "Now we have received not the spirit of the world, but the Spirit which is from God."[66] And to others again he writes about the Jews, "To them belong the promises, to them the fathers, and from them, according to the flesh, is the Christ, the blessed God who is over all forever. Amen."[67]

And who was it that Thomas touched after the Resurrection from the dead, and then uttered those words supremely wise: "My Lord and my God!"[68] Are we to think that the Word from God the Father can abide even the touch of a hand? Surely one would say, I think, that we were uttering sheer nonsense, did we dare to speak thus foolishly. What it was, then, that he touched is not hard for anyone to understand.

Following all these other persons, though, let the leader of the holy disciples, Peter himself, come forward; when the Savior once asked, "Who do people say the Son of man is?" he cried aloud, "You are the Christ, the Son of the living God."[69] He did not say: In you is the Son; but knowing him to be one and the same, both before and with the flesh, he said, "You are the Son of the living God." And what was the result? The disciple was blessed for what he said: "Blessed are you, Simon Bar Jona! For flesh and blood has not revealed this to you, but my Father who is in heaven."[70] And as a gift matching his thought, and a recom-

64. Phil 2.10–11.
65. Jn 20.22.
66. 1 Cor 2.12.
67. Rom 9.4–5.
68. Jn 20.28.
69. Mt 16.13,16.
70. Mt 16.17.

pense for his orthodox faith, he was given the keys of heaven, as is written.[71]

Let us follow this faith too, and, refusing absolutely to share the Jewish mentality, let us not say with them to Christ, the Savior of us all, "Why do you who are human make yourself God?"[72] Let us rather worship and confess one Christ, the same who is both Word from God and "man from woman,"[73] as is written. For since we were involved in many sins, and the bitter array of the pleasures in us had ravaged the souls of each of us, "God, having sent his own Son in the likeness of sinful flesh," as Paul says, "condemned sin in the flesh,"[74] and with it death, sprung from it, that he might restore everyone to the life of old. For those wretched Jews, obedient to the devil's plans in everything, crucified the Lord of glory. But it was impossible for him who is by nature life and God to be held by the bonds of death. Having looted hell accordingly, and emptied the devil's lair completely, he rose on the third day, having become the way, the beginning, and the door for human nature, in order to return to life and to triumph over the snares of death. For we were all in Christ, inasmuch as he became a human being without sin: "And he took for himself the descendants of Abraham,"[75] as is written, in order that "having been made like his brothers and sisters in every respect,"[76] he might conquer death when he became a human being. For this is the whole purpose of the economy of the Incarnation.[77] Rising from the dead for us and because of us, he appeared to his own disciples, and, having bade them baptize in the name of the Father, the Son, and the Holy Spirit,[78] and to illuminate the whole world with their message,[79] he ascended "into heaven itself, to appear finally in the presence of God on our behalf,"[80] as is written, so that "having him as an advocate with the Father, and an expiation for our sins,"[81] as John says, we might hurry "toward the prize of the upward call,"[82] rejecting all sin resolutely, and being eager rather to make every effort to

---

71. Mt 16.19.

72. Jn 10.33.

73. Gal 4.4.

74. Rom 8.3.

75. Heb 2.16; Cf. Is 41.8.

76. Heb 2.17.

77. Cf. n. 59, above.

78. Mt 28.19.

79. Mk 16.15.

80. Cf. Heb 9.24.

81. 1 Jn 2.1–2.

82. Phil 3.14.

achieve that virtue which is dear to God. This means practicing moderation, embracing continence, "presenting the members of our body to God as instruments of righteousness,"[83] remembering the unfortunate, supporting orphans and widows, relieving prisoners in the distress of their captivity, and, in a word, holding to mutual love.

It is then, then indeed, that we will achieve a fast which is supremely pure and the mother of all good. We begin holy Lent on the twelfth of the month of Phamenoth, and the week of the salvific Paschal feast on the seventeenth of Pharmuthi. We break the fast on the twenty-second of Pharmuthi, late on the eve of Saturday. We celebrate the feast on the eve of Sunday, the twenty-third of Pharmuthi,[84] in Christ, to whom be the glory and the power, now and for endless ages. Amen.

83. Rom 6.13.
84. April 18, 420.

# FESTAL LETTER NINE

## A.D. 421

NCE AGAIN we display the radiant signal for the holy feast, crying out in a loud and piercing voice, "It is time to act for the Lord!"[1] For once again there has come to us, come indeed through the yearly cycle, the time for fasting. For just as when the sun begins its flight over the earth from its eastern regions, but still holds within itself its splendor, its bright rays rise up to transform the dejection of darkness into the vision of the pleasantly laughing beauty of its colors, so also, I think, now that the announcement of our holy feast is being sent around, and the Church is persuading us to let this solemn proclamation of it shine forth, everyone's mental energy somehow brightens to a more cheerful condition. And it seems to me, and I do not think that I am veering from the subject in saying so, that one might feel resentment toward the time for the competition to begin, if it continually delayed its arrival. For the mind, being industrious, naturally suffers and is wearied when it does not see the competitions starting when they are announced. Just so, the divinely inspired Scripture quite rightly compares those affected by desires so keen, to a war-horse, when it says, "Afar off he smells the war with prancing and neighing."[2] For the frightful uproar of battle, the clash of arms, the sight of the glittering steel, and the sound of the battle-trumpet, so freighted with fear, rouses in the high-spirited horse the longing for battle, while the description of those things which are the fairest of all incites the soul of the holy man to take part in the divine contest, disposing him quite effectively to the love of

1. Ps 119.126.
2. Jb 39.25.

155

God. I am sure that anyone will acknowledge that this sort of language is illuminating and estimable.

Now the fact that we appear in no way suited to this business might well have made us somewhat afraid, and made silence seem utterly desirable (for, as it is written, "they that are judges of themselves are wise"),[3] had not the divine law driven us to the necessity to speak. For it says, "Hear, you priests, and testify to the house of Jacob, says the Lord Almighty."[4] And he reveals through another prophet what it is that we are to discover and testify about to the house of Jacob when he says, "Sanctify a fast, proclaim a service, gather the elders and all the inhabitants of the land into the house of the Lord our God, and cry earnestly to the Lord."[5]

For of course one would never say that it is permissible to enter the inner tent[6] with feet unwashed; one must rather be cleansed first with all due care, and then, and then only, once one "has put to death what is earthly in one"[7] by the efforts of asceticism,[8] should one hasten beyond the divine curtains,[9] examining carefully the deep mystery of our Savior. For it is not possible, not at all possible, to share richly in the blessing given us from above, unless we choose to do what we are told here, and do it with great zeal. Thus we are brought to our present discourse: that we wage war at the signal given by the law, bearing arms in the company of the holy fighters, and keep festival with those who feast, present with them as an initiate. And what is the proof of this? The very Master of all, speaking to us thus through Moses: "If you shall go forth to war in your land against your enemies that are opposed to you, then you shall sound the trumpets; and you shall be had in remembrance before the Lord, and you shall be saved from your enemies. And in the days of your gladness, and in your feasts, and in your new moons, you shall sound with the trumpets at your whole-burnt-offerings, and at

---

3. Prv 13.10 (LXX).     4. Am 3.13.

5. Jl 1.14.     6. Cf. Heb 9.2; Ex 26.33.

7. Cf. Col 3.5.

8. For a discussion of the ways in which Cyril was impacted by asceticism, see the introduction.

9. Cf. Lv 16.2; Heb 6.19; 9.3; 10.20.

the sacrifices of your peace-offerings; and there shall be a memorial for you before your God."[10]

2. And "the Law, having but a shadow of the good things to come instead of the very image of these realities,"[11] bids those invested with the priesthood to use the trumpets when the time for battle looms, sending forth a mighty blast to stir the man at arms to remember his courage; while for those at the feast, they are to match the music to their joyfulness.[12] But we who transform what is from the darkness here into the power of truth busy ourselves with the words of instruction, instead of with that trumpet of old and its useless braying, words which urge to a prudent boldness those who muster the practice of continence against the movements of the flesh as they battle against their own passions, once they have decided to strap on the weapons of justice.[13] They are indeed words which are wont to leap with joy with those who make merry and render spiritual thank-offerings to the sovereign nature of all, and which acclaim the achievements of our Savior, which pass all wonder.

It is now springtime, a season which I think someone of ready tongue and outstanding intelligence could crown with an abundance of words. For it has washed off the dour sight of winter like dust, brightening it with the clear light of the sun, and it restores to mountains and vales, copses and thickets, their fairest form. For they are rejuvenated, and bloom with new verdure. The shepherd too rejoices, piping pleasantly, and, sending forth a clear song from his instrument, leads his flock to graze in the newly-grown grass, all lovely with flowers. The herdsman drives to pasture the heifer bouncing beside its mother. The vines put forth shoots quite new which run out and with their tendrils curl around the rushes like fingers, leaping upon the plants fixed next to them. They strive always to rise upwards, that the splendid beauty of the grapes may be seen. The meadows, for their part, wrapped in the multiple fragrance of their flowers, gladden the husbandmen with their accustomed generosity. And one who was paying honor to the season which brings forth flowers

---

10. Nm 10.9–10.
11. Heb 10.1.
12. Cf. Nm 10.1–10.
13. Cf. Rom 6.13; 13.12.

might add countless other details. I do not, however, think that the glory accruing from these things amounts to much at all, when that which is worth more than all the rest is the following. I mean that together with the plants, that nature which is sovereign over everything on earth has also returned to life: man himself. For the season of spring presents us with our Savior's Resurrection, through which we are all refashioned unto newness of life,[14] having escaped the intrusive corruption of death. For it would be quite unbelievable, that while the plants in their species and kinds were restored to their original appearance by the power of God, who gives life to everything, the one for whose sake the birth of plants itself was contrived should be lifeless, from want of any concern from on high. The renewal of the nature (as well as of all else) which is superior to all others on earth, takes place for us therefore concurrently with this very same season. And Christ is the Artificer of this. God the Father spoke indeed through one of the prophets: "Be of good courage, Zion; let not your hands be slack. The Lord God is mighty in you; he shall save you, and he shall renew you in his love."[15]

For in the time of his love for us, that is, when he became man for us, he refashioned in himself the whole of nature unto newness of life,[16] restoring it, as God, to what it had been originally, and thus showed us a supernatural spring, but he also rendered spiritual through piety those who were unspiritual because of the sin which had held dominion over them from of old. If anyone would like to learn, and is particularly eager to know clearly, what is meant by these two words, and in what way and to what extent the two terms differ, I will let Paul explain: "The unspiritual man does not receive the gifts of the Spirit of God, for they are folly to him, and he is not able to understand them because they are spiritually discerned. The spiritual man judges all things, but is himself to be judged by no one."[17] For those who engage in entertaining indiscriminately whatever may come into their minds, and who allow full play to the desires of the soul, cannot stand the laws of the Spirit, which urge self-control and

---

14. Cf. Rom 6.4.                    15. Zep 3.16–17.
16. Cf. Rom 6.4.
17. 1 Cor 2.14–15; cf. 1 Cor 15.44–46.

the cultivation of a well-disposed and well-rounded life. Those, however, who entrust to the laws of the Spirit the need to conquer, will not proceed incautiously to the performance of anything that must be done, but will always assess what is naturally of benefit, and will prefer profit to pleasure. Determined as they are to put what is beneficial over what is not, they are condemned by no one; they themselves rather discern everything. For anyone who would say that those who had chosen such a life were wicked, would simply condemn his own malice, and call down upon his own head the worst possible shame. It seems to me that to dare to mistreat witlessly those who ought rather to be admired, is to show utter wickedness, and those who do not refuse to support such evil people testify themselves to their own beastliness. It is precisely by that which they should have condemned as wicked, and which they have decided to honor, that they will clearly acknowledge themselves to be worthless in character.

It is a weakness than which there is none greater, declares holy Scripture, to be unable to discern correctly the natures of things. "Woe to them that call good evil," it says, "and evil good; who make darkness light, and light darkness."[18] For in my opinion one could as easily distinguish what is good from what is bad (one could make the judgment in either case without effort) as one might declare the difference between light and darkness. Woe, therefore, he says, to those who have so far departed from their senses as to confuse what is perfectly observable, and who do not blush to give the name of darkness to the light, and to the darkness that of light. One might say, however, that it is not those who are good and spiritual who have such weaknesses, but the unspiritual and the wicked. For since the pleasures of the present life hold sway over their mind, they are so far from wanting to do what is good, that they no longer even know what it is. But since we, unlike they, are God-loving and spiritual, "let us present ourselves as men who have been brought from death to life"[19] to Christ who died and was raised because of us and for us, and, as the divine Paul bids us, "if we live by the Spirit, let us also walk by the Spirit."[20] Let us not be drawn away to strange

18. Is 5.20.                    19. Rom 6.13.
20. Gal 5.25.

pleasures, nor let us venture from home out of destructive desires to dwell in sin as in a place which is a pit. Let us rather keep in view the fair city of the saints, the heavenly Jerusalem, which is our mother, and thus illuminate our own life with all forbearance and sobriety. Let us in addition render due honor to our own Master with that faith which is right and unwavering, keeping in mind what is written: "You shall love the Lord your God with your whole soul and with all your strength."[21] Now in bidding us offer up the full measure of love without ever dividing it or diverting it elsewhere, he orders us to render honor with a complete faith, never giving thought to what is of minor import in the faith and does not contribute to piety, nor paying any honor to those who are not gods. He therefore goes on to say, "You will not have other gods besides me."[22] For the tendency to apostasy and aberration, and the inclination to what is unlawful, is a clear sign of a completely shrunken soul, and makes one appear ridiculous and quite worthless.

3. Now even I realize that we are not at present saying much that suits the needs of those whose conduct has been perfected through their practice of the highest degree of compassion, who are already used to being filled with solid food;[23] "for these things are the elements and first principles of God's words,"[24] as Paul says. But I will not speak for long of that to which they are used, and I will crave indulgence for the present, having recourse to what our Savior says, "It is not the healthy who need a physician, but the sick."[25] For those whose mind is at bottom healthy, even if they do not have the assistance of [physicians], will recover all the same; but those whose heart is weak may need a great deal of help, for otherwise they may not fend off the attack of their illness. Let me show what I mean by examples. Those plants which are well rooted, and assured of being firmly set by the stoutness of their trunks, shoot up tall and strong, paying no heed at all, since they are firmly fixed, to the bluster of the winds, even when these mount an attack from round about

21. Dt 6.5; Mt 22.37.    22. Ex 20.3.
23. Cf. Heb 5.14.    24. Heb 5.12.
25. Lk 5.31.

with whistling blasts of unendurable force. Those trees which are not quite mature, however, and which are still rather delicate and newly planted and have only recently overtopped the ground which bore them, may need quite a few props. For they are as weak as they are young, and so completely unsteady, that any blast of wind is enough to topple them out of their holes. Now youths on the edge of adulthood are the same way, I think. Some there are who, having already attained an understanding that is secure and really God-loving, and being rooted in faith in God, remain resolutely unshaken, even when pressed by Satan's temptations. Others, though, who are still more delicate of heart, may easily slip, I think, and yield to the destroyer's will in everything, unless they receive the word of correction with great frequency. If such folk were not among us, I would have had to proceed immediately in my discourse to those parts of doctrine which are well rehearsed, and which entail a deeper exposition. But since there are many, one may see, who for some reason like to be tossed about hither and yon, and to waver in their minds between the One who is God by nature and those who are not, whatever they may be called, why should we thoughtlessly abandon the side that is sick and go right to the one that is not? It is time, therefore, it seems, to speak to these folk in the words of the divinely inspired Paul: "Take care, brethren, lest there be in any of you an evil, unbelieving heart, leading you to fall away from the living God."[26] If it is necessary for us to speak clearly as well, without dressing up our words in any way, then if you approach the faith,[27] come to it honestly, that is to say, unconditionally, and not with hesitant mind or divided heart. Rather, if it behooves us to speak yet more truly, let your heart be wholly inclined toward those things by means of which grace ransoms those who are truly converted. "For no one can serve two masters; either he will hate the one and love the other, or he will be devoted to the one and despise the other."[28]

Let us consider our subject as follows, using what relates to

26. Heb 3.12.

27. This is possibly a reference to unconverted pagans considering coming into the Church. See SC 392, 142, n.1.

28. Mt 6.24.

ourselves. Someone has happened to become a barbarian, captured by barbarians when young. Reared among them, he has borrowed their ways and been molded, as it were, to savage customs and laws. Then, as he has matured in age and understanding with the passage of time, he has realized that he has been deprived of his native place, and thenceforth has grieved, and missed his homeland, so dear to him, and yearned to be made gentle by its native laws. Then, having restored his way of thinking, and with it his way of life, to the mildness which was his originally, he has approached the emperor, and having explained the reasons for his situation—that he was deeply in love with his homeland and longed for civilized laws—he has been granted honor and gifts. Now then, I shall ask my listeners in regard to him: do you not think that if such a one continued to live as a barbarian, sharing their mentality, he might fairly be chastised by every sort of evil, and that there would be no kind of punishment that suited him? While if he remained true to what he had spoken when prompted by the correctness of his thoughts, and preserved his goodwill without dispute by the honor [shown him], he would be worthy of still greater things?

But I think what has been said is clear. Surely, then, we should proceed to the truth itself from what we have just presented in the form of an image. Let us then return to the beginning of our race and examine the case of him who was the first created,[29] arranging our considerations according to the same analogy as before.

4. For he had an abundance of everything good, including the grant of that which is our deepest desire, possession of which he would have enjoyed unceasingly, had he not transgressed the divine commandment when deceived. But even if this happened to him, he will be in a sorry plight if he has suffered the loss of his worship and reverence of the One who is the one God by nature.[30]

29. That is, Adam.

30. The construction here is confusing, but Cyril means that Adam's fall would have been far worse if he had lost God along with his life. The French translation suggests that Adam may have fallen into idolatry (SC 392, 144, n. 1), which seems to be a misreading.

The first pair of sons to be born to him, accordingly, offered him the first-fruits of what they found. For nature knew how to honor God, and needed no law for that. Abel from the herd and Cain from the produce of the earth[31] made their thank-offerings. For the one kept flocks, while the other thought husbandry good, and did that work.[32] Since our race, however, kept deteriorating little by little, and was suffering from the illness of a vice far worse than that preceding, the law which had been sown in nature perished utterly and was trampled, even as it kept urging recognition of the one and only God. But the error of polytheism was devised before all other evils: a frightful doctrine, my brothers, and the one which holds the fullest measure of the devil's bitterness. For he thought he ought not only expel us from friendship with God by means of the sin which was introduced, but render us as well reviled and repulsive when we were suffering the sickness of deprivation of true knowledge. For it was thus, and not otherwise, that he could bring our affairs to complete ruin. But he feared, as one might understand, lest we approach the One who is by nature God, and strive to know the Artificer of all, and so shake off the yoke of his oppression, and choose to run back to the original beauty of our own nature. It was for this reason that he darkened the eye of our understanding,[33] and, having bound man by false and alien forms of worship, made him who is free to be like a prisoner, reduced to the condition of a captive. But "a deceitful man shall catch no game,"[34] as it is written. For his plan did not have the result he had intended. For the wretch was mad enough to fight with God, and he seems to me to have suffered what happens to sailors on the sea who strive unskillfully against headwinds, and perish with their ship. For the only-begotten Word of God shone upon us, removed us from his bonds, and rendered us free instead of captive.[35]

5. These are the observations which it seemed necessary to us to make for the moment. For I thought it would be of benefit to show how ancient the knowledge of the one true God is, and

31. Cf. Gn 4.3–4.
32. Cf. Gn 4.2.
33. Cf. Eph 4.18.
34. Prv 12.27.
35. Cf. Is 61.1; Rom 8.2.

how it is shown to be inherent in nature, and how alien and per-
verse a device the sickness of polytheism is.[36] But even if, when
conquered by his tyranny and unable to bear his unbearable oppression, we once erred, and worshiped the creature instead of
the Creator, bestowing the name of divinity upon the sky, the
sun, the moon, the stars, the earth, and the water, listing gods
beyond number, let us from now on reject the shame attached to
them, and having been ransomed by Christ from this horrid deceit, let us remain faithful and true worshipers of the Redeemer;
let us not be found to have faith only on our tongue, but disbelief in our mind; let no one behave as a Christian outwardly,
while concealing idolatry within. For if one is still completely
barbarian in attitude, why does one pretend to side with the
king? The law of freedom knows that the best defender of the
ruler is not the traitor, dear sir! Nor is it the one who sides with
the enemy, but the one who shares valiantly in the contest, and
for whom the victory of the foe would be an abomination; and it
would say that the one who is duplicitous in manners and behavior is abhorrent and quite repulsive: beyond all evil. And in fact
even the pagan poets have said as much, and one may acknowledge that they have spoken quite rightly; they call such characters fickle cheats and buffoons, and other names, and are, I
think, quite right in so doing. I have even learned that one of
them says clearly that he would put on a level with the gates of
hell those whose tongues spit out things other than what they
have heaped up in their minds.[37] For fraud and deceit are really
most unholy, easily convicted on their own terms, a conviction
indicating a wickedness beyond all others. For why do you think
you need to be silent? Why do you hide in darkness the things
that you value in your mind? Will you not admit that the only
reason is that you are anxious to conceal the shame attached to
them? For one conceals, my friend, the things for which one
might be justly chastised, the things which do not enjoy the
brightness bestowed by frankness in speech; one certainly does
not hide what ought to be admired. If, then, you think that your

36. Cyril's predecessor and uncle, Theophilus, was militantly anti-pagan.
Cyril inherited some of these tendencies.

37. *Iliad* 9.312–14.

ideas are worthy of admiration, why are you not known to everyone for what you really are? But if you blush at what you have hidden inside and cover it over with language unlike it, as with a curtain before what is unseen, seeking thereby a reputation higher than that of those who are considered upright, then why not say farewell to all this, and thus be found completely bright, speaking in a way that is akin to what is within you and assured that your speech is cognate to your thought? For such is the simple man, filled with praises reaching high. And I think that with this I have defeated those inclined to be argumentative, those who think they must take issue with what we have said about this.

For when it is everywhere agreed that something is good, who will doubt that it is so, and not be accused of folly? But since I consider it right and good to confirm these things from the divinely inspired Scriptures, let me quote the divine utterances which show clearly that the hypocrite is completely displeasing, or rather abhorrent to God, and liable to be accused of being double-minded. Some of the Israelites of bygone times suffered from this illness; they made a show of honoring the commandments of the Law with extraordinary care, forever quoting the Legislator; but extended reflection persuaded them that their thoughts should be otherwise, and each of them hastened to secure by his own decision that which seemed to him alone to be indisputable. What, then, has God said about them through the prophet? "This people draws nigh to me; they honor me with their lips, but their heart is far from me. For in vain they worship me."[38] For will one not admit that people worship in vain, and offer to God an honor which is entirely feigned and spurious, when their thoughts are otherwise, and they adore creatures instead of him,[39] and only speak in a Christian way while pretending reverence for God with their clever language? Who is it, then, that will agree with them? If someone, then, thinks that he will not pay the price for his deceitful language, and does not expect to undergo bitter punishment for lying to God, then let him honor duplicity, and let him believe that the one

38. Is 29.13.
39. Cf. Rom 1.25.

who urges improvement has gone mad! But if a frightful punishment hangs over those with this attitude, and penalty, judgment, and every sort of torture, and fire unquenchable await them, even in their defiance, then how can I myself not look even more foolish in putting the realm of illicit pleasure ahead of my own soul? For it is the love of pleasure, and nothing else, that is the polytheistic disease. And indeed it seems good to say what a perilous thing it is.

What I mean is that one may repel the attack of someone like us, or slightly superior, either by opposing one's own strength to the other's, even if it is a bit less than his, or by contending with unequal resources that boost one's power, or by having recourse to some other means. But tell me, is there any way that one may escape God when he is vexed? Where could one run to unnoticed? Let us even add to that person, if you like, such brilliance in life that anything surpassing it could not be seen. Let his possessions abound so greatly that even the famous and unrivaled riches of Croesus could not compete with them. Will he have any enjoyment from them? Will they remove the punisher, even against the latter's will? Far from it! Sacred Scripture tells no falsehood at all when it says, "Treasures shall not profit the lawless."[40]

Is it not, then, a dangerous thing to give offense? Let us show once again that God considers the duplicitous person unholy, and that he treats the fickle with insolence, as being themselves pretentious and insolent. For he says somewhere to Jeremiah, in charging the Israelites with madness, "Have you seen what things the house of Israel has done to me? They have gone on every high mountain, and under every shady tree, and have committed fornication there."[41] He put "have committed fornication" instead of "have consecrated themselves to the demons." For this is how sacred Scripture is accustomed to speak. For they would go up to the wooded summits of the mountains, and under the lofty trees thickly covering them would erect sacred precincts and altars, sometimes with only a small stone, and the wicked folk would offer libations and sacrifices and who knows what

40. Prv 10.2.
41. Jer 3.6.

other shameful things to the woodland demons and perhaps to the country nymphs, and even to the one they call Baal. And what was the result? Their audacity grieved God. For, having been educated by the law given by him for attainment to the truth, they went over to the devil, catering rather to their own pleasures, and banishing from their hearts the commandment that chastened. What, then, does the Master of all say about them to the prophet Jeremiah? "Cut off your hair, and throw it away, and take up a lamentation on your lips; for the Lord has reprobated and rejected the generation that has done these things."[42] In order, that is, to show clearly the punishment that those who have transgressed in these matters will undergo, he orders the prophet to be shorn. For in the same way that hair, when cut by the hand of the shearer, is alienated from the body that grew it, so also those who have lapsed when deceived by the demons and are cut off from friendship with God because of the divine anger will depart into nothingness, no longer accorded any concern from above.

Indeed, if one cares to examine how great the divine anger is in their regard, one may consider the sequel. For even though he usually treats the prayer of the saints with the highest regard, in the case of these people alone he did not accept it. For thus he speaks: "And you, do not pray for this people, and do not ask that mercy may be shown them, in supplication and prayer, for I will not listen."[43] But since this so greatly grieved the Spirit-bearing man, and the situation seemed so bitter to the prophet—having his prayer rejected and unable to accomplish anything—God defends himself in a certain manner, and teaches him in forceful terms that not even if he were approached by persons still greater and more ancient would he assent: "Though Moses and Samuel stood before my face, my soul could not be toward them."[44] But perhaps one of those who have dared to engage in this behavior will say in reply: What of it, my dear sir? When certain people were caught committing this same deed without concealing it, and being openly provocative, it was for that reason that they caused grief.

42. Jer 7.29.  43. Jer 11.14.
44. Jer 15.1.

But tell me: is there any sensible person who would not rightly and justly rank impiety done in secret among the acts of unholiness, and would say that there was nothing about this dreadful deed to grieve the God who sees what is hidden? Away with this ill counsel, my friend! Even if one may perchance escape human eyes, no one who exists will escape God. "For in his eyes everything is open and laid bare,"[45] as Paul says. It is useless, therefore, to speak of "done in secret" or "without concealing it" in his case. But if you would care to learn the nature and extent of the wrath hanging over those who choose to act impiously in secret, I will cite one of the passages of sacred Scripture. Give me your attention once again! Some of those of olden times fell into error, then, even though they recognized the Lord of all, and had been piloted toward a grasp of the truth through numerous writings. They in fact fashioned a swarm of idols of many forms, and stashed them away in dark and lightless places. Little by little, though, the illness, as it worsened, fed upon even those entrusted with the priestly offices; and the situation was quite grievous, and intolerable to God. As he was considering punishing those who were so offensive to him by their worship of other gods, he relates to the prophet their audacious acts, or rather he shows them clearly: "Hear, therefore, says Ezekiel. And it came to pass in the sixth year, in the fifth month, on the fifth day of the month, I was sitting in the house, and the elders of Judah were sitting before me, and the hand of the Lord Adonai came upon me. And I looked, and behold, the likeness of a man: from his loins and downwards there was fire, and from his loins upwards there was as the appearance of electrum.[46] And he stretched forth the likeness of a hand, and took me by the crown of my head; and the Spirit lifted me up between the earth and the sky, and brought me to Jerusalem in a vision of God."[47] And after some other things he goes on at once, "And he brought me to the porch of the court, and I looked, and behold, a hole in

45. Heb 4.13.

46. According Lampe, *Patristic Greek Lexicon, electrum* can mean "amber" and was a symbol of spiritual perfection. It is also a compound of gold and silver and was seen by some as a symbol of the humanity of Christ, compounded of body and soul.

47. Ezek 8.1–3.

the wall, and he said to me, Son of man, dig in the wall. And I dug in the wall, and behold a door. And he said to me, Go in, and behold the evil iniquities which they practice here today. And I went in and looked, and behold, every sort of likeness of reptile and beast, vain abominations, and I saw all the idols of the house of Israel portrayed upon it round about; and seventy men of the elders of the house of Israel, and Jechoniah the son of Shaphan stood in their presence in the midst of them, and each one held his censer in his hand; and the smoke of the incense went up."[48]

Do you hear how they thought they could escape notice when they deprived God of the honor befitting him and offered it to the demons instead, but God revealed everything to the prophet? For after he had shown him their insolence, he continues, "Son of man, have you seen what the elders of the house of Israel do here, each of them in his secret chamber? Because they said, The Lord has forsaken the land, the Lord does not notice."[49] For none of those who do not refuse to insult him by devoting themselves to the demons acknowledges that he watches over our affairs. "For the fool has said in his heart: There is no God."[50] Or again, as the Psalmist says elsewhere, "They said, The Lord will not see, nor shall the God of Jacob understand."[51] But then he immediately ridicules them with the words: "Understand now, you fools among the people, and you senseless ones, be wise at last! He that planted the ear, does he not hear? And he that formed eyes, does he not perceive?"[52] For it would be most ridiculous, and I would say of an extreme absurdity, if God could not think or see or hear, when it was he who implanted just that knowledge given through the senses in us ourselves, or rather in all others.

Since, then, God made clear to the prophet the insolent acts of those who offended, and the deeds done in the secret chamber, he also shows immediately the inescapable punishment to follow upon them. For he says further, "And he cried in my ear with a loud voice, saying, The punishment of the city has drawn

48. Ezek 8.7–11.                    49. Ezek 8.12.
50. Ps 14.1.                         51. Ps 94.7.
52. Ps 94.8–9.

nigh; and each had the instruments of destruction in his hand. And behold, six men came from the way of the gate that looks toward the north, and each one's axe was in his hand, and there was one man in the midst of them clothed with a robe down to his feet, and a sapphire sash was around his waist. And he said in my hearing, Go after him into the city, and strike: and let your gaze spare no one, and have no mercy. Slay without exception old man and youth, and virgin, and infants, and women; but do not go near any on whom the sign is."[53] Do you hear how violent and implacable is the punishment he assigns to those who decide to practice a secret impiety? For God observes and investigates the heart of each person;[54] and he rids himself completely of those who are offensive and those who are liable to charges of duplicity. But he seals with supernal grace those who are devoted to him wholeheartedly, and who know only him as God. But enough of this for now. Let us next speak of the right way to dedicate ourselves to God.

6. I say, then, that there should be held fast within our souls, before all else, a pure faith, one that is true and which lacks nothing in its conception of the One who alone is God by nature. Paul in his supreme wisdom leads one there with the superb words, "One Lord, one faith, one baptism, one God and Father of all, who is above all and through all and in all."[55] For the One who rules as sovereign over all things, and governs them, giving life continually to everything and maintaining them in existence,[56] is God the Father, through the Son, in the Spirit, not as though by means of some instrument taken up by chance to serve his purpose; for he has God the Word, begotten from him, sitting by him and sharing his throne, and his own Spirit reigning with him. But since the Son is the Father's power and wisdom,[57] effecting everything in the Spirit, it is as though through his own power and wisdom that God the Father maintains everything in existence and rules over the universe. When, therefore, there is already settled in us the blameless and irreproachable faith that has been laid

53. Ezek 9.1–2, 5–6.          54. Cf. Wis 1.6; Jer 17.10.
55. Eph 4.5–6.               56. Cf. 1 Tm 6.13.
57. 1 Cor 1.24.

down in our hearts as a foundation, it is then, then indeed, and most opportunely, that we shall do the things through which we will be illustrious, and that means virtuous acts of every sort, and achievements springing from an attitude of love of God.

For just as "faith without works is dead,"[58] so also the works, when faith is not already present in us, have no way of benefiting our souls. "For no one is crowned who does not compete according to the rules,"[59] as it is written. For a man who is not well versed in the skills of the wrestling ring, even if he believes that he is superior in strength to the others, will find no way to where he may pride himself on the honors of the crowns if he does not first enter upon the contests for the purpose of acquiring renown, and have the stadium president as spectator to his own achievements. Let us contend, then, as if in God's sight, honoring his divine law, and steering our own life in the direction of what pleases him by being thoroughly submissive, and let us show an ardent and invincible desire for all that is best, presenting ourselves as a fragrant odor to God,[60] the contest judge of the saints. And let us keep impure pleasure as far as possible from our soul, and as for the desires for what is utterly shameful, let us reject them as an indelible stain and consider them a defilement that cannot be washed away. Let us reflect in addition on what God has said: "You will be holy because I am holy."[61] For thus it is that we will be presented to God as having been brought from death to life;[62] thus it is that the One who is pure will welcome us when we are pure; thus it is that, when we come to share in the mystical blessing, we each will fill our own soul with all that is good.

For thus says God, the Master of all, through Moses: "This is the law of the Passover: no stranger who is a sojourner shall eat of it, and a hireling shall not eat of it, and every slave of someone and servant bought with money—him you shall circumcise, and then he shall eat of it."[63] Do you hear how and in what man-

---

58. Jas 2.26.
59. 2 Tm 2.5.
60. Ex 30.7; cf. Ezek 20.41; Eph 5.2; Phil 4.18.
61. Lv 11.44.                              62. Cf. Rom 6.13.
63. Ex 12.43–45.

ner we will be with the Lord in purity and blamelessness? For he shuts out the stranger, and sends away the sojourner and hireling as unholy. The "stranger" you may regard as the one who is still completely alien to belief in Christ, while the "sojourner" is the one whose belief is not firm, but who, as it were, returns home and goes back to his own city or country, which is unbelief. "Transient" is what we usually call such folk, and that is why they have been allotted a position next to the strangers. For those who have denied the faith are near to those who have never believed at all. But let me correct myself: their case is far worse, as the disciple of Christ testifies as follows: "For it would have been better for them not to know the way of truth than, after knowing it, to go back from the holy commandment delivered to them."[64] Again, he speaks of them as "hirelings," concerning which we have already spoken to you fully and at length. For they say that there are some who go to share in the divine mysteries, not because their disposition toward God urges them to do so, nor because they are prevailed upon by respect for the faith; it is rather because they are cultivating the good will of those who see them, and are anxious to have their own affairs prosper. For as a kind of payment of the love for God in which they trade, they seize the aid supplied by those who love with a pure intention, that they may gain something worldly. The hireling is therefore a hypocrite and a wretch, and is among those rejected with good reason.

Now as for the slaves and the servants bought with money, he does not dismiss them as completely unholy, but orders them first to be circumcised, and then bids them approach. What does this mean? Christ redeemed us when we were slaves of the wicked demons, or of our own passions, and made us servants bought with money, giving in ransom for the life of all his own blood,[65] and the flesh which he bore for us. We must then be circumcised in advance, as it were, and, having cut off the shame of that ancient slavery, rise swiftly to a free and God-loving state, and thus cleave to Christ,[66] who purchased us, for we owe him

64. 2 Pt 2.21.
65. Cf. Eph 1.7; 1 Tm 2.6; 1 Pt 1.19.
66. Cf. Rom 12.9; 1 Cor 6.17.

our very life. Paul testifies to this in the words: "For one has died for all, that those who live might live no longer for themselves but for him who for their sake died and was raised."[67]

For let us reflect that even though he is God the Word, and has all of creation, the sensible and the intelligible,[68] under his feet, and is in every way equal[69] to the One who begot him, "dwelling in unapproachable light"[70] with him and surpassing the eminence of all renown and glory on high, in his burning love for us "he has humbled himself for us, taking the form of a slave, born in our likeness."[71] This was so that he might rescue everyone from death and corruption, "nailing to his own cross the bond which stood against us, and triumphing in it,"[72] as is written, "over principalities and powers, and the world rulers of this present darkness,"[73] so as to shut the mouth[74] of all lawlessness and render us pure through faith, and thus bring us to the honor of adoption.[75] For he underwent the cross,[76] and death in the flesh, with the iniquitous Jews raging against him. But "it was not possible for him to be held by death,"[77] as is written. For being by nature life,[78] he rose on the third day, having pillaged Hades, thrown open to those below the gates forever locked,[79] and said "to those in bonds, Come forth! and to those in darkness, Show yourselves!"[80] as the prophet says. Having preached the message of faith, then, even to the spirits in prison,[81] he rose on the third day, and having appeared to his disciples and ordered them to baptize "all the nations in the name of the Father and of the Son and of the Holy Spirit,"[82] he ascended again to the heavens,[83] bringing us into them through himself; from there we expect that he will come again as Judge in the Father's glory with the holy angels.

Since, then, we are to give an account of our own life, "let us

67. 2 Cor 5.14–15.
68. Cf. Ps 9.7; 1 Cor 15.27.
69. Phil 2.6.
70. 1 Tm 6.16.
71. Phil 2.7.
72. Col 2.14–15.
73. Eph 6.12.
74. Cf. Rom 3.19.
75. Gal 4.5.
76. Cf. Heb 12.2.
77. Acts 2.24.
78. Cf. Jn 11.25; 14.6.
79. Cf. Rv 1.18.
80. Is 49.9.
81. 1 Pt 3.19.
82. Mt 28.19.
83. Cf. Jn 20.17.

cleanse ourselves from every defilement of body and spirit, and make holiness perfect in the fear of God."[84] For then it is that we will fast in purity, beginning holy Lent on the twenty-seventh of the month of Mechir, and the week of the salvific Paschal feast on the second of Pharmuthi. We end the fast on the seventh of Pharmuthi, the eve of Saturday, as the gospel message says. We celebrate the feast on the following day, the eve of Sunday, the eighth of that month,[85] adding then the seven weeks of holy Eastertide. Thus shall we inherit the kingdom of heaven,[86] in Christ Jesus our Lord, with whom and through whom be glory to the Father without beginning, together with the coeternal Spirit, for endless ages. Amen.

84. 2 Cor 7.1.                          85. April 3, 421.
86. Cf. Mt 25.34.

# FESTAL LETTER TEN

## A.D. 422

EHOLD, ONCE again we take it to be our duty to obey the voices of the saints, and in our eagerness to follow as it were in the footsteps of the custom they practiced, to extend a hand of mutual affection to those who are as brothers and at the same time all but children, addressing them in the following sacred words: "Grace and peace to you from God the Father and the Lord Jesus Christ."[1] He it is who once again has proclaimed to us this time of the holy feast, so deeply longed for and ardently desired, which the great and illustrious chorus of the holy prophets itself announced previously, instructed as it was in the divine mysteries through the illumination of the Holy Spirit, and taught in advance about what was to happen to us through Christ. Thus the divinely inspired David struck up a divine melody for us as though from a spiritual lyre; the song goes as follows: "Let the heavens be glad, and the earth exult; let the plains rejoice, and all who are in them, before the face of the Lord, for he comes, he comes to judge the earth, to judge the world in justice, and the peoples in his truth."[2]

But he of whom it was foretold of old that he would come and would render a just and faultless decision in our regard has made gladness known to us no longer in its expectation but in its reality. For he has sojourned [among us] in the last days of this age, as is evidenced by the sacred and divine Scriptures: "He has judged the world in justice,"[3] as the Psalmist says. How has he judged it? By condemning those in error or punishing those who have long disregarded the divine laws. But then, how is it

---

1. Rom 1.7.  2. Ps 96.11–13.
3. Cf. Ps 96.13.

that he can still be speaking truthfully when he cries out concerning himself, "For God did not send the Son into the world that he might judge the world, but that the world might be saved through him."[4] And indeed, anyone of good sense would, I think, agree that to pass a severe judgment on those who have sinned, and to condemn them to punishment, is not the act of someone who is a savior, but of one who wants to cause affliction, someone who without any mercy demands an account of sins already committed. How is it, then, that he has not come to judge the world but to save the world,[5] if the sentence he has passed on it is so severe? But I do not suppose that anyone would be so foolish as to think that the Truth could lie about anything. How, then, has he judged the earth? For that is what the Psalmist has cried out to us.

A fearsome tyrant had risen up against us, and Satan, driven by greed,[6] had seized power, he who had been thrust from the throng of the holy angels like lightning, and been shown to be quite deprived of the glory which was in him, and of the preeminence of his honors, for he had dared to say, "I will be like the Most High."[7] But since he could not go against the decrees from on high, and could not otherwise grieve the holy chastiser, he undertook to wage war on us. He immediately took man out of the straight way, turning him away toward what he himself wanted, and that alone, and, having removed him from the true knowledge of God, made of him who was fashioned in the image of God his own worshiper and adorer. This he did in the grip of an unjust jealousy of us, crowning himself with a glory equal to God's, for he was under the control of his old passion: more deeply infected by that for which he was being punished, he now aimed openly at achieving universal rule. And as though he had taken over the whole earth, and as though God were completely unconcerned about his own creatures and no longer deigned to take any account of our life, the barbarian became scornful, despising human weakness as he spoke: "I will seize in my hand all the earth like a nest, and I will take it like eggs that have been abandoned; and there is none that shall escape me, or contest

4. Jn 3.17.
6. Cf. Is 14.12–13.

5. Cf. Jn 12.47.
7. Is 14.14.

me."[8] And while he was saying this, he heard God, the universal sovereign, reply, "As a garment defiled with blood shall not be pure, so neither will you be pure; because you have destroyed my land, and have slain my people. You shall not endure forever."[9]

God therefore, having threatened to bring his tyranny to an end, when he became man for us, since the time had now arrived in which the murderous charlatan had to be delivered over to severe punishment, "he judged the world in justice."[10] For he passed judgment on him and on us; and finding him to be unjust and grasping, "cast him into hell and committed him to pits of nether gloom" to be kept for punishment "until the judgment" of the great day, as is written.[11] But those throughout the whole earth he released from the bonds of sin,[12] having justified them by faith[13] and restored them once again to their original holiness. For if you pay attention to the words of the Psalmist, you will observe clearly how we are seen to be asking, for so long a time, that he be called to account for his transgressions against us: you will notice how he has introduced the person representing humanity in general as falling before God while saying, "Awake and attend to my judgment, even to my cause, O Lord my God."[14]

But that the Savior has once again condemned the devil's tyranny,[15] having won us for himself[16] once he had set us free,[17] must be clear to everyone, since he cries aloud in the Gospels: "Now is the judgment of this world; now will the ruler of this world be cast out, and I, when I am lifted up from the earth, will draw everyone to myself."[18] He who has just said that the reason he came to us, or was sent to us by God the Father, is not that he might judge the world, now has said that it is the judgment of the world.

It is evident, then, and quite beyond doubt, that he has justified us, but has condemned the murderous beast to perdition.

---

8. Is 10.14.
10. Ps 96.13.
12. Cf. Rom 6.18–22.
14. Ps 35.23.
16. Ti 2.14.
18. Jn 12.31–32.

9. Cf. Is 14.20–21.
11. 2 Pt 2.4.
13. Gal 2.16; 3.24.
15. Cf. Heb 2.14.
17. Cf. Gal 5.1.

For he has been cast out, and that means into complete worthlessness, ejected from his dominion over those who have been unjust. For Immanuel, crucified for everyone and because of everyone, redeemed the life of everyone by his own blood, and through himself joined to God the Father the race that had shied away from its original intimacy with him. For "he is the mediator between God and man,"[19] as is written, mixing together in an ineffable combination that which is held in thought, being at once man and God.[20] It is for this reason that he is by nature attached to the substance of the One who begot him, and to ours as man. For it was not otherwise possible for that which by nature perishes ever to be saved, and for that which has been shaken to rise to a firm desire for virtue, unless the reflection of the substance of God the Father,[21] that is, the Son, who is above all corruption and change, or rather whose nature is quite inaccessible to such things, had come down to enter into communion with it.

All of these things, then, form the themes of our feast, and "the heavens rejoice, and the plains exult,"[22] as the Psalmist says. For the heavenly ranks rejoice with the things on earth. Indeed, we will find the holy angels saying, when Christ was born, "Glory to God in the highest, and peace on earth, good will to men."[23] For Christ is "everyone's peace,"[24] as Scripture says, having willingly undergone being emptied for us. Having been born because of us in our situation, he did not disdain the limits of our nature, nor was he ashamed of the poverty of the form of a slave.[25] This was so that we too, having come through faith in him and through holy baptism to share in the Spirit,[26] and having been transformed into his manner of conduct and life, might flash forth the image of the One who made us. For that the true

19. 1 Tm 2.5.

20. While Cyril will later abandon this terminology to describe the union of the two natures in Christ, he will continue to maintain that the distinction between the natures is grasped intellectually; it is not discernible in the one Christ after the union. Cf. SC 392, 192 n., and Cyril's *Second Letter to Succensus* 92.14–16, ed. L. Wickham.

21. Cf. Heb 1.3.                    22. Ps 96.11.

23. Lk 2.14.                         24. Eph 2.14.

25. Phil 2.7.                        26. Cf. Heb 6.4.

and genuine faith molds us in a way upon God, and the imprint of the divine nature is marked on our souls by our manner of life in Christ, you will learn from what Paul says to those who had returned to the commandment of the Law after the divine and heavenly baptism: "My little children, with whom I am again in travail until Christ be formed in you!"[27] For Christ is formed in you in no other way than through an irreproachable faith and an evangelical way of life. For it is "not under the old written code but in the new life of the Spirit"[28] that those who long to walk toward God must make their way.

That is something which, I think, may be realized quite well in our case as well, when in our desire for every possible good we, as it were, brace up our own mind, and thus welcome this most holy fast as that which will be for us the mother of all purity; in our moderation we are satisfied with a light diet, and we keep our table free from fancily dressed dishes, in order that we may refine the eye of our understanding.

In addition, however, we know quite well that the effort made by the flesh does not suffice for the sanctification of our souls, nor is the fact of abstinence from food enough in certain cases to prove the presence of virtue, if purity in deeds and dignity of life do not go along with them in some way, and accompany the prestige of fasting. For what is necessary, I think, or I should say most urgently required, is complete and utter devotion to the worship of Christ. And this means not turning aside stupidly in another direction and leaving the straight way, and, having departed from the well-trodden road on which one may go toward God, taking the steep one and ending up heading foolishly in the direction that the devil wants. For "no one," the Savior says, "can serve two masters; for either he will hate the one and love the other, or he will be devoted to the one and despise the other."[29]

The one, therefore, who is not the master, Satan that is, is to be rejected, so that we may love him who is really and truly Lord. But what the manner of that love is to be for us, the Lord illuminates by his own words when he says, "Those who love me keep

27. Gal 4.19.                    28. Rom 7.6.
29. Mt 6.24.

my commandments."[30] Those who genuinely keep the Savior's commandment have an abiding piety, and, refusing to bear the devil's domination, they shake off the yoke of sin and aim at a disposition which is free, mastering all improper and vicious pleasures, and mortifying the desires of the flesh by the efforts of asceticism. You may hear Paul himself crying aloud this very thing: "For those who belong to Christ Jesus have crucified the flesh with its passions and desires."[31] I will therefore once again quote from Paul: "If we live by the Spirit, let us also walk by the Spirit,"[32] "putting to death what is earthly, that is, fornication, impurity, passion, evil desire, and covetousness,"[33] presenting ourselves rather as "an odor of sweetness,"[34] as is written, and offering our very life like a kind of spiritual sacrifice[35] to the God who loves virtue. For the fruit of good labors will be completely glorious. For let none of those among us suppose that they will achieve what is good without effort, or triumph over sin without arduous work. For Satan is a formidable opponent, capable of impeding with the obstacles of deceit the mind of those who are set on living rightly and irreproachably, and enervating those who are already aiming at the achievement of virtue.

We will take as the clear and indisputable proof of what we have said the things that have been done and written about in Exodus (this is a book of Moses). For God establishes the things that are visible as something like images and completely manifest figures of what is invisible, and one will not go wrong in thinking that whatever one notices has happened to those of old is evidence of what is concealed and intelligible. Indeed, the divinely inspired Paul agrees with what we say about this, crying out concerning those of old: "These things happened to them as a figure, but they were written down for our instruction."[36] It is, then, possible to see finely drawn in a history of old, as on a tablet, the domination of the devil, which he so easily acquired over us in his supreme boldness, and the fierceness with which he encounters those who are making their way toward freedom

---

30. Cf. Jn 14.15.
32. Gal 5.25.
34. Eph 5.2; Ezek 20.41.
36. 1 Cor 10.11.

31. Gal 5.24.
33. Col 3.5–6.
35. Cf. 1 Pt 2.5.

of disposition and intention, not allowing them to leave the realm of sin, but forcing them to dwell there, and ordering them not to pay full reverence to God. And who, then, would choose to adopt the right frame of mind? It is time, then, it seems, to tell what the history says.

2. It happened[37] upon a time that Israel was robbed of the honor and glory of its ancient freedom. This occurred when the most cruel tyrant of the Egyptians placed upon them the hard yoke of slavery, and maltreated the Jews with ceaseless work making bricks from clay.[38] But when God took pity on them, seeing them now crushed and exhausted by the inhumanity of the ruler, and decided to restore them to their ancient and original freedom, he ordered the all-wise Moses to go to the Egyptian tyrant in person and say, "Thus says the Lord, the God of the Hebrews: send my people away, that they may serve me in the desert."[39] Why did he not order rather that he be served in Egypt? Why did he call them into desert places? Does it not seem reasonable to consider that he thought that those who were to serve God, the Ruler of all, must first take off the yoke of enslavement to others, must begin by putting off, so to speak, their obedience to the devil's commandments as though they were of necessity, and stop making bricks from clay? That means once again to refrain from and henceforth avoid the impurity of earthly works, in order to depart from the entire region of the usurper, as it were, and thus at last to approach in purity the acts of service offered to God, having arrived at a frame of mind that is, like a desert, free and unencumbered.

Now the divinely inspired Moses, truly great as he was, gave these orders, and called Israel to a desert of utmost purity. Pharaoh did indeed take up weapons recklessly, and defied the divine glory, saying, "I do not know the Lord, and I will not let Israel go."[40] But when he had been overcome by the plagues from on high, he then consented unwillingly, since his whole land was

---

37. Cyril's interpretation of Exodus against the background of ascetical discipline is similar to the approach taken by Gregory of Nyssa in the *Life of Moses*.

38. Cf. Ex 1.14.                    39. Ex 5.1.

40. Ex 5.2.

in danger. Then he thought up various ways of hindering them, and, without releasing them from the yoke of slavery at all, he tried to prevent them in another way, saying, "Go and sacrifice to the Lord your God in my land."[41] You see how even when God's law draws us somehow from sin, Satan rises up to counter this. It is true that when Christ our Savior strives on behalf of the life of all, he[42] reins in his greed reluctantly, finding no way to tyrannize over those he wants. But he does not therefore release us from his own land completely, but orders us to be divided, as it were, in two ways: toward what he wants and toward what the Master of all wants.

But it is impossible for the manner of our service to be blameless, unless we have fled from the entire territory of the devil, as it were, and thus are found to be quite free from subjection to his servitude. That this is true I will show you from the words of the all-wise Moses. What does he say to Pharaoh when the latter tells him, "Go and sacrifice to the Lord your God in my land"?[43] "That cannot be."[44] "For no one can serve two masters,"[45] as I have just said. And among the most unseemly things to see are those whose acts are both immoral and tending toward virtue, and who devote themselves with equal zeal to things which are so far separated from each other that there are times when their mind is weakened from being sick with what the devil esteems, and others when it again recovers unto what pleases God, calling down upon itself a most well-deserved outcry, as it were.

For how can it not denounce vehemently the shamefulness attaching to the other kind of acts by means of those it has decided to esteem, and which alone it should have chosen? How can it avoid being accused, when it has been convicted of being the wicked author of deeds thus condemned? We need a generous and vigorous outlook if we are to be able to succeed in making our way to God by means of every good deed, perfectly and completely. And that we will do, and quite easily, if we decide to follow the ancient figures.

You will see, then, those from Israel who have decided that

---

41. Ex 8.25.                    42. That is, Satan.
43. Cf. Ex 8.25.                44. Ex 8.26.
45. Mt 6.24.

they should shake off their most ignominious slavery and prevail over the power of those who dominated them of old, that they would have been powerless to do anything of the sort, had they not sacrificed in Egypt the lamb as a figure of Christ, and been anointed with the blood, and eaten unleavened bread with it.[46] Through the truer and mystical blessing,[47] then, we must build up our souls, if we are to refuse to be enslaved to sin any more. For one cannot otherwise escape the irresistible attacks of our earthly passions, except by participation in Christ,[48] who can disable the power of Pharaoh, that is, of Satan.

It is for this reason above all that, even though he is God by nature, appearing as the Only-Begotten from God the Father, he voluntarily "came down to be emptied, taking the form of a slave," as is written, "and being found in human form,"[49] that he might raise the lowliness of our nature to a great height, bestowing on it his own stability. For, being unchangeable by nature, and unacquainted with the experience of being pushed down toward sin, he mingled himself ineffably with that nature which is most apt to be pushed down toward every sort of wickedness—human nature, that is; he bestowed upon it in its weakness the stability of his own nature, as I just said, that our mind might from then on be seen as committed to good deeds, and the passions of the flesh chastised, put to death utterly by the power of the One dwelling in it, God the Word. Paul, at any rate, writes in his letter, "For God has done what the Law, weakened by the flesh, could not do: sending his own Son in the likeness of sinful flesh, and concerning sin, he condemned sin in the flesh, in order that the just requirement of the Law might be fulfilled in us, who walk not according to the flesh but according to the Spirit."[50] Sin has therefore been condemned, put to death first in Christ in order to be put to death in us as well, when we settle him in our own souls through faith and participation in the Spirit, who conforms us to Christ through his quality of sanctifier, to be sure.

For his Spirit is like a kind of form of Christ our Savior, im-

46. Cf. Ex 12.
47. I.e., the Eucharist. Cf. *Letters* 8.5 and 9.6.
48. Cf. Heb 3.14.    49. Phil 2.7.
50. Rom 8.3–4; cf. Rom 7.7.

pressing through himself our divine likeness in a manner. It is for this very reason that [the Spirit] is named as he [Christ] is in the divinely inspired Scriptures, being not other than he when it comes to identity of substance and to divine activity. Indeed, when our Savior himself says, "I am the truth,"[51] John writes, "The Spirit is the truth,"[52] and Paul, nourished as he was on the sacred Scriptures, also writes, "The Lord is the Spirit. And where the Spirit of the Lord is, there is freedom."[53] You hear how elegantly the teacher of mysteries has preserved for the Son and the Holy Spirit both their identity in substance and their being regarded as distinct in subsistence;[54] I mean that [reality] that each of the two is said to be, and is in truth. For the Spirit would be regarded as Spirit, understandably, and not as Son, or rather as the Spirit of the Son, fashioning and conforming[55] to him that in which he comes to be by participation, in order that when God the Father sees conspicuous in us the features of his own offspring, he may thenceforth love us as his children, and may adorn us with transcendent honors.

The following prophecy given of old through the all-wise Moses may again be the clearest proof of this. What does he say to him? "Sanctify to me every firstborn, first-begotten opening the womb." He says "sanctify" instead of "inscribe and offer" as sacred and owed to God. For I doubt that anyone would say that it is possible that Moses could appear as the one who bestows the gifts of the divine Holy Spirit, and that he who is employed as a servant and minister could pride himself on what belongs to his Master's higher station, and could achieve what pertains properly to God alone. What, then, does Moses signify? And what does he say to the children of Israel? "And it shall come to pass that when the Lord your God shall bring you into the land of the Canaanites, as he swore to your fathers, and shall give it to you, you shall set apart everything that opens the womb, the males to the Lord."[56] He orders every firstborn who opens the womb to be

51. Jn 14.6.    52. Jn 15.26.
53. 2 Cor 3.17.

54. Although the contrast is clearly between *ousia* and *hypostasis*, Cyril does not use the latter term, but rather a cognate, the infinitive *hypestanai*; cf. SC 392, 211, n. 4.

55. Cf. Gal 4.19.    56. Ex 13.11–12.

sanctified. For all of those are holy in whom the image of the holy Firstborn, I mean Christ, appears radiant. The Law, having begun with the corporeal similarity as a figure of an intelligible reality and of the conformity which the spirit conceives, has shown what the eternal will of God the Father is. It is for this reason that Paul, in understanding this great mystery by means of this legislation, I think, speaks as follows: "For those whom he knew, and predestined to be conformed to the image of his Son, those he also called, and those he sanctified; and whom he sanctified he also glorified."[57] But come, let us again, in treating, as deftly as may be possible, the meaning of what we are contemplating, consider more clearly what kind of form one may reasonably bestow on Christ without departing from the bounds of what is appropriate.

3. But there can be no doubt that it is certainly the supernatural beauty which would be regarded as pertaining to the transcendent substance itself, that substance that is divine and above the mind. The imprint of this substance may appear in our souls only if we are rendered sharers in the divine nature,[58] having received the Spirit of the Father and the Son, and, as Paul said, "being changed into his likeness from one degree of glory to another, for this is from the Lord who is the Spirit."[59] The transformation takes place in us in our acts, to be sure, and in the energy we devote to the practice of virtue, and the remolding [takes place] in a sanctification which carries us toward everything that pleases God, rids us of every weakness in our understanding, and reforges it, as it were, into a henceforth secure and invincible tool of thought. For I think that it is for this reason above all that God, the giver of the Law, did not speak simply of sanctifying every firstborn, but added that it was to be the males. For what is the reason why the female gender is unholy, and is not sanctified, even if it is the firstborn?[60] Well, if no one else wants to an-

---

57. Cf. Rom 8.29.                     58. Cf. 2 Pt 1.4.
59. 2 Cor 3.18.

60. Cyril's attitude toward women is quite common in Christian antiquity. Counter-examples, like that found in Augustine's *City of God* 22.17, are more the exception than the rule.

swer, I will speak on, since the occasion and the necessity summon me to do so.

We will contemplate that which is manly and vigorous in all things as a sort of part of the form regarded as in the divine and incomprehensible nature, fixing upon it the eye of our thought. For that is how the nature of divinity is: it yields to nothing, but rather is victorious, and in a completely virile way, over that which is called into being, and shows the most enormous strength, impossible to describe, in the achievement of its own works. The one, therefore, who in all good deeds is like someone of manly spirit and vigorous, may fairly be regarded as conformed to Christ. But that cannot be said of the one with, so to speak, a female attitude, cowardly and easily subdued. For the female race is timid and powerless, declining battle and deeds of daring.

I will present you with an image of the matter taken again from Moses' writings. He says that the tyrant of the Egyptians, who in sacred Scripture is a figure of the devil,[61] armed himself against those being born to the Hebrews, fought against those still in the womb, and set himself to slay at once their infants who had scarcely seen the light. His cruel decree was drafted with a skill suiting him. For the murderer ruled that the females might be preserved alive, while the males were to be drowned in the waters and marshes.[62] What meaning, then, are we given here to contemplate? What does the passage present to the thoughts of those quick to understand?

The devil likes ways of thinking that are cowardly, unmanly, and effeminate. Thus he allows what is female to grow, since the evil one does not expect ever to be dominated by them. The male person, however, he considers quite warlike and hard to defeat. He knows that, when he is nourished on the doctrines of truth, if he comes to maturity in Christ and grows "to adult manhood,"[63] as Paul says, there will be no way to vanquish him, and so he slays him before his youth. For what may be inferred from this attack upon the male offspring from the very womb? That all that God holds dear is abhorred by the devil. But the converse will also assuredly hold true. What the devil abominates

---

61. This interpretation appears to go back to Origen; cf. SC 392, 219, n. 1.
62. Ex 1.22.                    63. Col 4.12.

is required by God. Along with other kinds of good conduct, there is nothing that carries a higher recommendation with him, as it were, than to be hated by the devil. And it is quite easy to show you from the sacred Scriptures that this is so.

Thus in what is called Numbers (one of Moses' books is named such), at the very beginning God says to Moses, the teacher of mysteries, and to Aaron: "Take the sum of the whole assembly of the sons of Israel ('sum' meaning the computation or count) according to their kin, according to their ancestral houses, according to their number by their names, according to their heads: every male from twenty years old and up, everyone who goes forth in the forces of Israel, take account of them."[64] You see how he orders what is male to be listed, and the multitude already in the prime of youth and in full vigor: "from twenty years old and up," it says. But he quite ignores the female gender and the age of boyhood. For with God the frame of mind that is weak and too immature to understand is to be rejected. What is manly and at the same time intelligent, by contrast, is fully recognized and listed in the book of life, as now being capable of resisting the devil's wickedness. For when intelligence is yoked to vigor of thought, it has what is needed to perform whatever befits those of pious life.

4. The Spirit therefore (I must sum up now the point of what I am saying) renders us conformed to Christ; and through the practice of virtue the divine features radiate from within us in full brilliance. But the contrary will happen to those who are otherwise. I will make utterly clear the meaning of my words. I am saying that just as the male gender has been taken as a figure of manliness, in the sense of the manliness conceived of in connection with God, which renders one conformed to Christ, along the same lines the female character is presented as a figure of softness and weak temperament, which falls quite easily into the enjoyment of pleasures. Holy Scripture in fact represents sin itself, and those who commit sin, in female form. For just as we say that those who love Christ are conformed to him, so also the hideous features of sin are engraved in the souls of those who love sin.

64. Nm 1.2–3.

Let me once again cite the blessed prophet Zechariah; he has the ability to explain this very thing to his listeners quite lucidly. This is what he says: "And the angel speaking in me went out and said to me, 'Lift up your eyes, and see this thing that goes forth.' And I said, 'What is it?' and he said, 'This is the measure that goes forth.' And he said, 'This is their iniquity in all the earth.' And behold, a talent of lead being lifted up. And behold, a woman sat in the midst of the measure. And he said, 'This is iniquity.' And he cast her into the midst of the measure, and he cast the stone of lead into her mouth. And I lifted up my eyes and saw, and behold, two women coming forth, and the wind was in their wings; and they had wings like the wings of a hoopoe; and they lifted up the measure between the earth and the sky."[65] You hear how iniquity appears to the prophet in the form of a woman. And the souls who try to lift her up high have the same kind of ugliness that is in her. For they too are seen as women. The prophetic word, in fact, has asserted to us that they had the wings of a hoopoe growing from them, in order to show thereby how prone unholy souls are to impurity, and how ready they are for pleasures of the flesh. For the sparrow, that is, the hoopoe, is unclean, feeding for the most part on worms and excrement from the stomach. And this is how every soul appears which loves sin and pleasure. For the mind which is pure feeds on the doctrines of truth, and Christ is regarded as the truth. But the earthly mind, wallowing in filth, when it sees the desires attached to every vicious thing crawling within itself like worms, gathers them and feeds on them, paying no attention at all to the stench arising from it.

If then we consider it pleasant and attractive to bear the most glorious image of the Savior, and to be conformed to that divine and heavenly beauty, let us reject the horrid imprint of sin. Let us flee from that feebleness of mind that falls such easy prey to the devil's evil ways. Let us rather act manfully, like Christ, that we may be found[66] to be sharers in his life,[67] having been brought into the presence of God the Father[68] through him and in him.

For thus it is, thus indeed, that after shaking off the corrup-

---

65. Zec 5.5–9.
67. Cf. Heb 3.14.

66. Cf. Phil 3.9.
68. Heb 9.24.

tion dwelling in our bodies like some intolerable burden, we will put on instead the glory of incorruptibility, not by denying the nature of the flesh, but by being refashioned unto the honor of incorruptibility, radiant together with our flesh with an ineffable glory coming from Christ. For "he will change our lowly body to be like his glorious body,"[69] as is written. But the doctrine that, when we have come into the presence of God the Father, we shall remain incorruptible, having put on the Savior's glory,[70] even though we are by nature corruptible, is one which sacred Scripture shows us no less by the example it offers.

For the all-powerful God wanted to teach that even that which is by nature corruptible changes its form to something other than what it is, and endures the alteration to a better state, if he should grant it his providential care. For "the eyes of the Lord are upon the just,"[71] as is written in the Psalms. He therefore said to the holy Moses and to Aaron, "'Fill a homer with manna, to be laid up for your generations.' And Moses said to Aaron, 'Take a golden jar, and cast into it one full homer of manna, and you shall lay it up before God, to be kept for your generations.'"[72] And even though the manna would perish, according to its own nature, and was found to be perfectly useless to those wanting to keep it even for the next day, it nonetheless remained incorruptible when placed in God's presence by Aaron's hand and contained in the golden jar.[73]

That this is what will happen to us, too, I think no one will doubt. For he who is really the holy High Priest of our souls, Christ that is, will wrap our body with divine glory as with something of gold. And having placed it, as it were, in the presence of God the Father, he will change it to incorruptibility. For we will no longer be subject to corruption, but rather will remain forever. The manna was taken as an example of this reality.

Since, therefore, this lamp so bright has been laid up for the saints, let us push away as far as possible the drowsiness that comes upon us from laziness, and with all due sobriety work out our own salvation.[74] And by our eagerness to achieve ev-

---

69. Phil 3.21.
71. Ps 34.15.
73. Heb 9.4.

70. Cf. 1 Cor 15.52–54.
72. Ex 16.32–33.
74. Cf. Phil 2.12.

ery kind of virtue and to follow the gospel precepts with all our strength, let us repay the Savior in this beautiful way, and let us offer in thanksgiving spiritual sacrifices to him who contended for the life of all and redeemed us by his own cross, as the Psalmist somewhere says, "I will enter your house with whole-burnt-offerings; I will pay you my vows, which my lips uttered."[75] For we who have accepted the faith unreservedly, acknowledging that Christ is Lord and God, have promised our service and engaged ourselves to obey; we owe him our submission.

Let us reflect, then, that being by nature God, since he even appeared from God, shining forth ineffably and incomprehensibly from God the Father's very substance, he is for this reason quite reasonably regarded as completely in his form and in equality with him, as is in fact true; and yet "he humbled himself," as Scripture says, "taking the form of a slave,"[76] becoming, that is, as we are, that we might become as he is, refashioned by the activity of the Spirit into his likeness by grace. Since, then, he is one of us, he is a human being like us because of us; but he is God because of himself and the One who begot him, both before the Incarnation and when he became a human being. For it was not possible that he who is from God by nature should not be God, even if "he became flesh,"[77] as John says.

Indeed, when his close disciple (Philip it was) besought him, "Lord, show us the Father and it is enough for us,"[78] he placed himself in view of the Father's substance and glory, and said, "Have I been so long with you, and you do not know me, Philip? Those who have seen me have seen the Father. Do you not believe that I am in the Father, and the Father in me?[79] For I and the Father are one."[80] For he showed us in his own nature that of the Father, and through the divine activity exercised everywhere, he presented himself to us as both image and substance of the One who begot him, that we might know him, and thus he showed us the one true God.

He accordingly ordered the dead to return to life, even when they were already corrupt and smelly.[81] He also spoke command-

75. Ps 65.13–14.
77. Jn 1.14.
79. Jn 14.9–10.
81. Cf. Jn 11.1–45.

76. Phil 2.7.
78. Jn 14.8.
80. Jn 10.30.

ingly to the sea and the winds: "Silence, be still!"[82] He made the sweet and dearly desired light to shine in those blind from birth,[83] and in addition he worked countless other wonders. For "no one has ever seen God,"[84] as the holy evangelist says. For what sort of bodily eye could gaze upon that which is regarded as being, and truly is, the divine and incomprehensible nature? Or how can that be seen which is by essence invisible? Who will stare at that inaccessible light, when the sunlight glares too intensely for our eyes? But it was, finally, necessary for us to see God himself. That sight, therefore, became possible through the miracles, and, in the marvels that were accomplished, the beauty of the divine nature will be presented to the mind. And Wisdom, further, has said that from the beauty of creatures their Creator is contemplated by analogy.[85] In order, therefore, that he might be recognized when he worked wonders, might show us the Father in himself, and might be believed to be God by nature and the Lord of all, he became as we are, a human being that is, and having put on our likeness, "he appeared on earth," as one of the wise has said, "and dwelt with men."[86]

And since he was under obligation to the Jews by promise, "he was born in Bethlehem of Judea,"[87] as Scripture says. He taught them first, and he granted his listeners an incomparably better knowledge of Moses' writing, composed as it was of old in figures; "for the Law made nothing perfect."[88] But the glory of piety reaches its fullness through the precepts of our Savior. When the time therefore arrived which urged that what had been foretold in figures should be transformed at last into truth, Christ declared to those of the blood of Israel, "I am the truth,"[89] all but saying thereby: Let Moses' precept pass away at last, and let the type and the inane form of worship in shadows cease,[90] but let the power of truth shine forth at last, and let the grace of virtue in action be seen as now fulfilled in the realities themselves. For "God is Spirit, and those who worship him must worship in spirit and truth."[91]

82. Mk 4.39.
83. Cf. Jn 9.1–11.
84. Jn 1.18.
85. Wis 13.5.
86. Bar 3.37.
87. Mt 2.1.
88. Heb 7.19.
89. Jn 14.6.
90. Cf. Heb 8.5.
91. Jn 4.24.

But the relentlessly hard-hearted Jewish people, who look only toward what is inane and are infected by a bestial madness, did not reckon that they ought to welcome him whom the Law and the prophets had announced would come and would save our entire race; the wretches fell instead to such a depth of insanity that they senselessly ridiculed him when he taught them and expounded doctrine which is above the Law. They thought his teaching, so venerable and valuable, worth nothing, and hurled the most absurd abuse at him, not hesitating to call him a glutton, a drunkard,[92] and a Samaritan;[93] I decline to repeat what was even more hurtful. That is why the voice of the holy prophets laments this people, found to be so fearfully insolent: "The house of Israel has fallen, and there is no one to raise it up; the virgin of Israel has fallen upon her land, and there is no one to raise her up."[94] For the synagogue of the Jews has been uprooted from its very foundations, as it were, having recklessly squandered the Savior's supreme forbearance. For the Jewish people and their leaders somehow thought that their impiety toward the prophets was in no way reprehensible. That is why, having no fear of raising their irreligious hand against him as well, they condemned Christ, and the wretches departed from eternal life through this insane behavior. One of the prophets indeed says of them, "Woe to them! for they have departed from me; they are wretched, for they have acted impiously toward me. Yet I redeemed them, but they spoke falsehoods against me."[95] Cruelly did they repay him, returning evil for good,[96] as is written: not only did they speak falsehoods, but, adding to their original impieties that crime which is greater than all the others, they spoke to each other about Christ those words which are of course written in the Gospels: "This is the heir; come, let us kill him, and the inheritance will be ours."[97] Then, carrying out their most odious plan, and taking Satan as their collaborator in the deed, or rather as their leader and commander, they bought the most venal of the disciples for a few silver pieces. For concerning such folk the divine

---

92. Mt 11.19.  
94. Am 5.2.  
96. Ps 35.12.  
97. Mt 21.38.  

93. Jn 8.48.  
95. Hos 7.13.

word says somewhere, "May they be erased from the book of the living, and may they not be enrolled with the just!"[98] But why extend my discourse about matters so plain to view? For everyone knows the audacious deeds of the irreligious Jews. The wretches handed over for crucifixion the Master of all, inscribing the charge of impiety upon their own heads, and upon the whole race. For in their madness they dared to say, "His blood be upon us and upon our children."[99] Not only that, but, looking at him nailed to the precious cross, they had the supreme insolence to deride him, and were persuaded by their own father, I mean Satan, to say, "If you are God's Son, come down now from the cross, and we will believe you."[100]

But the Lord Jesus Christ, seeing that the death which had long tyrannized over us was already trembling and falling (for it was to be completely destroyed by the death of the holy flesh), took no account of the reproaches of the Jews. For his purpose was to remove from sin both the living and the dead, and to renew once again for human nature the ascent to incorruptibility; and that is what happened. For he despoiled Hades with his divine and gracious command, saying to those there, "Come out and show yourselves!"[101] And having raised himself on the third day, the first-fruits of those fallen asleep,[102] and the firstborn from the dead,[103] Christ was taken up[104] to the Father,[105] an intercessor for us.[106] For as Paul says, "We have not a high priest who is unable to sympathize with our weaknesses, but one who in every respect has been tempted as we are, yet without sin."[107] And again, "For because he himself has suffered and been tempted, he is able to help those who are tempted."[108] But that he will also come, according to the Scriptures, and will render to each according to his deeds,[109] once he has set up the divine tribunal for everyone,[110] there can be no doubt.

98. Ps 69.28.
99. Mt 27.25.
100. Mt 27.40.
101. Is 49.9.
102. 1 Cor 15.20.
103. Col 1.18.
104. Cf. Mk 16.19.
105. Cf. Jn 14.12; 20.17.
106. Cf. 1 Jn 2.1.
107. Heb 4.15.
108. Heb 2.18.
109. Mt 16.27; cf. Ps 62.12.
110. Cf. 2 Cor 5.10.

For all these reasons it is understandable that we celebrate the radiant feast, living no longer for ourselves, as sacred Scripture says, but for Christ,[111] who redeemed everyone. Come, then, let us bend our necks to him and be courageous in undertaking every good deed, keeping the body chaste and rejecting defilement in the soul. Let us keep to love of each other, remembering the poor, and "those who are in prison, as though in prison with them; and those who are ill-treated, since you also are in the body."[112] For it is then, then indeed, that in our purity we will celebrate this all-holy fast purely. We begin holy Lent on the nineteenth of the month of Mechir, and the week of the salvific Paschal feast on the twenty-fourth of Phamenoth, breaking the fast on the twenty-ninth of the month as evening ends, according to the gospel tradition, and celebrating the feast on the following day, the eve of Sunday, the thirtieth of Phamenoth.[113] We add to it the seven weeks of holy Eastertide, according to the precept of the divine law. For it is thus that, made perfect by right faith and good works, we will inherit the kingdom of heaven in Christ, forever and ever. Amen.

111. 2 Cor 5.15.                    112. Heb 13.3.
113. March 26, 422.

# FESTAL LETTER ELEVEN

## A.D. 423

"COME, THEN, COME now, let us exult in the Lord,"[1] and through the all-holy fast, "come, let us worship and fall down before him,"[2] and in complete submission let us honor the King of heaven and earth, knowing what is written: "It is good for a man when he bears a yoke in his youth."[3] For who would not be overjoyed to be yoked under the Law, and to be reared in the precepts which come through Christ, counting it among the highest marks of honor? For virtue, dearly beloved, is something precious and valuable, and among all the things held in admiration in this life, it would, I think, be preferred by those who are in the habit of viewing matters rightly. One would with very good reason commend the good and honest man who would be willing to undergo countless labors for it with enormous diligence, filled with that best sort of zeal. I for my part say to those who have achieved such exceptional glory, if any of them should need a purpose, that they must never slacken, but must accustom themselves to fight manfully against hesitancy and cowardice, and all laziness, so as to consider no path as steep or hard to travel, but regard even what is rough as quite well-trodden, and even what is hard to put into practice as quite easy to accomplish.

For it would really be a shame to see those who typically vaunt their bodily strength, and who polish a skill which is prized in the wrestling ring and suits the gymnastic exercises in the cities, or which displays itself in combat and is invincible against attack, showing such eagerness to crown their own heads with preeminent glory, while we ourselves, upon whom God the Word

---

1. Ps 95.1.     2. Ps 95.6.
3. Lam 3.27.

has shone, and who are keen to acquire not a worldly happiness, nor joy that is measured in time, but, as the all-wise Paul has said, are receiving a kingdom of heaven[4] that cannot be shaken, look askance at the brief labors in this life, and do not seek the relief that comes at the proper time, even though Paul cries out most clearly and plainly, "The sufferings of the present time are not worthy to be compared to the glory to be revealed in us. For the creation waits with eager longing for the revealing of the glory of the children of God."[5]

That the life which is most law-abiding reaches at last the goal of a most glorious hope is something of which we are assured by the divine words: "For glorious is the fruit of good labors."[6] But what surprises me is the following. If one of our enemies were caught trying to take from us this glory so radiant, we would understandably consider it no minor injury and an intolerable affront, thinking ourselves deprived of what is best of all. But since there is nothing to keep us from appearing radiant, it can only be quite ridiculous to find it unbearable when we suffer from the evil ways of others, and to show ourselves oppressed by their cruel slanders, and yet to draw down upon our own heads the loss of these good things, and to contend against our own lives by the attitude we adopt.

It is, therefore, the time for reflection, dearly beloved, for sobriety and self-control, and for the all-holy fast; the season brings it around to us, and leads us now to its doors. Following the prescriptions of the law, accordingly, and all but lifting up the trumpet which so perfectly suits those with the priestly office,[7] we have hastened to make the proclamation resound loudly and piercingly, as a sound most conspicuous, announcing to those everywhere that "it is time to act for the Lord,"[8] as is written, a time of contests and labors and victory over the passions of body and soul.

2. We are incited to this proclamation by the divine and sacred Scripture which runs as follows: "If you go forth to war in

4. Cf. Heb 12.28.　　　　5. Rom 8.18–19.
6. Wis 3.15.　　　　7. Cf. Nm 10.8.
8. Ps 119.126.

your land against your enemies that are opposed to you, you shall sound your trumpets at your whole-burnt-offerings and at the sacrifices of your peace-offerings; and there will be a memorial for you before your God. I am the Lord your God."[9] Since, therefore, the law of the fast persuades us that we should do battle against the flesh and the passions at the present time especially, come, let us arm ourselves courageously with the weapons that are suitable, and let us put on the spiritual armor.[10] Let the soldier of Christ come forward to us, the one who is to fight not with a breastplate of bright iron, nor with the dread crest aloft, nor with a bronze shield and spear in hand, but rather, as the divinely inspired Paul says, "dressed in the armor of God,[11] faith, hope, and love,[12] and patience, perseverance in doing good." He will be vigorous and unbreakable in spirit, with a heart not easily shaken, but, rather, firm and unswerving; peaceable toward his brothers, but experienced in war against his adversaries. This I think is what is rightly signified by what the prophet says, "Let the meek become a warrior."[13]

For let no one suppose that the cruel horde of demons will remain quiet, or that Satan will let die his rage against us. It was said somewhere to the Jews, "If the Ethiopian will change his skin, and leopardess her spots, you also will be able to do good, having learned evil."[14] But this saying, which is so fair and right, one might repeat, and quite understandably, to the wicked, hostile powers that go about this world, prying into the life of each person in it, staring at the saints with their fearsome, savage eyes, and inciting those already inclined to evil to that apostasy which is still worse, and which now tends toward the very last measure of all wickedness. But against those who have chosen to do good, and to take pride in accomplishing just deeds, they range themselves as against their very worst enemies, directing against them the cruelty of that malice which is inherent in them. For it is not blood and flesh that fight against us, but the completely implacable rebel multitude of the demons, although it is true that added to it is the innate yet untamed law of the movements of

9. Nm 10.9–10.
11. Eph 6.11.
13. Jl 3.10.

10. Cf. Rom 13.12; 2 Cor 10.4.
12. Cf. 1 Cor 13.13; 1 Thes 5.8.
14. Jer 13.23.

the flesh, which pulls and forces one to do as it likes, and lifts its stiff neck against the spirit. For their concerns are mutually opposed, and are widely separated due to their antagonism. And it seems to me that the souls of the irreligious suffer something like that which may well happen to cities or countries when a war from without is declared with their barbarian neighbors. But there is no peace within the gates; a civil war is devastating those inside. And that which would defeat those outside, even if with difficulty, if only it enjoyed some measure of harmony, crumbles of its own accord because it is rent by divisions. For that the difference of wills in us can be seen, one that is not unimportant, is something that the divinely inspired Paul testifies to in the words: "For I delight in the law of God, in my inmost self, but I see another law at war with the law of my mind and making me captive to the law of sin which dwells in my members. Wretched man that I am! Who will deliver me from this body of death?"[15]

There is waged therefore in us a double war, not a single one. But I can imagine that someone who hears me saying this might ask: In that case, dear sir, are we to put down our weapons and yield the victory to our enemies without a fight, and bow our necks as though to masters most violent, knowing how perilous it is to fight? Is it necessary to serve the flesh and the demons, giving up hope of salvation? By no means! That is sheer nonsense, nothing else. Away with such ill counsel, sir! Turn your mind to the recovery of courage. And even if the carnal nature makes itself heard to you, that nature whose concern is so much with pleasure, do not fail to resist it. The slightest efforts are enough to subdue it, and even if you see it moved, and incited against the will of the spirit, put aside indolence as quickly as you can, and, in imitation of the best athletes, prepare yourself the more ardently. Putting on the weapons of chastity, show it your efforts of asceticism, and the law of sin will turn to flight, and the one you thought hard to vanquish you will suddenly see a fugitive.

This is how the divinely inspired Paul himself fought against carnal desires, saying, "I pommel my body and subdue it, lest after preaching to others I myself should be disqualified."[16] For a high-spirited horse is brought with the bit to run in a disciplined

15. Rom 7.22–24.     16. 1 Cor 9.27.

fashion by those in charge of such things. And those in charge of fleets get the ships to run straight by the way the helm is turned. A prudent and reputable mind is by no means fickle or easily carried off by deceptive arguments. But established, as it were, upon itself and irreproachably steady, it trains the flesh by the efforts of asceticism to choose the obligation to submit to God; it takes its course, without swerving at all, toward everything that is to be done. For "the thoughts of the righteous are judgments,"[17] as is written. And it would be in any case really inexcusable to apply oneself weakly to self-control. For it is certainly not mildness alone that will vanquish the flesh; rather, that which is divisive in it has already been put to death and done away with through Christ.[18] The Savior's disciple will again explain both the power of the interior struggle and the manner of putting to death. For he says further, "So then, I of myself serve the law of God with my mind, but with my flesh I serve the law of sin. There is therefore now no condemnation for those who are in Christ Jesus. For the law of the spirit of life in Christ Jesus has set me free from the law of sin and death."[19] And again: "For God has done what the law, weakened by the flesh, could not do: sending his own Son in the likeness of sinful flesh and for sin, he condemned sin in the flesh, in order that the just requirement of the law might be fulfilled in us, who walk not according to the flesh but according to the Spirit."[20] The flesh, accordingly, having been put to death—in what concerns its desires, that is—it is only reasonable to consider that it is truly shameful and ridiculous for those who have already achieved such glory, and have been called to receive the dignity of adoption, to appear as slaves of the flesh, rather than to be noble guardians of virtue, in order to preserve the glory they have found. For the following is directed at those wanting to win the victory: "We are debtors, not to the flesh, to live according to the flesh, as is written. For if we live according to the flesh, we will die; but if by the Spirit we put to death the deeds of the body, we will live. For all who are led by the Spirit of God are sons of God."[21] For on the day of judgment

17. Prv 12.5.
18. Cf. Rom 6.6.
19. Rom 7.25–8.2.
20. Rom 8.3–4.
21. Rom 8.12–14.

it is not possible, not at all possible, to counter the charge of negligence by babbling about having been oppressed and enslaved, when Christ, as it were, refutes us, and all but compels the law of freedom to shout down our explanations.

3. Let the trainer of the saints instruct us, therefore, and teach us the ways to struggle with the flesh, when he writes, "I appeal to you therefore, brothers, by the mercies of God, to present your bodies as a living sacrifice, acceptable to God, which is your spiritual worship. Do not be conformed to this age, but be transformed by the renewal of your mind, that you may assess what God's good and perfect and acceptable will is."[22] John indeed in his wisdom adds, "Do not love the world or what is in the world. For those who love the world do not have the love of God in them. For all that is in the world, the lust of the flesh and the lust of the eyes and the pride of life, is not from the Father but from the world. And the world passes away, and lust; but those who do God's will remain forever."[23]

Someone would lack good sense, then, who thought it more beneficial to abandon what was better and consider it of no account, and to choose instead what appears laughable and lasts only a short while. If someone therefore were to put gold and lead side by side, and bid one choose which one preferred, would we not be thought by ourselves and others to have decided for the best when we passed over that which is regarded as of quite little value, and without hesitation gave the decision to what is incomparably superior? If so, then it can only be quite ridiculous, and absolutely absurd, when we judge with such nice discernment and correctness what concerns corruptible material things and earthly matters, but when it comes to the good things of the soul, even though the natures of things must be examined as accurately as possible, we are seen to lose heart, and this so much so that we consciously neglect to search for what is fitting, to the point of quite ignoring what is beneficial. Or if we do know what it is, we disdain it, thinking of little value, or none at all, that which by nature is always profitable, and pouncing

22. Rom 12.1–2.
23. 1 Jn 2.15–17.

upon what is most shameful. Come then, let us show ourselves superior to a most loathsome love of the flesh, and let us grant a more suitable attention to that virtue which is our companion on the way, shaping our lives according to the model of every good work.

For in my opinion, those who choose an honorable life have need not only of that continence which is of the body, and not only of victory over the flesh, but also of that other moderation which is of disposition and manners. For the mind which has practiced the tranquility coming from gentleness is not controlled by anger. For "he who governs his temper is better than he who captures a city,"[24] as is written. It may in fact be added that it is the one whose thoughts are well ordered that is the most vigorous, unvanquished by unjust or superfluous gain, convinced that contempt for riches makes for unwavering justice, and determined to prefer voluntary poverty to the anxiety occasioned by wealth. For Paul in his supreme wisdom bids the Savior's disciple to appear content with as little as possible, and to be so in truth, when he says, "If we have food and clothing, with these we shall be content. But those who want to be rich fall into many useless desires that plunge people into ruin and destruction."[25] Away therefore with the search for what is superfluous! Let it be cast upon a mountain or a wave, as the expression goes, and let us concern ourselves with necessities rather than abundance: with food and cheap clothing. For these are quite easy to come by, and may be found with no trouble.

4. In addition to all these good things, let the law of brotherhood in Christ be honored, and let the precept of mutual love reign.[26] "For the fullness of the law is love,"[27] as is written.

And we hold that a fruit of love is pity for those in need and for those who lack what is necessary. Do not tell yourself, my friend: I am rich in faith; I know the One who by nature is truly God and Lord; I have come back from the devil's nets and from the deceptions of the demons; I have washed myself clean of any

---

24. Prv 16.32.  25. 1 Tm 6.8–9.
26. Cf. Jn 13.34; 15.12, 17; 1 Jn 3.11, 23; 4.7, 11, 12; 2 Jn 5.
27. Rom 13.10.

charges of idolatry. I may boast of the benevolence assured me. Remember the one who said, "What does it profit, my brothers, if one says he has faith but has not works? Can his faith save him? If a brother or sister among you is ill-clad and in lack of daily food, and one of you says to them, 'Go in peace, be warmed and filled,' without giving them the things needed for the body, what does it profit?"[28] Or do you not know, can you not realize, that it behooves those who believe to obey the divine laws unhesitatingly? For one would not, I think, fairly bring an accusation of lawbreaking against a barbarian who had dwelt outside of countries and cities and had no part in our customs and laws, not at any rate if one had any sense; but one might understandably, and not unreasonably, blame those brought up in cities and laws, if they happened to fail in what is fitting. Those therefore who have not yet achieved the esteem of which we speak, and for whom that achievement is generally regarded as improbable, have nonetheless the possibility of clearing themselves of the charges against them in that they are not being educated in the divine laws; and their defense is plausible. But the disobedience and rebelliousness of those who have chosen to believe is quite inexcusable, and their refusal to serve by shaking off God's yoke can only be wholly grievous. Let the pride engendered by works be joined to faith, therefore, and, as the Savior says, "Let us be merciful, just as our heavenly Father is merciful."[29] "For judgment is without mercy to one who has shown no mercy; yet mercy triumphs over judgment."[30] It is by no means difficult to show you from holy Scripture itself both the rewards of mutual love and the condemnation of what is opposed to it. For the blessed Job is admirable when he says of himself, "But the helpless missed not whatever need they had, and I did not cause the eye of the widow to fail. And if I ate my morsel alone, and did not share it with the orphan, and if I even overlooked the naked as he was perishing, and did not clothe him; and if the helpless did not bless me, and their shoulders were not warmed with the fleece of my lambs; if I lifted my hand against an orphan, trusting that my strength was far superior; then let my shoulder sepa-

28. Jas 2.14–16.  29. Lk 6.36.
30. Jas 2.13.

rate from the blade-bone, and my arm be crushed off from the elbow."[31]

5. Now the rich man in the Gospels is condemned and suffers an inescapable punishment; he is the one of whom the Savior says, "There was a rich man who was clothed in purple and fine linen and who feasted sumptuously. And at his gate lay a poor man, Lazarus, full of sores, who desired to be fed with the crumbs that fell from the rich man's table; moreover, the dogs came and licked his sores. The poor man died and was carried by the angels to Abraham's bosom. The rich man also died and was buried; and in hell, being in torment, he lifted up his eyes, and saw Abraham, and Lazarus in his bosom. And he called out, 'Father Abraham, have mercy on me, and send Lazarus to dip the tip of his finger in water and cool my tongue; for I am in anguish in this flame.' But Abraham said, 'Son, remember that you in your lifetime received your good things, and Lazarus in like manner evil things; but now he is the one to be comforted, and you are in anguish.'"[32]

If there is anything to be added briefly to this, one may say that the rich man was dressed in wonderfully fine purple clothing, perhaps shot with gold; he had a splendid house, beyond all wonder, the object of maddened envy; a great number of well-dressed servants; all sorts of carpets strewn on the floors; cup-bearers, cooks, and bakers attractively and elegantly turned out; a table always loaded with food. And one may also imagine a swarm of flatterers hanging on the rich man's every word, swearing that whatever he chose to admire, even if it was most absurd, was the best thing of all, and hastening to denigrate whatever he had denigrated, even were it virtue itself. And as for that vain abomination, the revelry that God hates, the applause, the table-songs, and the flute-players' dances: why say anything? One should keep silence, I think, about things which are harmful even when they are only remembered.

The other man, now, was quite wretched in his poverty, lacking clothing, hearth, and protectors. Deprived even of physical strength, his whole desire was to obtain what was indispensable,

31. Jb 31.16–21.            32. Lk 16.19–25.

and he was happy with just a few things. He thought he could reach the zenith of his hopes and prayers if he could get some bread and rags. The gospel account of the parable describes how he reached such a depth of misery that he even lay among noisome dogs, who were his only companions, and received their attentions with great pleasure when they wanted to assuage his distress by applying their gluttonous tongues to him; such was the remedy for their own hurts which they had discovered by the laws of nature, and with which they succored Lazarus.

But of none of this did that noble and ostentatious man take any notice; hard and unfeeling, he found it burdensome to have to take pity, and as for shedding a tear of compassion for the irremediable misfortunes of the sufferer, he called that a useless burden, impiously rejecting anything of the kind. He was for him a part of the rabble, no different from those in the tombs, loathsome and repulsive, and worth nothing.

And yet he ought to have had the wit to reflect that the Creator and Artificer of our nature did not provide one passage into existence for the rich and another for those in need: the insemination of the mother by the father is the same for all, the birth-pangs and the method of birth are not different, and of course the body which comes forth is similar in its features. And all of us are surrounded by the same sky; we have been granted the light of one sun, which does not shed better and brighter beams on those more illustrious by their wealth, while shining less brightly on those in need. Nature, then, knows no difference, nor, certainly, does God, the Author of all of creation; rather, it was invented by human avarice.

Now there seems to be no reason not to infer with great confidence the mind of God from what we have just said, and thus to steer our affairs toward a happy outcome when they are guided toward equality by the bond of love. For how could it be that the One who has dispensed equally all the good things of nature, granting no one a superfluity or advantage, has not wanted to do away with avarice towards others, and establish those with possessions as stewards, as it were, of those in need, that they might be able to share something of glory and eternal delight with those who are well off?

But I almost forgot something that it would be good to add. It happened that when Lazarus was in this distress, and was taken by death, he departed from this human realm and was transported by angels to Abraham's bosom. But he who was surrounded by the boundless delights of wealth, and often called enviable and blessed, and other things even higher than these by the acclamations of his flatterers, was subjected to the laws of nature, entered into death's snare, was shut up deep in darkness, and received in exchange for his earthly goods a sentence to hell in punishment for his lack of love.

But some of those listening might well say: What would you say if someone were to come forward and out of curiosity ask: Has poverty crowned itself with the prestige of piety toward God, and has it been honored by the law of justice, while the state of wealth is accursed, and has received a cruel sentence against itself? How can that be? One must, however, consider the following: wealth in this life is always somehow associated and linked with many harmful things, at least for the most part. The wealthy are more prone to arrogance, uncontrolled in greed, and dominated by pleasures as much as by luxury. But those worn down by poverty can hardly suffer from such things. They constantly grieve that they have nothing, and bewail and groan over themselves. They are as far removed from pleasure as from luxury. Their whole concern is to gather the little that they may, and to find some modest consolation in the face of necessity.

6. To all of these comments, I think the following should be added: that each person's character, in giving him the power to turn each thing in its nature in any direction he chooses, puts him either among those who are wicked or those who are admirable. And one might say that as the colors from dyes are to the things to which they are applied, so is the character of people to the natures of the things in which they are engaged. Thus I will say unhesitatingly that the one who manages to live in poverty prudently is the best of all. For if, when he is satisfied even with little, and earns with his sweat what is most available, so to speak, he then offers prayers of gratitude, how could he not be worthy of that epithet, and merit the highest praise? Necessity urges him

to evildoing, but he honors so highly the law of self-control that he is never caught behaving wickedly. Whereas he who is illustrious for the abundance of what he owns cannot but be censured, and quite rightly, if, when he might have disposed the God of the universe kindly toward him by showing pity toward others and by giving a little to those in need so that they might rise and recover somewhat from their incessant misfortune, he instead puts his temporary wealth at the sole service of his own pleasure.

While Lazarus, then, found himself among unexpected delights, the rich man found himself amid unwonted flames and lashes. If therefore someone went to him just at that time and spoke to him, asking how much he would be willing to pay to escape his punishment, if the judge allowed him to choose, would he not affirm with the greatest willingness that he would give all he had for that? Would anyone doubt it?

It is, then, stupid, and completely absurd, to expect to learn from experience what is dangerous, when those who wish may do so while keeping clear of traps and constraint. And if what we have among us is better than the Jewish religion, it must be quite clear to everyone that it would not appear logical to think that one ought not to outdo their practices by observances which are superior. The Savior himself said to us, accordingly, "Amen, amen, I say to you, unless your justice surpasses that of the scribes and Pharisees, you will not enter the kingdom of heaven."[33]

What was it, then, that the Law given through Moses revealed to those from Israel when it urged them through figure and shadow to honor equality among brothers? They were crossing that vast desert, and their food was running short, so that they cried out against the all-wise Moses; and as though they could no longer be saved from the grip of famine, they were already raising a funeral dirge. Having lost all hope, as it were, they said, "Would that we had been smitten and died in the land of Egypt, when we sat by the flesh-pots, and ate our fill of bread! For you have brought us out into this desert, to slay all this congregation with hunger."[34] The all-wise Moses was at a complete loss, with nothing at all that he could do or say in response to this; but he revived his courage, drawing it solely from the hope that comes

33. Mt 5.20.                    34. Ex 16.3.

from God, and a happy ending was promptly supplied that was different from what had been expected. For the Lord said to him, "Behold, I will rain bread upon you from heaven, and the people shall go forth, and they shall gather their daily portion for the day."[35] Now the blessed Moses interpreted the meaning of the Law to those from Israel, saying further, "This is the bread which the Lord has given you to eat. This is that which the Lord has appointed: gather of it, each man for his family, a homer for each person, according to the number of your souls. Gather each of you with his fellow-lodgers. And the children of Israel did so," it says, "and gathered, some much and some less. And having measured by the homer, he that had gathered much had nothing over, and he that had gathered less had no lack."[36] For the Lord of the Law never allowed more to be gathered than what was needed, but only what sufficed for the provision of the day. And if anyone collected more than this, putting the Law far from his mind, he turned it into a swarm of worms. The Law, I think, thus showed, and quite clearly, how pleasant and irreproachable is the acquisition of what suffices; while that which is stored away and heaped up insatiably beyond strict necessity will only breed worms.

It was to this that the Law summoned those of old. But to what does the Savior summon us ourselves? "Make friends for yourselves from unjust mammon, so that when it runs out they may welcome you to their tents."[37] And so that I may make clear to you the meaning of this declaration, I will add that it cannot be doubted, no, it cannot, that among the needy there is no small number of wise and just persons which probably escapes our notice, but is certainly not unknown to God. When therefore we admit them as sharers in earthly goods, no one must doubt that we will also share with them in the reward for their equity. "For they will receive you into their tents,"[38] as is written. The blessed Paul himself understood this perfectly when he said somewhere, "Your abundance supplies their want, that their abundance may supply your want."[39] "Let us be good to one an-

35. Ex 16.4.  
37. Lk 16.9.  
39. 2 Cor 8.14.  

36. Ex 16.16, 17, 18.  
38. Ibid.

other, and tenderhearted," as is written, "being generous to one another, as God in Christ has been generous to us."[40] And how can anyone not see what God has given us in Christ, or in what kind of goods we have come to share? We have been granted the remission of our transgressions, a forbearing love. For we have been saved, as though God had forgotten human pettiness. It is necessary, then, beloved, that we also practice forbearance, hastening to follow in the footsteps of the tranquility which is in the Master of all. And let us give prudent consideration to the following: human failings are countless, and there is no occasion which is free of our pettiness. But if, whenever that occurs, we are going to get upset seriously and enter into disputes with those who have grieved us, our whole life will be spent in bitterness and distress. And since "the ways of those who remember injuries lead to death,"[41] as is written, there is nothing to prevent anyone's soul from falling prey to death if it cannot nobly repel what causes grief, but is always incited to rise up fiercely against its attackers. As the blessed Paul says, therefore, let us bear each other's burdens, and thus we will fulfill the law of Christ.[42]

For this manner of piety is conspicuous as well. But there are some among us who are so far from wanting to be good, and distance their own souls so completely from the honor of being unmindful of injury, that if any of those called to brotherhood commits even the slightest fault, they shake out every reef, and, spreading their whole sail to their passions, as it were, are borne off by uncontrollable impulses and charge like bulls, thinking it the deepest dishonor if they do not commit some frightful deed. And if perchance some among those who have offended them are the stronger, then at once an enormous number of ministers of violence gathers around, inciting them to anger, goading them to act inhumanely, suggesting plans, and presenting paths by which the force of their appetite may take its course. The judgment upon such people is quite frightful, dearly beloved. And those who are provoked will certainly perish with those who have provoked them. I will again show you the proof of this from the divinely inspired Scripture itself.

40. Eph 4.32.    41. Prv 12.28. (LXX).
42. Cf. Gal 6.2.

7. The Idumaeans[43] and the Israelites were settled by turns, and were not allotted the same territory. But they were brothers and neighbors. Esau was considered the father of the one group, while the others were from Jacob. One group possessed the land of promise, the other the land of Idumaea; the latter borders on the former, but is a highland with frequent mountain prominences and rocky hills, hard to conquer for anyone deciding to plunder it, since the approaches to the region are quite unassailable; the inhabitants indeed took pride in that. These being the origin and the land of the aforesaid peoples, they differed greatly in their mentalities. The situations of the two groups were so separate as to lead to opposition in behavior, and their difference in religion became a pretext for war. For while the Israelites, taking pride in the laws given through Moses, worshiped the God of the universe, the Moabites or Idumaeans (they are the same), being under the sway of the deceptions of the demons, fashioned stones and wood and gave the title of gods to things that have no knowledge. The peoples therefore were separated from each other by religion, behavior, and place.

Then it happened that those from Israel fell, and grieved God by maltreating the Law; there arose against Jerusalem an impious and lawless man, the tyrant of Babylon. He ordered the whole people subject to him to be armed, and, intending to conquer at once those devoted to God, he gave the clarion signal for war. He arrived in Judea, and, encamping there with his whole army, he so terrorized those from Israel that they scattered to the neighboring lands, abandoning their native country as though jumping from a ship that was already foundering. And what did the Idumaeans do then? They ought to have taken pity on those in confusion and fear, and tried rather to protect them and to settle them in their own cities, forgetting the differences between them. But they did quite the contrary. Binding the suppli-

43. A reference to the inhabitants of Edom, in southern Judea. Idumaeans were the descendants of Esau, which, according to Gn 36.1, is synonymous with Edom. Cyril's summary is a conflation of narratives that appear in 2 Kings, 2 Chronicles, Jeremiah. His main source appears to be Jer 25–26 and 49. It is not unusual for Cyril (or other ancient interpreters) to interpolate historical material from the prophets into the basic timelines and narratives of Kings and Chronicles.

ant, they presented him to the Babylonians as though he were ready prey, and made the killing of their brother and neighbor a point of honor of their religion. They laughed loudly at those consecrated, and, rising up against the divine glory, said in their madness that the power of the demons had arisen, and had hurled the Babylonian down upon those who disrespected the religion practiced among themselves; this, they said, was the only reason for what had happened. But since the laughter directed against the Jews was no longer tolerable to people, and was hateful to God, the enemy army departed from the region of those consecrated, and, as it were, now flowed to Idumaea, the Almighty having reversed the nature of the situations and with good reason now shifted his wrath to those others. And that once extensive, hardy, and boastful people was so decimated by the arrows of the Babylonians, that perhaps one inhabitant might escape out of even a populous walled city. I will read you the divine text itself, which runs as follows. It is the word of God to the Idumaean: "Behold, I have made you small among the gentiles; you are greatly dishonored. The pride of your heart has elated you, dwelling in the holes of the rocks, as one that exalts his habitation, saying in his heart, Who will bring me down to the ground? If you should mount up as the eagle, and if you should make your nest among the stars, thence will I bring you down, says the Lord."[44] Then he explains the reason for his indignation when he goes on to say, "Because of the slaughter, and the impiety against your brother Jacob, shame shall cover you, and you will be removed forever. From the day you rose up in opposition, in the day when foreigners were taking captive his forces, and strangers entered his gates, and cast lots on Jerusalem, you also were as one of them. Do not look on the day of your brother on the day of strangers, and do not laugh at the children of Judah on the day of their destruction, nor boast on the day of affliction, nor go into the gate of the people on the day of their troubles. Do not look upon their gathering on the day of their destruction, nor attack their host on the day of their perishing, nor shut up their fugitives on the day of affliction."[45] You see, then,

44. Ob 1.2–4; Jer 49.15, 16.
45. Ob 1.10–13.

that because they did not think they had to defend those from Israel, but rivaled the inhumanity of their enemies, they themselves, contrary to what they had expected, perished with their whole nation. So it was, then, with the Idumaeans. But did the Babylonian boast against the holy land with impunity, and, triumphing over the miseries of those who suffered, prolong his happiness untouched? Hardly. I will show how he immediately paid the penalty most befitting his audacious behavior.

Having left Idumaea, that is, he thought to go back home, and, having decided to return, gave the signal for departure. No one opposing him, he made his way back. And when he was within his barbarian palace, he set off the festivities, and made of the sufferings of the consecrated ones a solemn narrative. He ordered those of high rank to gather for a great banquet, the feast being replete with acclamations and applause for him. Some there were who were notable for the madness of their language, and those who had done something particularly revolting sought to be honored far more highly than the others; the rewards they received were in proportion to the inhumanity of their behavior. And then it was, just then, that almighty God unleashed his wrath against the tyrant,[46] overwhelming that haughty man with unexpected calamities. For it was at that time that his subjects revolted against him, and the nations were divided against each other by dissensions. The most powerful among his officials now proceeded to rebel against their sovereign, and planned an undeclared war. Their chief aim was to burn the tyrant's palace, and to uproot that famous and boastful city, I mean Babylon, from its very foundations, as it were. And when the battle was joined, they won their prize, destroying Babylon by fire and its inhabitants with iron, and hastening to crown their brave deeds by killing the tyrant.

But since the prophet Jeremiah understood with perfect certitude, through the illumination of the Spirit, that this was going to happen, he is seen shouting loudly a portentous message. As though inciting a multitude to battle against that man, he says, "Set yourselves in array against Babylon round about, all you that bend the bow; shoot at her, spare not your arrows, and prevail

46. Cf. Jer 27.1–20.

against her. Her hands are weakened, her bulwarks are fallen, her wall is broken down, for it is vengeance from God, the vengeance of his people."[47] And almost as though he were not unaware of the groans of those who were falling, he adds, "A sound of war and great destruction in the land of the Chaldaeans! How is the hammer of the whole earth broken and crushed? How has Babylon become a desolation? Babylon among the nations, they will attack you, and you will be taken, Babylon, and you will not know it; you have been found, and taken, because you resisted the Lord."[48]

8. These are the stories I would put before you, not so that we may vainly applaud the empty speech we hear, but so that, in taking as our instructor the experience of past history, we may avoid imitating those who are evil. For since we have known the God of the universe, who is good and compassionate, we must not gloat over those who have fared wretchedly, but rather share their pain and offer them willing assistance, burying grievances under an affection that forgets resentment. To this end we must not rise up against those already prone, nor exult over the distress of those who fall, even if we may do all this without hindrance; we must rather have fear in either situation. Girded with zeal for the good, and distinguished for our vigorous spirit, let us prepare our own mind for the acquisition of virtue, once we have, as it were, sown and planted in our own souls the uprightness of the blameless faith.

The true and really God-loving Christian must believe in one God, the Father almighty, and in one Lord Jesus Christ his Son, and in the Holy Spirit, so as, namely, to think and say that God the Father is truly the source of his own offspring, and is as a root which has obtained the fruit from itself as co-eternal with itself. For of all other things, visible and invisible, he is the Creator, and, by his will, Father. For thus we say that everything is from God. But of his own offspring he is not the Creator, but the Father by nature. For he truly begot him, not by emanation or division or passion, as indeed may be seen in the case of our own selves as well. For a body comes forth from a body, and thus there

---

47. Jer 27.14–15 (LXX).          48. Jer 27.22–24 (LXX).

is division. But with God it is not so, since he is not corporeal, nor is he in a place or a form or circumscription; but as God he is incomprehensibly and ineffably what he is.[49] For it is not possible that the nature which surpasses everything should be affected as we are. The Father therefore has begotten the Son from himself, light from light, image and impress,[50] and radiance of his own subsistence,[51] as is written.

But when our situation was nothing short of desperate under the reign of death, with the evil rebel dragon lording it over the things on earth, and sin holding sway, he became a human being, that he might remove us all from the things just mentioned. For, having become this in truth, and taken flesh from a woman, from the holy Virgin that is, according to the Scriptures, "he appeared on earth, and dwelt among men."[52] For what was seen was a human being, according to the nature of the flesh, and one certainly perfect with respect to humanity. But in a truer sense he was God.[53] For the Word of God did not come to be in a human being as in the saints, but truly appeared himself and was called a human being. When accordingly we think rightly, we do not speak of two Sons, nor of two Christs or Lords, but of one Son and Lord, both before the Incarnation and when he had the covering of the flesh. For we do not worship separately, as God, the Word shining forth from the substance of God the Father, after making a division into two, regarding the human being as apart. No, we do not accept any division or separation at all after the combination with the flesh, at least as regards the Sonship. We honor and glorify, together with the holy angels, the one and only Son whom we have known, because he is indeed by nature God; he is only-begotten, since he alone was begotten from God the Father, and also, the same one, firstborn, when he came to be among many brothers.[54] For thus says the

49. Cyril uses standard Nicene categories when he writes about the divine persons, although he is generally dependent upon Athanasius. See Norman Russell, *Cyril of Alexandria,* 21–30.

50. Cf. Col 1.15.                              51. Cf. Heb 1.3.

52. Bar 3.37.

53. Here again the relative immaturity of Cyril's Christological thought is evident. This sentence seems to minimize Christ's humanity.

54. Rom 8.29.

divinely inspired Paul: "When he brings the firstborn into the world, he says: Let all the angels of God worship him."[55]

As the Psalmist says, therefore, "The Lord is God, and has shone upon us."[56] For he has truly shone upon those walking in night and darkness,[57] and, illuminating the heart of his listeners with words conducive to piety,[58] has ordered them forcefully to strike out toward God. And having demonstrated, by prodigies that surpass comprehension, that he is God by nature, he called everyone to a readier belief.

But those who do not fear to dare anything, those from Israel that is, while they should have been grateful and happily welcomed a benefactor, and called him Savior, Helper, and Lord, behaved impiously. For they were merciless in what they said, and, omitting no sort of rashly arrogant behavior, in the end they crucified him. For they probably said to themselves the oracle pronounced of old by Isaiah: "Let us bind the just man, for he is inconvenient to us."[59] But those who meditated these things, and dared to do them in their lack of love for God, drawing the wrath upon their own heads to which they had called it, perished and were utterly destroyed. But he, although he was by nature life, allowed the flesh to suffer death for us in the economy "that he might be Lord of the dead and of the living,"[60] as is written. For, having descended into hell, preached to the spirits there,[61] opened the ever-locked gates to those below, and emptied the insatiable recesses of death, he revived on the third day. And thus he ascended to the Father with the flesh he had assumed, a kind of first-fruits of our nature, and "firstborn from the dead, that in everything he might be pre-eminent,"[62] as is written. And he will come again to us from heaven as Judge, to render to each according to his works. "For he will judge the earth in justice,"[63] as is written.

It is to this end, beloved, that the signal for our holy feast, this very signal, announces to us the outset of the divine festival. Let

---

55. Heb 1.6.
57. Lk 1.79.
59. Wis 2.12.
61. 1 Pt 3.19.
63. Ps 96.13.

56. Ps 118.27.
58. Cf. Eph 1.18.
60. Rom 14.9.
62. Col 1.18.

us then put aside all hesitation, reject all indolence in our own thoughts, and so hasten with energetic and alert minds, and with fear of the divine mind, toward all that is good. Let us embrace mutual love, pursue chastity of body, reject defilement of soul, remember the poor who are mistreated, as being ourselves in the body, remember those who are in prison, as though in prison with them,[64] and do everything with the fear of God. Then it is, then indeed, that we will achieve a pure and blameless fast for Christ, the Master and Savior of all. We begin holy Lent on the ninth of the month of Phamenoth, and the week of the salvific Paschal feast on the fourteenth of Pharmuthi, breaking the fast on the nineteenth of the same month of Pharmuthi, late in the evening, according to the gospel message. We celebrate the feast on the following day, the eve of Sunday, the twentieth of the month,[65] adding thereafter the seven weeks of holy Eastertide, so that we may also enjoy once again the holy words through a right way of life, in Christ Jesus our Lord, through whom and with whom be honor, glory, and power to the Father with the Holy Spirit. Amen.

64. Heb 13.3.
65. April 15, 423.

# FESTAL LETTER TWELVE

## A.D. 424

"THE LAW HAS a shadow of the good things to come,"[1] and outlines the bright form of the truth, by figures and symbols, giving us a glimpse of the mystery of the things revealed through Christ. It bids the sons of Israel accordingly, "Blow the trumpet at the new moon, on the glorious day of your feast."[2] But let us, in leaving the figures as far behind us as we may, and ridding our present situation of the ancient forms, consider more important our education in the divine and evangelical precepts. And since the luminous and most glorious feast has shone upon us once again, bringing with it, as something in season, the struggles to achieve order in our lives,[3] allow then, allow the one who follows the voices of the saints to cry out to us as though from a spiritual trumpet: "Prepare the way of the Lord, make straight his paths!"[4] For to strive to live in friendship with God, and to be in the habit of priding oneself on the honors that come from one's virtue, is, I think—especially in the present time—what it means to prepare the way of the Lord and to receive the joy that befits those who keep festival with a good conscience. "For the impious cannot rejoice, says the Lord."[5] For how or whence does that suit them, when the penalty assigned them as their punishment looms over them? For to live in spiritual enjoyments and to feast upon rich hopes belong in justice to them who have lived as rightly as possible, and who have declared that the divine law was like a norm for their own life.

---

1. Heb 10.1.                    2. Ps 81.3.
3. See the discussion of asceticism in the introduction.
4. Lk 3.4; cf. Is 40.3–5.        5. Cf. Is 57.21.

"Therefore, holy brothers, who share in a heavenly call,"[6] "let us consider how to stir up one another to love and good works,"[7] as is written, remembering the one who says, "Iron sharpens iron, and a man seasons his friend's face."[8] For it is like those who rise up against barbarian attacks and want to resist them as strongly as possible: they urge each other to be bold and strive to encourage a show of strength and skill, convinced that the right moment for war has come; and thus, made fearsome and irresistible, they fall upon their foes now that they are above hesitation and fright and have mastered the gravest dangers, whatever they may be. In the same way I hold that those who love holiness, whoever they may be, must accustom themselves to oppose the devil's wiles without the slightest hesitation, and to put up such a stout resistance that they can then speak these very words in truth: "Who shall separate us from the love of God? Shall tribulation, or distress, or persecution, or famine, or nakedness, or peril, or sword?"[9] For there is nothing at all that can make us cowardly, if, in following closely the virtue of the saints, we have the same attitude as they when they act manfully and say, "The Lord is my light and my Savior; whom shall I fear? The Lord is the defender of my life; of whom shall I be afraid?"[10] "Come, therefore, let us exult in the Lord," as is written, "let us make a joyful noise to God our Savior."[11] For it is just the present moment that calls us to the thrice-longed-for feast. For if death, hateful to all, has been abolished by Christ's power, and the age-old corruption, fearful and invincible, has been destroyed through his Resurrection, then come, let us send forth loudly everywhere the resounding proclamation in the words, "The Lord reigns, let the earth exult!"[12]

And in what way may those exult who have chosen to do so in Christ? The most fitting way is to abandon as soon as possible that pleasure which is earthly and base, and, in a word, all carnal desire, to choose rather the things that are of the better sort, and, in attending to what is superior to the former things,

6. Heb 3.1.                          7. Heb 10.24.
8. Prv 27.17.                        9. Rom 8.35.
10. Ps 27.1.                         11. Ps 95.1.
12. Ps 97.1.

to strive to fulfill, with all zeal, what has been said to us so rightly and well by the blessed Paul: "Forgetting what lies behind and straining forward to what lies ahead."[13] Let what is past, then, be, as it were, buried in thick oblivion, and, having abandoned the thoughtlessness of old, let us strain forward to what lies ahead; let us, that is, hasten to make our way to him whose wisdom is perfect. We worshiped "the creature instead of the Creator,"[14] and "we were once darkness, but now we are light in Christ,"[15] as is written. For we have been called to the recognition of God, and the light of truth has flashed upon our understanding. For truth is the basis of every good, and the foundation in us of all virtue. God the Father himself, accordingly, indicated this very thing to us from on high through the voice of the holy prophets, saying, "Behold, I am setting for the foundations of Zion a choice stone, a cornerstone, precious. And those that believe in it will not be ashamed."[16] The divinely inspired Paul understood this perfectly when he told us, "Like a skilled master-builder I laid a foundation."[17]

And what the foundation is, or what sort of basis there is for our situation in life, you may learn from him when he cries aloud, "For no other foundation can anyone lay than that which is laid, which is Jesus Christ."[18] Having therefore our Lord Jesus Christ as a support and foundation of the true knowledge of God, "let us hold fast our confession,"[19] as holy Scripture somewhere says, and let us examine our own heart, lest some remnant of unbelief, so hateful to God, may, like a snake in a hole, have escaped notice; "for fear that any 'root of bitterness' spring up and cause trouble,"[20] as is written. For one could say that ignoble duplicity[21] is a wicked thing and a grievous illness of mind, and one would not be wrong, since its effects on those disposed to it are indeed most shameful, even when they do not want to experience them. One may observe that a house which has slid away from its original support is most liable to collapse, having

13. Phil 3.13.
14. Rom 1.25.
15. Eph 5.8.
16. Is 28.16.
17. 1 Cor 3.10.
18. 1 Cor 3.11.
19. Heb 4.14.
20. Heb 12.15; cf. Dt 29.18.
21. Cf. Jas 4.8.

been brought to the greatest state of weakness, so to speak, and is extremely vulnerable. And one may see the human soul in the same situation with Satan, the tempter, if it is so insane as to be caught leaving its own foundation, which is Christ, and treating the support of faith insolently with its duplicitous behavior.

It seems to me that Christ's disciple spoke correctly and irreproachably about these matters when he said, "It would have been better for them not to have known the way of truth than, after knowing it, to turn back from the holy commandment delivered to them. For what has happened to them is what the true proverb says, 'The dog turns back to his own vomit,'[22] and 'the sow is washed only to wallow in the mire.'"[23] For just as it is the worst of things, brothers, to see a soiled dog gulping down its own vomit, and anyone who acts that way causes immediate revulsion—and it goes without saying that someone well-bred is horrified to see a sow, because, foul and ill-smelling, it jumps straight from the spring-waters back into the filth and settles into the marshes which defile it utterly—so also, it seems to me that it is true to say that the crime of duplicity is completely shameful and wicked, or rather it surpasses all wickedness, since it persuades one to return to one's original imbecility, and bids one revert to that illness of impiety which through faith in Christ we had marvelously rejected when we laid hold of spiritual strength and possessed a healthy and undamaged mind.

It is fitting, therefore, that we consider this matter again. If one of the members of our body has been maimed, and a serious illness has consumed it, and a doctor has beguiled the sickness away with his skill, taming it and, as it were, checking the headlong course of the malady or even stopping it altogether, would anyone be so foolish as not to consider this beyond all praise, and to want to fall sick again? Is there any man so senseless and lacking in wit that, when he can choose to be healthy, he desires the contrary? Seeing that it is not what is carnal about us, which is from earth, but precisely that which is best, the soul and the mind, which has been freed from the ancient, loathsome diseases, and we have made our way through the illness of polythe-

22. Prv 26.11.
23. 2 Pt 2.21–22.

ism, do you not regard health as extremely desirable, dear sir? Does it seem so utterly pleasant to you to remain sick, even though you could avoid it, if only you wanted?

But someone will surely come forward with an outcry and loose from his heart this silly remark: What harm does it do you to believe that there is one Father and Creator of all, but to pay honors to the demons of the world as well, since the sacred and divinely inspired Scripture itself names them for us Thrones, Principalities, Powers, and Dominions?[24] To these silly, nonsensical words I think one should again reply as follows: namely, that it is beyond belief and utterly illogical, or rather quite dangerous, to seek to crown with the highest and equal honors both him who sits upon the throne of the earthly realm, and those who, lying beneath his feet, submit their necks to him as slaves. For will not universal domination be accorded to those who obtain it as something special? And would not one say that submission suits the others best? I do not think anyone will doubt it. And if there are those among the subjects who are well-disposed and most noble, they will be granted gifts and glory. But those who are disobedient, rebellious, and disdainful of the others will be ranked among the most hostile and will be issued the very worst punishment. But in connection with this, the following should be considered.

Now I admit that it belongs to the highest intelligence to be able to see perfectly well that those as well who have received the prestige of a noble birth, and have testified to it by their deeds, may sometimes share in glory and in the highest honor; but they do not obtain it on their own, nor from their own power; it comes from the free decision of the ruler. The emperor's will is the source of honor and glory for everyone. The latter are not among those who possess these gifts by nature, but among those who receive them. And as long as they remain firm in loyalty to the emperor, their power remains secure and they are in a fair

---

24. Cf. Col 1.16. Adopting the proper attitude toward angels and demons was a key component of the ascetical struggle. See the discussion in Harmless, *Desert Christians*. In Cyril's day, cultic veneration of angels seems to have been an ongoing problem: cf. SC 434, 36, n. 1, and the discussion in Theodoret, *A Cure of Greek Maladies*, SC 57, 196–202.

way to obtaining glory. But when they change to the opposite, they are no longer to be envied, but will be found most wretched, having fallen into the worst of evils. And certainly if someone has come to the point of making such wicked decisions, and, after being incited to rebellion by an uncontrollable madness and recklessly taking up the practices and the very weapons of a tyrant, has destroyed cities and countrysides, forcing his yoke upon others and seizing the glory of sovereignty for himself, he is not thereby deemed worthy of honor, not at least according to the wise; neither will he be ranked among the supreme sovereigns. Far from it. On the contrary, an account of his madness will be demanded of him, and satisfaction will be required of him for these so impious projects, and, with perfect justice, a punishment both matching and, so to say, equal in magnitude will be imposed.

It may be hoped, then, that our description and representation of these things from our world, like a painting on a tablet, is useful. But come, let us give our attention to concepts that go beyond the visible realm, and so examine with greater perceptiveness the divine beauty itself; and, in contemplating, as far as may be, the nature regnant over everything, and accurately reckoning, as far as possible, its power and potency, let us realize the state of servitude of the things made by it and lying under it. For there is one Master of everything, and Creator and Lord of the universe. And since he is by nature good, in order that he might be known to be so not by himself alone, but that others might also share in the kindness inherent in him, he brought into being things which once were not. And he created a multitude of holy spirits beyond number. But in assigning the highest rank to the things that came to be, he called one "Principality," another "Dominion," still another "Throne," while some he called "Archangels" and still others "Angels." For he measured out to each of the things made the honor suiting it alone; he intended only what was completely and absolutely good and beyond reproach.

2. The multitude of the holy angels in the heavens is therefore innumerable; some have been established by God as Principalities, and Powers, and Thrones, playing, as it were, the part of

a father or teacher for the others. For it was thus, and not otherwise, that matters could proceed as though with a fair wind for the beings that had been made. When therefore you hear the sacred Scriptures calling certain ones "Powers," "Thrones," and "Dominions,"[25] do not assume thereby that the error of polytheism is being preached, dear sir, and do not let yourself be borne away from true doctrine upon a tide of arguments proceeding from ignorance. For what I have just said, I will say again, for as the blessed Paul writes, "To say the same things to you is not irksome to me, and is safe for you."[26] There is one Creator and Lord of all, and ten thousands of myriads of holy angels attend him, and there is not one of the things made by him that does not bear the yoke of servitude. And if there were some who rebelled, and, as it were, withdrew their necks from the harness, they have been punished, have fallen, and, having with good reason lost the city on high, they have led into error some of those upon earth when they tried to seize for themselves the glory of God. One of them, and the first, is Satan. By no means should it ever be surmised that they are truly gods. For there is one nature which is truly sovereign over the universe. And all the rational creatures called into being by it, and holding the rank of slaves, take pride in the proportions which suit them best. And this is the dignity and excellence which is theirs: to be able to preserve the office assigned and given them.

For all things worship the Creator, and one may see them throughout all of the divinely inspired Scripture honoring the Master of the universe with unceasing acclamations. Indeed, the divinely inspired prophet Isaiah says, "I saw the Lord Sabaoth sitting on a high and exalted throne, and Seraphim stood round about him; each had six wings; and with two they covered their face, and with two their feet, and with two they flew."[27] And he says that, replying in turns to each other, they invoked as holy the Lord of powers.[28] For that is what "Sabaoth" means. Observe, then, how the highest powers, holy and rational, the Seraphim, keep to the limits befitting slaves: they surround the divine throne as though paying a debt by their acclamations. Now I ask,

25. Cf. Col 1.16.
26. Phil 3.1.
27. Is 6.1–2.
28. Cf. Is 6.3.

my friends: whom does it befit to sit upon a throne high and exalted, and whom, furthermore, does it befit to stand in attendance and serve? I think that, persuaded by the reality itself, you will certainly reply that being seated is a sign of the sovereign's dignity, while the position in attendance is that to which slaves are properly limited. And we will find blessed David himself in agreement with Isaiah's words when he says, "The Lord has prepared his throne in the heaven; and his kingdom rules over all."[29] Then he orders those under his rule: "Bless the Lord, all you his angels, mighty in strength, who do his word, ready to hear the sound of his words. Bless the Lord, all you his hosts, his ministers that do his will. Bless the Lord, all his works." Notice that in this passage too it says that the divine throne has been made ready in heaven, and that all must give glory unceasingly, naming them for us angels, ministers, and powers. And to all this it adds, "Bless the Lord, all his works."[30]

It is therefore stupid, or rather it is quite the last degree of impiety, to number the Maker with what he has himself made, and to enclose the Master of the universe within the bounds of a slave. For to raise something that has been made to the glory of its Maker is nothing other than to bring the Maker down to the rank of things made. For being ranked with the things he has produced is against his will and is completely hateful to him, and a most frightful punishment looms over those who attribute the divine glory to the impure demons: that is something you will understand well if you consult Moses' writings. For you will find: "Hear, Israel, the Lord your God is one Lord,"[31] and again, "You shall worship the Lord your God, and him alone shall you serve." And he bids them further, "And if the Lord your God shall utterly destroy from before you the nations into which you go to inherit their land there, and you obtain them as your inheritance and dwell in their land, be careful lest you seek to follow them after they are destroyed and eliminated before you. You shall not seek their gods, saying, 'How do these nations act towards their gods? I will do likewise.' You shall not do so to the Lord your God. For the abominations which the Lord hates they

29. Ps 103.19.    30. Ps 103.20–22.
31. Dt 6.4.

have performed for their gods; for they burn their sons and their daughters in fire to their gods."[32] And again: "And if there arises within you a prophet or one who dreams a dream, and he gives you a sign or a wonder, and the sign or the wonder comes to pass which he spoke to you, saying, 'Let us go and serve other gods which you know not,' you shall not listen to the words of that prophet, or the dreamer of that dream, because the Lord God is testing you, to see whether you love the Lord your God with all your heart and with all your soul. Follow the Lord your God; and that prophet or that dreamer of a dream shall die; for he has spoken to make you stray from the Lord your God."[33]

Death is therefore the punishment for those who divert the mind of the pure to those unholiest of things which are foreign to it. And the one who rebukes those who fall to such a depth of insanity quite clearly does not tolerate being worshiped with others, but claims the rule over the universe for himself alone. He spoke accordingly through the voice of the saints, "I am God, and there is no other; just and savior, there is none beside me."[34] Confessing therefore that there is one God, the one who is over all and through all, let us not reckon that there is any other beside him. Neither let us be caught imparting the crown of sovereignty either to visible creatures or to certain others. For we will not destroy God's glory even if we try to do this; we will rather plunge ourselves into the pits of perdition.

But there may perhaps yet be a secret and hidden worshiper of the devil and of demons, who all the while adorns himself with the forms of reverence and feigns to be frank in his speech. Let him listen therefore to the divinely inspired Scripture when it cries, "God is not mocked!"[35] and also indeed the divine David when he sings, "Understand now, you senseless ones among the people, and you fools, be wise at last! He that planted the ear, does he not hear? He that formed the eyes, does he not perceive? He that disciplines the nations, shall he not punish?"[36]

---

32. Dt 12.29–31.
33. Dt 13.2–6.
34. Is 45.21.
35. Gal 6.7.
36. Ps 93.8–10.

3. Since, then, God knows and at the same time observes everything about us, let us have a faith that is sure and stable. And let us rid ourselves of the shame coming from duplicity, remembering what the blessed Paul writes: "Therefore, my brothers, be steadfast and immovable, always abounding in God's work."[37] Come, then, while offering to God a genuine faith as a spiritual sacrifice, let us say from a heart free of suspicion, "Behold us, we will be yours, because you are the Lord our God."[38] And again, "Lord our God, take possession of us. Lord, we know not any other beside you. Your name we name."[39] For those who choose to think rightly must believe that the God who is over all and through all is the one and only God. He did not bring himself into being, nor of course did he receive that from another. But being and existing always, he is eternally before every age and time. Incorruptible and indestructible, "dwelling in light inaccessible,"[40] the source of wisdom and life, he is conceived of as being, and is, by nature, that which is good in itself, the root of all power. And while he is known to be, it is not known what he is by nature.[41] For that must be our attitude, as the Savior's disciple said in speaking as follows: "Those who approach God must believe that he is, and that he rewards those who seek him."[42] But they must not search further. Do not doubt within yourself, my friend, nor allow yourself to be pushed into a perilous curiosity by arguments springing from ignorance, so that you venture to say: I have been initiated and have believed, and have been taught to worship the one God. But why should I not learn the nature of the one adored?

Away with you and your ill-advised attempt to investigate matters which surpass the mind and its reason! What, after all, is human thought in comparison to that ineffable and inexpressible nature? Who would be of such intelligence as to be able to measure that beauty? Listen to what the divinely inspired prophet

---

37. 1 Cor 15.58.          38. Jer 3.22.

39. Is 26.13.          40. 1 Tm 6.16.

41. Cyril's views here have much in common with those of Gregory of Nazianzus in the *Theological Orations*. See the discussion in Russell, *Cyril of Alexandria*, 23.

42. Heb 11.6.

Isaiah says in indicating this to you in riddling language: "Who has measured the water in his hand, and the heaven with a span? Who has weighed the mountains in scales, and the forests in a balance?"[43] Do not therefore concern yourself with what surpasses nature, but accept it by faith, admitting and agreeing that he is and exists, and rules all things; but be wise enough not to let your mind go beyond the limits of what is human, as it were. For this is how the divinely inspired Moses received the faith as well. For when God said, "Speak to the children of Israel, and you will say to them, 'The Lord, the God of your fathers has sent me to you,'" he inquired, "Behold, I am going to the children of Israel, and I will say to them, 'The Lord has summoned you.' But they will ask me," he says, "'What is his name?' What shall I say to them?"[44] And what does God answer? "This is what you will say to the children of Israel: 'He who is has sent me to you.' This is my name, and an eternal memorial to generations of generations."[45] For to be and to exist forever belongs to the One who is by nature God. But what is and exists without beginning or ceasing will escape the defilement that comes from having been made, and will itself testify through itself that it does not have its existence from another.

For God the Father is uncreated and ingenerate, having the Son begotten from his substance as connatural and coeternal, [the Son] "through whom he made the ages as well."[46] And he grants the passage into being to things which once were not, and gives life to everything which can receive life, while illuminating again, with the divine and intelligible light, that which is in need of light. The divine David knows and teaches us this when he sings to God, the Father of all: "How you have multiplied your mercy, O God! So the children of men shall trust in the shelter of your wings. They shall be satiated with the fatness of your house; and you will give them to drink of the torrent of your delights. For with you is the fountain of life, and in your light we shall see light."[47] John indeed in his supreme wisdom says, "It was the true light that enlightens every human being coming

43. Is 40.12.
45. Ex 3.14–15.
47. Ps 36.7–9.

44. Ex 3.13.
46. Heb 1.2.

into the world."[48] For the Only-Begotten is, he is indeed, the genuine imprint of God the Father's substance,[49] possessing all of his Begetter in his own beauty. And from what he himself is, he portrays perfectly the nature of him who brought him forth. He says accordingly, "I am in the Father and the Father in me."[50]

Now when you hear of Father and Son, withdraw from the corporeal. Hasten away from any thought concerning bodies, and employ your thought as one must here; understand that we are not now speaking of something in the realm of generation and corruption. The nature which exercises authority over everything is incorporeal and above being. Let the mind, then, depart from the corporeal when you learn something about God. That which is regarded as beyond and above all corporeal substance cannot be circumscribed by place, nor can it be subject to the forms of shapes. Not only that, but when it is said to "beget," it will not be found to be subject to effluences or divisions—far from it! For human beings, or any other kind of corporeal living things, give birth from themselves and have offspring from themselves by ejaculation into another in their own way. But God, who is incorporeal and beyond all conception which we have, brings forth without being divided; begets without being cut.

But if someone wanted me to describe the manner of the divine begetting, and approached me to ask: How did the divine nature beget? I would say, with no embarrassment: And what kind of mind will conceive for you what is above the mind? Or what kind of language will interpret for us what is above language? For the blessed Paul writes, "The peace of Christ, which passes all understanding, will keep your hearts."[51] And Solomon in his supreme wisdom showed that such things are quite inexpressible when he said, "The glory of the Lord conceals language."[52] And that the manner of the Son's begetting escapes the holy angels themselves, even though they are so far above us, the blessed Isaiah persuades us when he says, "Who will recount his generation?"[53] The prophet Habakkuk, further, explains it more clearly when he says, "His virtue has hidden the

48. Jn 1.9.
50. Jn 10.38.
52. Prv 25.2 (LXX).

49. Heb 1.3.
51. Phil 4.7.
53. Is 53.8 (LXX).

heavens."[54] What could it mean to say that the Son's virtue hides the very heavens, if not that the language which concerns him is greater than even the multitude above and the holy orders? Christ's begetting is therefore ineffable and quite inconceivable to every creature. But following the divine Scriptures, and looking "as though in a mirror darkly,"[55] we say that he was begotten and coexists eternally in the following ways. I know that the examples are unimpressive and cannot suffice to signify to us the nature of God and the manner of his generation. But it is sensible to realize that there is nothing among the things that have come to be that would not be seen to fall short of God's glory.

4. Starting[56] therefore by using example as a sort of sensory figure preliminary to our considerations, let us leap up to what is incomparably superior, and, in making our way to the very beauty of the divine nature in the best way possible, as far as we can at least, let us realize that human language, and indeed even the form which may be thought of as happening to exist in bodies, are insubstantial and do not in any way subsist on their own. But the divine and supramundane Offspring, the Son, does subsist, having been begotten personally from the Father who subsists without having been engendered.

But let no one be disturbed by the difference in the terms. For we will not entertain the rashness of those "who speak from their hearts, and not from the mouth of the Lord,"[57] as is written. One might address them with the words, "Awake, you drunkards, from your wine!"[58] Or perhaps one might say—and actually, it would be the truth—that while they do not know

---

54. Hab 3.3.                    55. 1 Cor 13.12.

56. From here to the end of the letter Cyril rehearses a set of fairly standard arguments against Eunomius and other later "Arians." The technical sophistication is unusual for these letters, but it does parallel themes developed more systematically in his *Dialogues on the Trinity*. The compressed nature of the discussion, however, results in a diminishment of clarity. Cyril may have been working on these dialogues at the time this festal letter was composed; see G. Jouassard, "L'activité littéraire de saint Cyrille d'Alexandrie jusqu'à 428: Essai de chronologie et de synthèse," in *Mélanges E. Podechard* (Lyon, 1945). For a short discussion of Cyril's Trinitarian theology, see Russell, *Cyril of Alexandria*, 21–30.

57. Jer 23.16.                    58. Jl 1.5.

what concerns themselves, "they raise their horn aloft and speak unrighteousness against God,"[59] as the divine David himself sings to us. For they string together witlessly the inventions of human thoughts, and with their feeble arguments "weave a spider's web,"[60] as is written, and thus in their unholy way they plunder the souls of the simple, carrying them off into error and thrusting them into the depths of perdition. Let them listen therefore to the divinely inspired Scripture as it cries, "This wisdom is not such as comes down from above, but is earthly, unspiritual, devilish."[61] For what is it that the wretches say when they pull the Son out of consubstantiality with God the Father as far as they can? "How can what is begotten be the same in nature as the unbegotten Father? For the difference between the terms is enormous."

I at least would reply at once to this that while that which the terms suggest to us is admittedly different, this does not mean that the Son is cut off from consubstantiality with God the Father. No language will persuade us to acknowledge that what is begotten is completely different in nature from the begetter, as though that were necessary. On the contrary, as long as it is believed to be begotten at all—granted that the true manner of begetting is meant—it will be of the same nature and substance as the begetter. If then the Father has begotten in truth—and these people too acknowledge that such is the nature of the case—then in what way will the Son, who by nature has shone forth from him, be foreign and different in kind? For if these people's nonsense is true, then the divine nature will be proved to have suffered what creation itself has not had to suffer. For the offspring of a human being is a human being. And in fact any of the things which have been given the ability to beget will certainly produce offspring from themselves which are the same in species and substance. A human being will not give birth to a horse, nor a horse to a dog. And since God the Father is far superior to us and our state, he will certainly be far above us in this respect as well, and will be regarded as having his own Son consubstantial to himself. He can by no means experience what the nature

59. Cf. Ps 75.4–6.     60. Is 59.5.
61. Jas 3.15.

of generate things itself deems it shameful to experience. If then, when he was fashioning all things in the beginning, he judged it best that each of the things made should have its own offspring consubstantial to itself, why would he deprive himself of what is most excellent in not being likewise himself? But if it is ridiculous to think or say so—for it is right that he should have a claim on all that is most excellent—then this will certainly belong to him as well.

But if they think that God did not truly beget, why do they put forward the difference among the terms as something compelling, and try to negate the glory of the offspring, saying that it is other in nature than the ingenerate Father? For if God the Father did not beget at all, then neither is the Son begotten, according to them. Let the question then be resolved, and let them stop holding up to us the difference in terms as though it were an insuperable obstacle. And if the Father has not begotten, let them explain who the Only-Begotten is about whom God the Father says, "From the womb before the Day Star I begot you."[62] He says, "from the womb," for the language about these matters was composed as though it concerned human beings, in order that, by proceeding from our own situation to an understanding of what is above us, we might believe that the Son has been begotten from the Father's very substance.

And I am amazed that the following point has also escaped these folk, so very disputatious as they are and, as they suppose, wise. What I mean is that the divinely inspired Paul, even though he is the steward for us of the divine mysteries,[63] and was ordained thereunto, "for he was set apart for the gospel of God,"[64] when he shows that God is truly the first and only Father, and that it is by their likeness to him that the things produced by him have been honored with the title of "father," writes about him, "From him all fatherhood in heaven and on earth is named."[65] But these exacting investigators of what is above mind and reason, when they dismiss God, the Father of all things, from their own good things, say that he has not truly begotten the Son, that

62. Ps 109.3 (LXX).          63. Cf. 1 Cor 4.1.
64. Rom 1.1.                   65. Eph 3.15.

he is falsely named "Father," and that the Only-Begotten is his by
adoption.

It would be perfectly reasonable, therefore, dear friends, to
address them as follows: if God is not Father by nature and in
truth, and if he has not begotten his own Son from himself, from
his own substance that is, while we are fathers in truth, having
our own children from ourselves, then how is it that "all fatherhood" will still be from him, as is written? For he has been called
"Father" by resemblance to us, and we are no longer fathers because of him. For all of logic will compel our opponents, and
quite rightly, I think, whether they like it or not, to admit that it
is always somehow true that what is by convention is second to
what is by nature; and with respect to that which is in truth, that
which is by imitation and likeness to it is younger. It is we who
are the first fathers, accordingly, who are seen through the facts
to be such in nature and truth; God is in second place after us,
in likeness and imitation. In that case, how is it that all fatherhood in heaven and on earth is still named after him? One
should not attend to their impudent loquacity, however, but to
the voices of the saints. The divinely inspired Paul will never lie,
then, which means that God is truly the first Father, and has as
consubstantial the Son begotten from him. This is what is meant
by the manner of the true generation.

Perhaps, however, they will muster other arguments against
us, and, adding sins upon sins,[66] as is written, they will say that it
is what is ingenerate that is indicative of the substance of God
the Father, and what is generate of that of the Only-Begotten,
and that the ingenerate is not by nature like the generate.

5. I must say, dear friends, that I am astonished at the depth
of their idiocy; it will not take me long to show that they do not
know what they are saying or the matters about which they make
their affirmations.

What I mean is that if they do not say that the word "ingenerate" in the case of God the Father indicates that he has not been
begotten, and "generate" in the case of the Son indicates that he

66. Cf. Is 30.1.

has been begotten, but say rather that the names are indicative of substances, then whence have they learned the difference between the Father and the Son? For if the term indicates nothing other than that there is a substance, then who is it that has shown so clearly that the Son is alien to the Father, according to identity in substance at least, since he is in no way joined to him? If therefore they do not wish to regard "ingenerate" as indicative of not having been begotten, nor "generate" as having been begotten, but regard both terms as simply indicating substance—no difference being perceptible from that quarter—then whence will the otherness appear? For if a substance is compared to a substance, inasmuch as they are only regarded as substances, they will have nothing contrary to each other. What is there then to prevent the Son from being like the Father in substance, if the things indicated by the terms are not opposed to each other?

But since, having given over simplicity in their way of life and an unquestioning manner of belief, they join the party of the pagan elite, whence they arm themselves against us in the manner of the boastful Goliath, and like him heap reproaches on the Lord's assembly, let us also remove ourselves from worldly wisdom and entangled arguments, saying as the blessed David did, "I am not used to these things."[67] And let us approach these angry folk, taking Christ as a staff of power, and as a chosen stone in our mind as in a pouch. Let us in fact sally forth a short distance from ecclesiastical simplicity, since that is necessary, and let us convict them of raving about the matters in which they think they are so formidable and hard to withstand. Thus since they neither have the understanding that is from God, nor have they attained the external wisdom in accordance with reason, they may rightly hear the words: "How long will you hobble on both your hams? If on Baal, then on Baal; if on God, then on God."[68] For it will be evident from what follows that it is out of ignorance that they say that "ingenerate" signifies a substance; allow me to speak briefly of those matters which are widely aired among students of philosophy.

67. 1 Sm 17.39.
68. 1 Kgs 18.21.

6. They say, from what I have learned, that the things by means of which the substances of beings are signified are definitions, as they call them; and they hold that they compose the definitions from genus and difference or differences.[69] For they say that the genus is the substance signified simply, as for instance "living being," while the difference is the term which shows what kind of living being it is, rational or irrational. For if one wants to define "human being" or "horse," one will simply say that it is a living being. For human beings and horses are alike living beings. But if one adds the difference to the genus, then when it comes to a human being one will certainly say that it is a rational, mortal living being, while of the horse that it is a living being that neighs. If therefore the name "ingenerate" defines for us God's substance, and the term has the meaning of a definition, then let it fall under genus and difference. What do they say to that, then? Under which genus will they place the God who is over all? Or what sort of difference will he receive from them?

In addition, substances are signified clearly and logically not by means of what they are not, but from what they are considered to be. If one, for instance, asks what fire is, the proper answer is that it is what is hot, dry, burning, and illuminating. The explanation is made from what it is. But if one says that fire is what is not cold, one indicates it not by means of what it is, but from what it is not. But that is inept and quite illogical. If therefore, in regard to God, the name "ingenerate" indicates that he has not been engendered, then it designates God not from what he is, but from what he is not; for the name signifies that he has not been engendered. How, then, according to them, can the term function as a definition, that it may signify a substance, and not rather some one of the things which are considered attributes of substance?

That will be our reply to them. You, though, will be told that the Church's message is simple. We have been baptized, that is, in the Father and the Son and the Holy Spirit. And believing that the Holy Trinity is consubstantial,[70] we worship one godhead

69. The French translator sees here an Aristotelian influence, perhaps through philosophical handbooks; SC 434, 74, n. 1.

70. According to the French translator, this is the first time in these letters

in it, thanking God the Father for having sent from heaven his own Son for the sake of our salvation and life, the Son born of a woman,[71] the Son who put on our likeness and truly became a human being, in order that, having triumphed over the Principalities and Powers,[72] he might nail to his own cross, as is written, the bond that stood against us,[73] and might render us pure, freed from all guilt, once he had washed us of the defilement of our failings of the past. His purpose was also that he might preach "also to the spirits in hell, who formerly did not obey,"[74] as is written, in order thus at last to abolish death, the enemy of all, once he had been raised from the dead, and indeed, when he had opened the gates above to those on earth, to make the former runaway a citizen of heaven. For he will come, he will come indeed when the time arrives, and, as he himself said,[75] he will take with him all of us who are distinguished by right faith and illustrious for an evangelical way of life.

Knowing this, beloved, "let us cleanse ourselves from every defilement,"[76] once we have washed away every stain, and "let us be merciful, as our heavenly Father is merciful."[77] Let us assist those in need as far as possible; let us refresh widows and orphans;[78] let us bring the naked and homeless into our house. In a word, let us practice every kind of virtue. For thus it is, thus indeed, that we will keep a pure fast, beginning holy Lent on the thirtieth of the month of Mechir, and the week of the salvific Paschal feast on the fifth of Pharmuthi. We break the fast on the tenth of Pharmuthi late in the evening, according to the gospel proclamation, and we celebrate the feast on the following day, the eve of Sunday, the eleventh of Pharmuthi,[79] adding thereafter the seven weeks of Eastertide. For thus it is, thus indeed, that we will once again delight in the divine words, in Christ Jesus our Lord, through whom and with whom be honor and glory and power to the Father with the Holy Spirit for endless ages. Amen.

---

that the word "consubstantial" is used in reference to the Trinity. It is fairly common in other works of Cyril's. Cf. SC 434, 77, n. 1.

71. Cf. Gal 4.4.  
72. Cf. Col 2.15.  
73. Cf. Col 2.14.  
74. 1 Pt 3.19–20.  
75. Cf. Jn 14.3; cf. 1 Thes 4.16–17.  
76. 2 Cor 7.1.  
77. Lk 6.36.  
78. Cf. Jas 1.27.  
79. April 6, 424.

# APPENDIX
## INDICES

# APPENDIX

## The Dates of Easter Announced
## by Cyril's *Festal Letters*[1]

| Festal Letter | Alexandrian Date | Equivalent | Other Churches |
|---|---|---|---|
| | (19 pharmouthi) | April 14, 412 | |
| | (11 pharmouthi) | April 6, 413 | |
| I (1) | 26 phamenoth | March 22, 414 | |
| II (2) | 16 pharmouthi | April 11, 415 | |
| IV (3)[2] | 7 pharmouthi | April 2, 416 | |
| V (4) | 27 pharmouthi | April 22, 417 | March 25 in some Western churches |
| VI (5) | 12 pharmouthi | April 7, 418 | |
| VII (6) | 4 pharmouthi | March 30, 419 | |
| VIII (7) | 23 pharmouthi | April 18, 420 | |
| IX (8) | 8 pharmouthi | April 3, 421 | April 10 Elsewhere |
| X (9) | 30 phamenoth | March 26, 422 | |
| XI (10) | 20 pharmouthi | April 15, 423 | |
| XII (11) | 11 pharmouthi | April 6, 424 | March 23 in Africa (Roman) |

1. The following chart is taken from Évieux, 92–93. It shows the dates of Easter for the whole of Cyril's episcopate and illustrates some of the confusion surrounding the dating of Easter that continued to exist even in the fifth century.

2. Although the twenty-nine letters run in uninterrupted sequence from 414–442, a scribal error has resulted in the omission of a letter three in the manuscript tradition.

| Festal Letter | Alexandrian Date | Equivalent | Other Churches |
|---|---|---|---|
| XIII (12) | 24 pharmouthi | April 19, 425 | March 22 in some Western churches |
| XIV (13) | 16 pharmouthi | April 11, 426 | |
| XV (14) | 8 pharmouthi | April 3, 427 | |
| XVI (15) | 27 pharmouthi | April 22, 428 | |
| XVII (16) | 12 pharmouthi | April 7, 429 | |
| XVIII (17) | 4 pharmouthi | March 30, 430 | |
| XIX (18) | 24 pharmouthi | April 19, 431 | |
| XX (19) | 8 pharmouthi | April 3, 432 | |
| XXI (20) | 30 phamenoth | March 26, 433 | |
| XXII (21) | 20 pharmouthi | April 15, 434 | |
| XXIII (22) | 5 pharmouthi | March 31, 435 | |
| XXIV (23) | 24 pharmouthi | April 19, 436 | |
| XXV (24) | 16 pharmouthi | April 11, 437 | |
| XXVI (25) | 1 pharmouthi | March 27, 438 | |
| XXVII (26) | 21 pharmouthi | April 16, 439 | |
| XXVIII (27) | 12 pharmouthi | April 7, 440 | |
| XXIX (28) | 27 phamenoth | March 23, 441 | March 30 in some Western churches |
| XXX (29) | 17 pharmouthi | April 12, 442 | |
| | (9 pharmouthi) | April 4, 443 | |
| | (28 pharmouthi) | April 28, 444 | March 26 in some Western churches |

# GENERAL INDEX

# INDEX OF HOLY SCRIPTURE

## Old Testament

*New Testament*

7.22–23: 102
7.22–24: 198
7.23–25: 126
7.25–8.2: 199
8.2: 163
8.3: 153
8.3–4: 183, 199
8.12–14: 199
8.18–19: 196
8.23: 55
8.29: 150, 185, 213
8.32: 134
8.35: 217
9.4–5: 152
9.5: 99
9.7–8: 93
9–11: 20
10.21: 80
12.1: 126
12.1–2: 200
12.9: 172
12.12: 100
12.16: 35
13.8–10: 140
13.10: 201
13.12: 35, 157, 197
13.12–14: 137
13.13–14: 136
13.14: 85
14.9: 214
15.16: 16

1 Corinthians
1.20: 91
1.24: 170
2.9: 40
2.12: 152
2.14–15: 158
3.1: 120
3.2: 103
3.16: 77
3.19: 107
4.16: 127
5.7: 57
6.17: 172
6.19: 77

7.7: 62
7.19: 116
8.6: 99
9.16: 38
9:16–17: 54
9.24: 36
9.27: 103, 128, 198
10.8–9: 43
10.11: 180
10.13: 74
12.31–13.3: 129
13.4–8: 129, 141
13.5: 141
13.13: 197
15.20: 51, 84, 193
15.27: 173
15.44–46: 158
15.52–54: 189
15.55: 51
15: 55–56: 39
15.58: 57

2 Corinthians
2.11: 111
2.15: 55
3.17: 184
3.18: 185
4.4: 86
4.16: 42
5.5: 67
5.10: 193
5.14–15: 173
5.15: 62, 194
5.17: 55, 83, 115
6.5: 128
7.1: 51, 125, 174
8.9: 86
8.14: 207
9.8: 58
10.4: 197
11.27: 128

Galatians
2.16: 177
2.17: 16
3.5–7: 93

3.8–10: 93
3.15–16: 94
3.24: 177
3.27: 111
3.27–29: 94
4.4: 135, 153
4.5: 173
4.19: 179, 184
4.21–31: 93
4.22: 70
4.22–26: 24, 89
5.1: 177
5.24: 180
5.25: 159, 180
6.2: 208
6.10: 136
6.14–17: 16

Ephesians
1.4: 97
1.7: 172
1.18: 214
2.14: 136, 178
2.14–15: 66
4.2: 67
4.5–6: 170
4.6: 75
4.8: 99
4.18: 163
4.22–24: 36
4.32: 208
5.2: 171, 180
5.14: 64
6.11: 197
6.11–14: 71
6.12: 71, 173
6.14: 138
6.16: 71

Philippians
2.6: 173
2.6–7: 135
2.7: 30, 50, 81, 173, 178, 183, 190
2.8: 25, 97, 99
2.10–11: 152